The author has lived in East Anglia for over 30 years and had a career in banking, including Head Office finance function.

He is married, and has two sons and two grandchildren.

He says writing and research has provided a rich vein of human contact with a generous spirit shown by all to talk and to share.

Other than writing, his interests include gardening, family history, walking, watching sport, code-breakers of Bletchley Park, economics, music, art and reading—favourite topics: real-life exploits (especially at sea), war stories (particularly POW escapes) and amusing fiction.

But, he says, family always comes first.

To the memory of Bill Tutte

and

all who contributed to breaking the German code that
Bletchley Park called 'Tunny'.

Tom Williams

BILL TUTTE CODEBREAKER

and His Battle with Hitler's Secret Cipher

AUSTIN MACAULEY PUBLISHERS™
LONDON • CAMBRIDGE • NEW YORK • SHARJAH

Copyright © Tom Williams (2019)

The right of Tom Williams to be identified as author of this work has been asserted by him in accordance with section 77 and 78 of the Copyright, Designs and Patents Act 1988.

All rights reserved. No part of this publication may be reproduced, stored in a retrieval system, or transmitted in any form or by any means, electronic, mechanical, photocopying, recording, or otherwise, without the prior permission of the publishers.

Any person who commits any unauthorised act in relation to this publication may be liable to criminal prosecution and civil claims for damages.

A CIP catalogue record for this title is available from the British Library.

ISBN 9781528911498 (Paperback)
ISBN 9781528949811 (ePub e-book)

www.austinmacauley.com

First Published (2019)
Austin Macauley Publishers Ltd
25 Canada Square
Canary Wharf
London
E14 5LQ

Principal acknowledgements must go to Richard and Susanne Youlden, the great-nephew and great-niece of Bill Tutte. Their support, help and guidance has been immensely important to me without which, the book could not have been written. I am truly grateful to them for their trust and for granting me the opportunity to join with them and others in seeking appropriate recognition for their great-uncle. Very sadly, Richard Youlden died in April 2019, before this book was published. I am also grateful to Helen May Williams (no relation) for sharing with me and allowing me to use extracts from her mother's wartime diaries and memoirs in the portrayal of the character Grace. Her mother was a graduate recruit to Hut 6 at Bletchley Park and interestingly, even her personal diary entries of that time held true to her vow of total secrecy. Helen's mother was a wordsmith and poet and Helen, also a poet, kindly penned two poems for me in her mother's style, a lovely counter-balance to the serious themes of the book. I must also express my heartfelt thanks to Helen for willingly employing her considerable expertise in reviewing, editing and suggesting improvements to my manuscript. There are many others who have contributed in various ways, too many to thank individually. I would, however, single out three. Firstly, I mention Jim Reeds, a distinguished American mathematician and cryptography historian, who is one of the editors of a significant academic work, *Breaking Teleprinter Ciphers at Bletchley Park*, which incorporates the 500-page General Report on Tunny (GRT). The GRT was compiled by key players at Bletchley Park over several months at the end of the war in 1945 but was only declassified in the year 2000. I used it a great deal in the writing of this book. On occasions, I consulted Jim Reeds, who willingly shared his considerable knowledge and expertise on the subject. I am indebted, too, to Frederica Freer, who, on my behalf, posed questions to her husband, Stephen Freer, on his association with Bill Tutte at Bletchley Park. Their ready responses were both most helpful and encouraging. Sadly, Stephen Freer died in April 2017. Lastly, I offer my thanks to Ken Halton for his time and conversation. Ken was a young GPO teleprinter engineer in the Newmanry at Bletchley Park in the final 12 months of the war. He took a great interest in Tunny and in his later years, contributed to a number of books on the subject. His entertaining reminiscences provided me with many 'nuggets' of everyday life at Bletchley Park.

For quotes reproduced from the speeches, works and writings of Winston S. Churchill: Reproduced with the permission of Curtis Brown, London, on behalf of The Estate of Winston S. Churchill © The Estate of Winston S. Churchill.

Attributions

'Where Shore Meets Ocean' and 'When We Are Old and Grey' by Helen May Williams are reproduced with permission. © Helen May Williams 2017. Used by permission of the author. Extracts from VIA VERITAS VITA: The forgotten diary of Valerie June Dennis (née Hepburn), covering a period circa 1940-52. Predominantly written while she was working at Bletchley Park 1943-45 are reproduced with permission. © Helen May Williams 2016. Used by permission of Helen May Williams. Additional materials from *A Memoir of Valerie June Dennis: 05 March 1922 – 09 February 2014* drawn on with permission. © Helen May Williams 2016. Used by permission of Helen May Williams.

A Foreword by Richard Youlden, Bill Tutte's Great Nephew

At the corner of the sofa, his nose buried in a book, sat Uncle Bill: he rarely spoke, but saw everything going on around him. His silent presence easily dominated. When he did say something, his voice was soft and thin, surprisingly so. Occasionally, if he wished to be heard, he would affect an amusing gruff booming tone: a voice which growled for attention; a voice which as children we teased him to do for us—it was so odd and funny.

It was only years later that we discovered this was his *lecture voice*. I simply can't imagine the shock awaiting students who met him back stage. Our great uncle was shy and unassuming, but he had a wicked dry sense of humour and wry wit. Every utterance was considered; Uncle Bill never wasted words.

Tall, with tousled white hair, he moved slowly like a stork: deliberate and reserved. He favoured shorts and t-shirt during the summer, but sported a Macintosh-style raincoat for those less clement moments. In the winter, his heavier coat was sometimes combined with a tea cosy style wool hat pulled down over his ears.

Uncle Bill and Aunt Dorothy came over from Canada and stayed with us periodically through our childhood: a wonderful, exciting pause from the mundane, filled with adventure. These were times when we would visit local attractions, play games and have far more fun than usual. Their visits often coincided with Christmas when we were small.

I recall laughing along with my brother and sister as Uncle Bill bounced us, all 3 together, on his knees, untunefully singing: 'The Little Old Lady Who Swallowed a Fly'… doing all the appropriate sounds as he chortled through the tune. Uncle Bill was a big happy child at heart. Aunt Dorothy loved that here 'Billy' could leave his work behind for a time and truly relax.

Aunt Dorothy, with her serene nature and soft Canadian drawl, was in many ways the antithesis of Uncle Bill. Lively and outward-going, she seemed to talk from the moment they arrived. Uncle Bill lingered patiently in the background, lost amid his thoughts…

As we grew, the visits were less frequent but just as magical. Our only true family holiday was a week staying with Uncle Bill and Aunt Dorothy in an Oxford town house—a property belonging to the college where Uncle Bill was teaching. We played Monopoly, we enjoyed a coach tour and explored the city, watching the boats on the Isis.

In the mid-90s, I had the great pleasure of attending the switching on of the Colossus re-build with Uncle Bill. We sat in a small courtyard eating lunch; it was a glorious sunny day. I took this opportunity to ask Uncle Bill about Bletchley. In reply to most of my questions, he smiled to himself, and hesitantly replied, very softly, "I'm sorry, I don't recall that."

During his later years, after Aunt Dorothy passed away, Uncle Bill returned to England for a few years; he moved in with us. We didn't see much of him during this time however. He spent his days working on a final book of Maths, and recalling his memories of Bletchley in a biography he left to us. He enjoyed long walks around his childhood haunts. His hopes for a greater involvement at his former college, Trinity Cambridge, dashed, he returned to Canada and passed his last few years happily back with his colleagues at Waterloo University.

Our favourite Great Uncle, Bill is peacefully sleeping with Dorothy in a small cemetery in West Montrose, Ontario, Canada, the land he loved. We miss his gentle presence…

A Foreword by Andy Clark, Trustee of The National Museum of Computing on Bletchley Park

Bill Tutte was an extraordinary talent. He was so talented that even the broadest detail of his work had to remain secret for more than half a century—even longer than the 30-year silence about the machine his work inspired: Colossus.

The Second World War has provided a rich theme for authors and artists and, as we have seen through films such as the two on Enigma, fictionalised accounts can have an extraordinary impact upon the general public. They can bring to life highly complex stories and bestow recognition on characters whose amazing achievements might all too easily be overlooked.

In reconstructing the Colossus computer at The National Museum of Computing, the late Tony Sale was determined that the achievements of the codebreakers should be not be forgotten. He knew their work could inspire future generations. The work of Tony and his team has indeed had a profound effect in publicising the factual story of the Breaking of Lorenz—from Bill Tutte's incredible re-imagining of a fiendishly complex cipher machine that initially enabled codebreaking by linguists like Major Ralph Tester and Jerry Roberts, and eventually the acceleration of the process with Tommy Flowers' Colossus. Without the work of Bill Tutte, none of the rest could have followed—and the war would have been drawn out for two years or more. Yet we know extraordinarily little of the character of the man behind the genius.

Setting out to re-imagine the life of Bill Tutte through fiction has playful parallels with Bill Tutte's reimagination of the Lorenz cipher machine (a machine which he never saw until the end of the war). Bill Tutte could authenticate his work by breaking the cipher. Tom Williams can't have that sort of satisfaction, but we should enjoy his story about one of the great achievers of the wartime years.

I look forward to this fictionalised account and hope it raises the profile of an unsung hero

Chapter 1
War Work

"Come in, come in," called Professor Duff at the knock on the door. The heavy panelled door opened and a young man entered the dimly lit and cluttered study overlooking the Great Court of Trinity College.

"Ah, Mr Tutte, come along in and take a chair," said the professor who was seated at a desk virtually submerged beneath piles of books and files and bound manuscripts.

Bill Tutte sat down on one of the two battered leather chairs. There was a slight pause as he waited uneasily for his tutor to begin. He was somewhat nervous; the note in his pigeon hole did not say why the professor wanted to see him. It was possible, considered Bill, the reason was to see how he was settling in after his recent move to the mathematics faculty, a move the professor had facilitated.

Following on from his honours degree in natural sciences and his submission of a scientific thesis for his Master's degree, Bill had embarked on a science doctorate; but all had not gone well. It was the professor who had suggested the change, knowing that for some time Bill had had a notable involvement with the Trinity Mathematical Society and with a small group of college mathematicians who had published a number of well received papers. Bill had readily seized the opportunity to switch disciplines, but there was little tangible progress to report on his new PhD topic.

"Now, your Master's result will come through in a couple of months," he began, "and I imagine you are getting stuck into your new research—on graph theory, wasn't it? But that's not why I asked you to come and see me."

The professor paused again, looking past Bill as if seeking the right words to continue.

"I've been asked to put forward a name from the college for some war work. It's all very hush-hush I'm afraid and I can't really expand much further."

At the phrase 'war work', Bill started to tense. Since he had been obliged to register for National Service, privately he had been in trepidation at the prospect of being called up; added to which he did not want to abandon now what he had only just started.

"From the little I know, your name came to mind. I'm told it is important work. The request came from an old friend whose word I do not doubt. There are a number of Trinity and Kings people, past and present, involved already so I think you would be in good company, if that helps. There would be an initial interview so you'd have the opportunity to find out a bit more." There the professor paused again.

"Is it in the military?" Bill could not help betraying his immediate concern.

In the run up to the war, as a student he had been exempt from conscription but that general exemption was withdrawn when war was declared. He was not a conscientious objector like his mathematician friend, Cedric, but neither was he the military type. He had always shuddered at the idea of pointing a gun at anyone, or indeed, at anything living. From an early age, he knew he was different from the other boys.

Professor Duff picked up on Bill's unease. "I think it's something to do with the Foreign Office, but more than that I don't know."

There was another awkward silence as the professor allowed Bill a moment or two for his words to sink in. He knew full well that Bill would be very reluctant to leave Cambridge. Bill, on the other hand, was uncertain how a refusal would be perceived. Ever since he had come under Professor Duff, he had sensed their relationship was not entirely comfortable, although he could not think quite why that was. The professor was one of the youngest of the college tutors, one who was willing to involve himself with the students in extra-curricular activities. Indeed, a couple of summers ago, the professor had joined a group of students, including Bill, who had taken some unemployed youngsters up to the Lake District for a holiday of outdoor activities and conservation work. Even so, Bill never felt close to the professor but now regarded he was under an obligation, the professor having facilitated his switch to Mathematics from Natural Sciences. He sought further confirmation.

"You believe I should go for this interview, don't you, sir?"

"Yes, I do. I know you are just commencing your new studies, but we'll keep your position open, if that's worrying you."

That was certainly a concern and the professor's words were reassuring as far as they could be in such uncertain times.

"I'd better go and see what this is about, then," Bill responded trying to be outwardly positive.

"Splendid!" said the professor. "I'll pass your name along. You'll probably get a letter in a few weeks' time. Let me know how you get on."

As Professor Duff got up from his seat to signal the end of the interview, he added as an afterthought, "Oh! And I guess you should not mention this to anyone, at least not for the time being."

Bill rose from the deep leather chair and said, "Thank you," more from an instinctive politeness than any specific gratitude.

He made his way back to his room in Nevile's Court and as he passed through the Common Room, his friend, Cedric, called him over.

"Bill, have you seen this?" Cedric was waving the local newspaper. The headline was 'Germans Bomb Cambridge—Perse School Firebombed'. "Were you fire-watching last night? Did you see any of it?"

"Oh, dear," said Bill not sitting down. "No, I wasn't but I heard it. Was it bad?"

"Pretty much; there is damage around Hyde Park Corner too."

He would normally confide in Cedric, his closest friend, particularly on something as important as his conversation with Professor Duff. But since he was told not to disclose anything, he was anxious to be on his own to gather his thoughts.

Cedric was a Quaker who had strongly-held pacifist views which he did not push but would air amongst his friends from time to time in his usual jocular manner. For Bill, now was not the time, though, to start a conversation on last night's drama; he had other things on his mind.

"Can't stop, must dash," he said hurrying off.

In his meagrely furnished room, Bill lowered himself slowly onto his chair and gazed at the wintry scene outside, his mind already beginning to go over this surprising turn of events. He was not questioning his decision to allow his name to go forward despite the stark lack of information. Logically, that was the right decision, given the situation. There was an interview available so he could base a decision on what he could learn then.

Did, however, today's turn of events offer an alternative to National Service? It seemed so. Bill started to go over the meeting with the professor, trying to recall everything that had been said and, by reading between the lines, what had been left unsaid. It was war work. It was important. Critically, it was not military, so the professor believed. What could it be? Why him? A chill came over him at his next thought. Was he selected because of his chemistry background? Was this something to do with explosives and armaments, or worse, with chemical weapons? But surely 'they', whoever 'they' were, would know his recent research was in the field of molecular infrared and ultraviolet spectra. He reasoned, however, that as it was 'something to do with the Foreign Office', he could hopefully dismiss anything to do with weaponry. Hopefully, it would not involve somewhere overseas. He preferred a set routine. Change tended to unsettle him and he simply could not face a posting abroad.

Bill placed little emphasis on Professor Duff's remark that it was all very hush-hush; pretty much everything was secret these days. What did intrigue him somewhat, though, was the nature of the approach. It smacked of an old boy network, the request coming from an 'old friend', 'an old friend whose word was not doubted.' A mischievous thought came to him—maybe this 'old friend' was a spy! Surely not, not with the impeccable background of Professor Patrick Duff. There was, nevertheless, one comment that really did resonate with Bill and that was a number of Trinity and Kings alumni were already involved. This carried a lot of weight in his deliberations.

The real misgiving he had was the obvious disruption to his doctorate should he leave Trinity at this juncture, even if it be by arrangement. Or would it, perhaps, be by 'coercion'? Since the onset of winter, he had come to realise that the practical side of his original doctoral research no longer held his interest and that he had rather lost his way. The move to his more favoured mathematics had re-invigorated him and he felt confident he was now on the right path. The last thing he wanted just now was any sort of interruption, whatever it was. In the background, however, there was the spectre of conscription and this war was not going to end soon.

Bill did not tend to introspection. His head was normally so full of mathematical matters that he took little notice of the world around him let alone looking within himself. He had been steered along the science route but he had always been more interested in mathematics and during his Master's, he had probably spent more time on mathematics than on his scientific thesis. But the spectre of conscription had not gone away. He could not escape the chatter around the university that a number of post-graduates and even under-graduates had volunteered for military service and some had already left. Even so, around the common rooms, there were all manner of opinions about the war, from Cedric on the one hand to the gung-ho rugby types on the other.

When younger, he had tended to be content with his own company, avoided the rough and tumble of the school playground, preferring instead the library and the fascination of an Encyclopaedia or of books on mathematics. In junior school, he always achieved high marks and could have gone to the high school at age 10 but his parents thought him too young. But he went a year later to the County High School for Boys in Cambridge where, again, he excelled academically but emotionally, it was an unhappy time. Too often, he was an object of ridicule; too clever, by half, for some of the rowdier pupils and too reserved to stand up for himself. He adopted a strategy of saying as little as possible. When at home, he had no real friends and was ostracised by some of the local boys because he was no longer one of them; he went to the 'clever boy's school'. The university offered him peers of equal academic ability but by then, he was really quite introverted and avoided the social side of campus life. He had come to prefer the quiet life; it was easier, less stressful. No wonder he felt National Service was an anathema, unable to see how he could possibly survive even basic training. What did that make him?

Bill's brother, Joe, was scathing that he was still in civvies. Joe, his only sibling, had, as a young man, spent several years in the RAF from the end of The Great War and had re-enlisted in the run-up to this conflict, although because of his age, he was put on the reserve list. He was nearly 17 years older than Bill and this significant age gap was one of the reasons there was never a great deal of brotherly love between them. On several occasions, Joe had made his views known in no uncertain terms that Bill too should have signed up straight away. Bill, on the other hand, had always argued, albeit with his usual modesty, that Joe did not understand or appreciate Bill's academic pursuits. Cedric, however, said that Joe simply did not want to understand, that he was just jealous of Bill's academic success and the recognition it brought. In contrast, Bill's father, a gardener, and his mother, a housekeeper, were full of parental pride. They had always given him every encouragement, supported by the local headmaster who had identified Bill's scholastic abilities from an early age.

The war news had been so desperate of late. He remembered the night, last November, when wave after wave of German bombers were heard overhead on route to Coventry. And now, even Cambridge, hardly a key military target, was not spared Hitler's bombs. His one contribution to the war effort, so far, had been stints of fire-watching at night on the college roof; quite exciting to start with on warm nights but no fun now. Morally, he accepted that, at some point, he should serve in some capacity greater than fire-watching. But doing what? It was the 'what to do' that was the problem and so, he had repeatedly shelved the issue. Would he, could he, follow Cedric's path who had vowed he would register as a Conscientious Objector? In principle, the answer was, 'no'. Actually, he thought, maybe this 'Foreign Office' position could turn out to be a safe desk job somewhere. At least if he did do something war related full time that would hopefully silence his brother.

Reflecting on all these issues, he reasoned he should approach this 'Foreign Office' role in all seriousness and definitely with a more open mind than he had first thought. Once the letter arrived, he would prepare.

Then, as if throwing a mental switch, Bill turned to his books.

As the train drew into Bletchley Station, where it terminated, Bill checked the appointment letter again. It had been sent from a strange address, Room 47, Foreign Office, London SW1. The train was punctual so he knew he had plenty of time. The appointment was at a place called Bletchley Park. The letter said he was to report to the gatehouse at the main entrance, a short walk from the station. He looked out of the carriage windows as the train slowed to a halt but his view one side was blocked by the carriages of another train and he could not make out anything likely on the other side. He alighted and looked around for a sign and finding none, approached a porter to ask directions.

"Over the bridge and out through the station entrance," he said in a rather bored tone as though he was repeating this for the umpteenth time. "You want the small gateway over the road and follow the perimeter path." Bill thanked him and headed as directed.

A few minutes later, the narrow woodland path gave way to the main entrance, a gatehouse for checking vehicles both in and out and a side gate for pedestrians, manned by a substantial and disquieting armed guard. To Bill, it all looked rather worrying, appropriate to a highly sensitive military establishment. After various checks and a phone call, he was allowed through and ordered to go straight to the Main Building, a big mansion house, and report to reception in the entrance hall.

During the walk along the approach road, Bill was on the lookout for evidence of what this place might be, the main entrance and gatehouse having offered no indication. As he neared a large Victorian country house, visible through the trees on the left, he could see away to his right a small lake and further ahead, incongruously, a number of single-story prefabricated huts, some with high blast walls of brick around them. Quite a number of people, some in uniform but most in civilian clothes, were walking purposefully from one building to another. More huts were under construction. Yet, nothing gave away what was happening there.

A uniformed receptionist checked his papers again and directed him to wait along a corridor where he sat down and looked around. The walls were oak panelled and the décor ornate but there were still no clues to the purpose of the place. He was early. His coping strategy when required to move outside his routine was to be early and well prepared. To kill time, he got out the letter and his notes. He was to be interviewed by a Mr C H O'D Alexander. He went over his notes which listed all his achievements and interests from his undergraduate days to date, and his justification for switching his doctorate research to mathematics. He had also brought a copy of *The Dissection of Rectangles into Squares*, a paper he co-authored with his Trinity mathematician friends, Cedric Smith, Leonard Brooks and Arthur Stone, published in America the previous year. It was an in-depth and complex solution to a long standing, well-known mathematical puzzle, convincing evidence he thought of his mathematical ability should it be needed.

He was uneasy, more nervous than usual. He did not enjoy interviews at the best of times. The waiting unnerved him. This place unnerved him.

He had sensed a rather strange atmosphere during the walk from the gates to the Main Building. Over recent years, the city of Cambridge and the university had become very familiar territory; he felt at ease there, maybe more so than around Newmarket and the nearby village where his family home was. Sitting, waiting, he had a rather disturbing thought that he may end up in this strange and somewhat mysterious place. At that point, he was suddenly shaken from his thoughts by a nearby voice.

"Is this where I should wait to see Mr Alexander?"

Bill looked up. The enquirer was a tall chap, square jawed and with a shock of brown hair, possibly a few years older than himself.

"Err, yes," said Bill, "I believe so."

The tall chap introduced himself. "Leslie Yoxall. Are we here for the same job, whatever it is? Do you have any idea? I was told virtually nothing!"

"Bill Tutte," said Bill standing up and shaking Leslie Yoxall's proffered hand. "Me neither. I guess we'll find out soon enough."

The two chatted, although the conversation was mostly one-sided. They were surprised to find they had a great deal in common. Leslie too had been at Cambridge, graduated in mathematics and was waiting for his doctorate award. Currently, he was teaching at Manchester Grammar School, where he had been contacted by his old tutor about some possible war work.

Shortly, a nearby door opened and a man called from the doorway, "Mr Yoxall?" Leslie stood up. "Come along in." Leslie followed the man into the room.

"Mr Alexander, I assume," Bill said to himself.

It was a long 25 minutes before Leslie reappeared. "In you go," he said with a shrug of the shoulders which seemed to imply he still had no idea what this was all about.

"Come in and make yourself comfortable," the man in the room said. "I'm Hugh Alexander, glad you could make it." The handshake was welcoming.

To people who met Bill for the first time, he often appeared abstracted. Not so on this occasion. Hugh Alexander caught Bill's attention immediately with his intelligent face and piercing blue eyes. He was not very much older than Bill, in his early 30s maybe, had smoothed-down dark hair with a high parting. Bill thought he detected a slight Irish lilt. He was not in uniform which pleased Bill, not even wearing a suit, just a sports jacket, flannel trousers and a slightly crumpled shirt and tie.

"Now, let's just check." Hugh Alexander consulted the file on his desk. "William Tutte, age 23. At Trinity, currently studying for a maths doctorate. Excellent, I took maths at Cambridge too, entered 1928. Interested in chess, are we?"

The interview proceeded in a surprisingly friendly manner with some very insightful questions about Bill's interest in mathematics and current area of research, during which Bill took the opportunity to present his co-authored paper. But when it came to Bill's turn for questions, Hugh Alexander gave very little away, saying he was unable to say more without Bill signing the Official Secrets Act. Yes, it was vital war work; it would certainly be interesting work for someone of his talents; it did carry a Foreign Office salary; it would be based here at Bletchley Park. He was really sorry but he could not say any more. Bill would hear in due course if he was needed but meanwhile, would he please wait outside for a short while. Again, he was politely warned to say nothing of his visit and interview.

Back in the corridor, Bill was surprised to find Leslie still there. They compared notes but neither learned anything new. While they were patiently waiting, Leslie caught a snatch of a conversation between Hugh Alexander and an assistant to the effect they should be interviewed by another person who was 'head of the hut', and whispered as such to Bill. Sure enough, the assistant came to advise them they would be driven to see a Mr Turing for a second interview, giving Leslie a sealed envelope to be given to the driver marked for Mr Turing, 'Private and Confidential'.

On their way out of the Park, Leslie Yoxall asked the driver what happened there.

"You coming to work 'ere, sir?" retorted the uniformed driver in a heavy East End accent. "If so, you'll pretty quickly learn you don't ask such questions, not even to nobody. Me? I keeps me mouth shut." Leslie and Bill exchanged sardonic looks and they drove on in silence until the driver pulled into the forecourt of The Crown Inn in a nearby village. He disappeared inside with the letter, only to reappear obviously annoyed.

"You'll have to wait inside. He's gorne off on his bike, the… I've got to go fetch 'im; if I can find 'im."

Not long afterwards, a somewhat flustered, dark-haired young man, not much older than Bill, came in, rather dishevelled, no coat despite the cold, his sleeves rolled up and his trousers still tucked in his socks. He came over to Bill and Leslie who politely stood up.

"Alan Turing. Sorry you've had to come over here." Bill and Leslie introduced themselves. "Let's see what this is about." He opened the letter and quickly read it. "Ah, yes," he said appearing a little awkward at the situation, adding, "Mr Tutte, perhaps you'd be kind enough to wait in the other bar, if you don't mind."

A little later, during his interview with Alan Turing, Bill was pleased to discover his interviewer was yet another Cambridge mathematician. The interview was fairly brief. After checking Bill's background in mathematics, Alan Turing explained he was really looking for someone who could turn theory into practice, implying that he saw Bill as a theoretician only. At that point, Bill began to sense he was not what this 'head of the hut' was looking for. Nevertheless, Alan Turing showed great interest in and appeared very impressed with his paper, *The Dissection of Rectangles into Squares*.

Hugh Alexander's note to Alan Turing had said that while there was little to choose between the two candidates, he recommended Yoxall was the more suitable for Turing's team and that Tutte could prove valuable to the proposed Research Section and should also be taken on. Alan Turing scribbled on the back, 'Agreed. Take on both—Yoxall to my team'. The driver took the resealed note and headed back, dropping Bill and Leslie off at the station forecourt.

On the platform, they bid farewell, Leslie saying, "Well, that last bit was pretty weird. Never had an interview in a Lounge Bar before! In fact, the whole affair has been somewhat bizarre."

"I wonder what Mr Turing keeps in his hut. His bike perhaps?" quipped Bill dryly, picking up on Leslie's somewhat comical view of events.

Underneath, though, Bill's mood was far less cheerful. If the job really was more practical than theoretical then maybe it was not for him. He was certain the confident and more experienced Leslie Yoxall would be offered the position.

There was an envelope in his pigeon hole, clearly not the usual letter from his mother. It was a large brown envelope, his name and address typewritten reminiscent of the letter inviting him to the interview at that rather odd place, Bletchley Park.

Bill's immediate reaction was that it contained a rejection because that is what he had been expecting; he had written off the idea he would receive an offer, almost forgotten about it. But as he took the letter from the pigeon hole, he became curious as the size and thickness belied a simple notification that he had been unsuccessful. He took it to his room with a mixture of apprehension and expectancy. The letter was from the same Foreign Office address but the content was not what he had expected at all.

First, he was requested to attend a course, the nature of which could only be disclosed on joining once he had signed the Official Secrets Acts 1911–1939 Declaration. On satisfactory completion of the course, he would be appointed to the position of Temporary Junior Assistant Officer at a salary of £350 per annum on a placement for important war work which would be advised to him at the end of the course. The letter further advised him this position would be in lieu of National Service. He should confirm his attendance by immediately signing and returning the enclosed form together with the personal details sheet duly completed. Now totally absorbed, he quickly scanned all the enclosures. He discovered he should report to an address in Broadway, London, SW1 on Monday 17 February to register for the course which would commence the following day.

Bill sat back in his chair. "I did get the job!" he said to himself, tickled pink and feeling quite smug, a rather unusual sensation for him as he rarely let his emotions surface to that extent.

His heart was beating faster as he read the main letter for a second time to ensure he had taken it all in. Whilst on first reading it appeared to be an offer letter, on second reading, the wording gave the distinct impression he was required to accept, although it was silent on the consequences of non-acceptance.

Once the warm glow of success subsided, reality set in. He was, unexpectedly, faced with a major decision. Having dismissed the possibility of being offered the job following the recent interviews at Bletchley Park, particularly the interview with Mr Turing, he was now forced to re-engage with the arguments for and against. He had a bit more information now than he had gleaned from the original meeting with Professor Duff, but not much more and certainly not enough on which to base an informed decision. He sat in contemplation for a short while.

Logically, his head was saying, on balance, he should go. Whilst the job title gave nothing further away and the salary was, well, modest, Bill felt he would be in highly regarded company, people whose participation surely validated the importance of the work. That the position was in substitution for National Service was a most significant piece of new information. If he had to leave the university at some point, now was probably as good as any since he had only just started seriously researching his graph theory ideas and he had been promised his position would be kept open.

His heart, though, was heavy. He just wanted the whole thing to go away. He just wanted to be able to carry on with his doctorate undisturbed. But it appeared he was caught in a cleft stick; accept this 'offer' or risk National Service.

Deep down, he had always known that mathematics was his field but for the last seven or eight years, he had been persuaded that science was the way to go. At last, he had broken out and was pursuing his true vocation. The thought of having to defer his doctorate weighed most heavily on his mind. Also, it seemed he was required to complete a course of unknown nature for an unknown placement of unknown duration, probably at that rather odd place Bletchley Park, unable to judge for himself his suitability or otherwise. It would be a huge wrench to leave the ambience of Trinity and the elegance of Cambridge not knowing when or even whether he would return. Heading into that unknown was very troubling.

In the end, two considerations tipped the scales. Primarily, he could not face National Service, could not risk that outcome. The other consideration was more positive. That there was the circle of alumni from Cambridge and probably from other universities too who were there already was significant. Very, very reluctantly, he would accept.

He went to see Professor Duff to advise him of developments. The professor was sure he was doing the right thing, a sentiment touched with some genuine regret at his leaving. A letter would be prepared confirming his position would be kept open and a copy kept on his file. It was agreed he stay on until the course commenced. Then, with no little trepidation at the venture upon which he was about to embark, he filled in all the forms requested and posted them off. Lastly, he wrote to his parents saying he would be home shortly for a few days but divulging nothing else.

There was an underlying tension throughout Bill's visit home, overlaid with the gloom of winter and of war. It was no surprise his parents were taken aback at his unexpected and dramatic news. He told them as much as he could of the little he knew, their misgivings only compounded by his vagueness. His mother was apprehensive about his going to London with all the bombing. His father questioned whether he was doing the right thing; concerned that Bill may never return to Cambridge to complete his studies. And his brother, who came over one evening after work, was again critical that Bill would still be a civilian, still not in uniform. But it was his mother who fretted most. Stories were rife of the devastation wrought by the almost nightly bombing raids over London. After they had all retired to bed, Mrs Tutte confided her further, unsaid concerns to her husband.

Since Bill was small, his parents had been very protective of him. They had worried he did not make friends, that he was noticeably withdrawn, preoccupied and solitary, that later, he was teased and taunted because he did not fit in. He became upset if his routine was disrupted. Change unsettled him. His junior school headmaster was well aware of the situation, kept a pastoral eye out and tried to reassure his parents this behaviour was not unusual in someone so academically gifted. They worried more when he went to the County High School for Boys in Cambridge not only because of the distance but also because there was inevitably less pastoral care. But once settled at Trinity, they became far less concerned for his welfare. University life obviously suited him. He could be 'a little odd' without standing out and they grew immensely proud of his achievements. He had made some very good friends. They liked the slightly eccentric Cedric who had visited them a number of times, although they were rather in awe of their son's very clever friend. His mother's worry now was that he might not cope well with this sudden change to his settled routine and surroundings. Mr Tutte shared her concerns but felt they could not interfere, only encourage and support Bill, and urge him to keep regularly in touch.

Notwithstanding these worries, it was Bill's mother who managed to arrange some lodgings for him in west London. He was required to organise his own accommodation for the course and had asked around at the college, even posted a wanted note on the college notice board, all to no avail.

"I'll go and see Mary Mitchell," said his mother. "Her husband works for the General Post Office and has to go to London a lot to mend telephone lines. He stays with a landlady in South Ealing." She paused briefly, and then conspiratorially said, "Mary has a telephone in the house, you know." Few ordinary households in the village of Cheveley had a telephone installed in their home and Bill's mother laid emphasis on the fact that the Mitchells were amongst this important and privileged group. Mrs Mitchell came around the next morning to say her husband had had a word with his landlady and she had a room free.

"The landlady told Mary you will be very comfortable there and that I shouldn't worry as South Ealing was far safer than the East End," said his mother adding, "At least I'll know where you're staying."

To everyone's great relief, it was all arranged but Bill knew his mother would worry nevertheless.

The Friday afternoon of his visit, he walked the two miles or so into Newmarket to his brother's house. A raw east wind was blowing off the North Sea across the flat Suffolk landscape but he was glad to have a little solitude. At his sister-in-law's suggestion, he walked down to the school gate to surprise his niece and nephew when they came out after lessons. Young Joey's greeting was somewhat cool. He had overheard a number of times his father's undisguised disapproval that Uncle Bill had not joined the military. But his mood changed rather when his Uncle Bill had a shilling for each of them. In contrast, his younger sister, Jeanne who was just nine years old, went wild with excitement at seeing her uncle whom she adored. She chattered relentlessly all the way home and she and Bill played snakes and ladders on the floor by the fire while sister-in-law, Lola, made some tea. Lola was not anti-Bill like her husband. She recognised how lovely an uncle he was to her children, and now, as she looked down at the domestic scene, she smiled with contentment.

"Must you go?" Jeanne pleaded with him when he said he had to get back.

"Afraid so," said Bill, not saying he really wanted to leave before his brother got home from work to avoid further tension.

"Aw!" moaned Jeanne.

"I bet you'll have a boyfriend by the time I come home again, perhaps even married!" he teased.

Sunday evening, Bill joined his parents around the radio to hear Winston Churchill address the nation. They listened intently. The Prime Minister's message was of hope without denying the very great dangers that lay ahead. Since the dark days of last summer and autumn, the country had prospered in several directions, he said, recounting successes in the Middle East and North Africa and saying how our forces had grown stronger. He praised the steadfast folk of London and the other big cities that had taken a pounding during the dark winter months, saying their plight would ease as the back of the winter had been broken and daylight hours were growing. But he would not encourage false hopes, warning the threat of invasion had not gone away and there was grave danger to our shipping in the Atlantic. He did, however, hold out the certainty of aid from the USA.

Even after nearly 40 minutes, they were still hanging on Churchill's every word as he began his conclusion.

"The other day, President Roosevelt gave his opponent in the late Presidential Election a letter of introduction to me, and in it, he wrote out a verse, in his own handwriting, from Longfellow, which he said, 'applies to you people as it does to us'. Here is the verse."

He quoted:
"…Sail on, O Ship of State!
Sail on, O Union, strong and great!
Humanity with all its fears,
With all the hopes of future years,
Is hanging breathless on thy fate!

"What is the answer that I shall give, in your name, to this great man, the thrice-chosen head of a nation of a hundred and thirty millions? Here is the answer which I will give to President Roosevelt: Put your confidence in us. Give us your faith and your blessing, and, under Providence, all will be well.

"We shall not fail or falter; we shall not weaken or tire. Neither the sudden shock of battle, nor the long-drawn trials of vigilance and exertion will wear us down. Give us the tools, and we will finish the job."

Bill's father leaned forward and switched off the radio.

"Well!" exclaimed his mother. "That's the grandest speech he's made." Her face was almost radiant as she sat back in her chair.

"Splendid," agreed his father in his quiet manner.

Bill too was caught up in the mood and had been particularly struck by Churchill's oratory. He had not listened to one of his speeches before, only read or heard about them; but actually hearing him talk was riveting and stirring. Like his parents, he was lifted by the whole broadcast, although he did not express himself so openly.

The following morning, as Bill prepared to leave, his mother seemed unusually quiet. His father, who had had already left for work, had genuinely wished his son well with his war work and told him to take care. But now, when it came to say goodbye to his mother, he could see how worried she was and sought to reassure her.

"Don't worry. I'll be fine. I'll write as soon as I know more. I'm sure Mr Mitchell will look out for me. Look, here is £10. I have an allowance and soon, a salary so I don't need this. Make sure you and Dad keep warm. And see if you can get Dad to take it easier; he looks tired these days. Can't he get someone else to do some of the heavier work?"

His mother initially refused the money, saying it was far too much but Bill insisted. He had deliberately not offered it to his father who he knew would be too proud to take it. His parents had never been in a position to help him financially through his studies but Bill's frugal upbringing meant he had fared well enough on grants and scholarships. He just wanted his parents to be a little more comfortable this winter and pressed his mother to accept. Reluctantly, she tucked the notes into her pinafore.

"Don't forget to write," she ordered after giving him a farewell hug. He told her to stay indoors but she insisted on coming to the garden gate where she waited till he had walked past the church to the end of the lane. He stopped and gave a brief wave before turning into the High Street. Normally, visits home were pleasant interludes. This one he had anticipated would be somewhat fraught. He was right and rather relieved it was over.

Chapter 2
The Course

The imposing modern building across the road must be the one, thought Bill. He had taken the train from Cambridge to London, Liverpool Street Station and the underground to St James's Park. It was sobering to see, from the carriage window, the increasing bomb damage as the train neared central London. The directions he had received read, 'At St James's Park Underground Station take the 55 Broadway exit and enter 54 Broadway opposite by the door with the Minimax Fire Extinguisher Company brass plate by it. Take the stairs to the 3rd Floor and report to reception.' The uninterested receptionist on the 3rd Floor directed him to the next floor and said to wait outside Room 405.

He took a seat in the corridor outside Room 405 and set down his small suitcase. He had had to steel himself several times to get this far. More than once, he had become so worked-up that he almost turned around. He had never done anything like this on his own before. And this place unnerved him even further. There was no one about and nothing to indicate occupation by the Foreign Office or any other organisation apart from the fire extinguisher company of which there was no other sign than the brass plate. He had obediently followed instructions not to tell anyone where in London he was going that day; similarly, he had kept silent about the events leading up to today. At long last, though, he was to find out what this was all about but sitting there waiting, he felt like Daniel about to enter the lions' den and hoped someone was looking over him.

The appointment was for two o'clock and as usual he was early. To help calm his nerves while he waited, he re-read his instructions to make sure he had missed nothing. Of course, he had not. Just one person walked down the corridor past him and disappeared through a non-descript doorway without saying anything. He tried to take comfort that at least there was someone else in the building. At two o'clock, the door of Room 405 opened.

"William Tutte?" enquired the smartly suited man, his dark hair slicked down. As Bill rose, the man added politely, "Do come in." Bill followed him into the modest, almost bare office with a single file on the desk.

"Let me take your coat. Sit yourself down. This won't take long," said the man opening the file. "We just need to register you for this course. A few details to check first, if you please." He opened the file. "First then, full name please?"

"William Thomas Tutte."

"Date of birth?"

"17 May 1917."

"Age 23 then. Home address?"

"45 Church Lane, Cheveley, Newmarket, Suffolk."

"Father's name and mother's maiden name?"

"William John Tutte. Mother's maiden name Newell."

"Current position or military rank and unit?"

"PhD student, Trinity College, Cambridge."

"Good. Now, before we go any further," he paused and looked Bill in the eye, "have you told anyone you were coming here?"

"No," said Bill firmly.

"Excellent! Now, you need to sign the Official Secrets Act Declaration. You were advised this was a requirement, were you not." He passed over a piece of official looking paper and a pen. "Read it all and ask any questions."

Bill read it and signed it. Again, the man looked Bill in the eye as he tapped a finger on the signed declaration.

"I can't emphasise too much that you must keep secret everything from now on, and I mean everything. Jail awaits those who defy the declaration you have just signed. So, no hints or clues to anyone, not to your closest friends, your family, girlfriend or the man in the pub who buys you ten pints and who may not be what he seems. This is serious. There is a war on and walls have ears. Understood!"

"I understand," answered Bill, anxious to get to the nub of why he was here.

"Right, now that's out of the way, we can concentrate on why we wanted you to come along. Oh by the way, have you arranged accommodation?"

Bill passed over a note with the name and address of where he was staying in South Ealing.

"Excellent! Right. Now then. You are about to join a cryptography course, learning how to break the enemy's military and diplomatic codes and ciphers. How long the course lasts will depend to some degree on each student's ability. As you can imagine, there is a lot to cover. Towards the end of the course, there will be an assessment to decide where best to place you."

"So, this is what it has all been about," Bill said to himself. Now, he understood why he had been chosen for this work; it sounded right up his street. He palpably relaxed.

"You seem pleased?" said the man.

"I think so," Bill replied. "I've wondered what I was being put in for. It sounds jolly interesting." He thought it politic to sound enthusiastic. And it crossed his mind that this was probably what they did at that Bletchley Park place.

"Splendid! That's the spirit. The course itself is being held round the corner at the St Ermin's Hotel in Caxton Street. We hire a few rooms there. You'll meet your tutor and the other students shortly and the course proper will commence tomorrow. Your tutor will outline the course content. You'll be given an allowance to cover travel and accommodation while you are on the course." He paused. "You have been especially selected for this vital war work. Intelligence of the enemy's plans and intentions saves lives. People might comment you are not in uniform. Don't be worried or get drawn into justifying your situation. The need for secrecy totally overrides any concerns others might have. Do you have any questions?"

"I can't think of any at the moment," said Bill.

"Ask your tutor if you do," said the man standing up and offering a hand. "The receptionist will tell you where to go. Good luck."

Bill could hardly believe what was happening to him as he walked across the courtyard of St Ermin's Hotel, an extraordinarily ornate red-brick building. 54 Broadway had a weird feeling about it. And now, he faced this surprising, imposing building that looked more like a Victorian mansion block than a hotel. On visits to London with Cedric and the others, his curiosity had often been aroused discovering historic and delightful hidden-away buildings and here was another. He was directed to Room 210 and knocked on the door which was opened by a stocky man in civilian dress who introduced himself as Lieutenant John Cheadle. He invited Bill to put his coat and suitcase in an anteroom before showing him to one of the vacant desks in the main room. There were 16 desks in all, set out as though for a school examination. Ten faces looked up to greet this latest student.

Two more students joined them during the afternoon which was taken up by yet more administrative matters. They were all reminded to be prompt the following morning when the course proper would begin. Later, Bill took the underground to Northfields on the Piccadilly Line, the underground station after South Ealing, and walked the short distance to his digs. His mind was so full with the day's events, he hardly noticed the people on the underground and in the streets all wrapped up, heads bowed against the cold and the grinding oppression of war. He was pleased, however, to find his landlady, Mrs Briggs, very welcoming and his room comfortable with facilities much superior to his rooms at Trinity. After supper, he excused himself saying he wanted to sort his things out. Sorting out his things only took him a few minutes and he then sat for a while reflecting on the day.

Cryptography! Codes and ciphers! What is the difference between a code and a cipher? Is it about letters or numbers? What languages? He was not a linguist but he had quite enjoyed French at school and had a smattering of Latin and German. It did sound intriguing though and hopefully, he would be able to bring mathematics to bear somewhere along the line. Tomorrow should be really interesting.

There was an electric meter in his room. He put a shilling in and turned on the one-bar electric fire before settling down to read a book.

"Good morning, gentlemen," Lieutenant Cheadle addressed the room. "This morning will be taken up with a brief introduction to codes and ciphers. I will then give an outline of the course and its content. First, though, it may be helpful for each of us to give a short introduction. I'm John Cheadle, Army Intelligence and I was brought in by Colonel Tiltman of the Government Code and Cipher School to deliver this course. It's a new course as there is an urgent need for more cryptographers. Despite the apparent military involvement, the course is for the Government Code and Cipher School which comes under the Foreign Office, hence civilian dress is in order. The Government Code and Cipher School has, of course, very close ties with the military."

Bill learned the majority of the other students were from intelligence units of the three main services. The remainder were, like him, from a university background.

Most of the morning was taken up with Lieutenant Cheadle's overview. Bill listened with interest. He learned codes and ciphers went back to Roman times; Caesar himself used them apparently. Essentially, Lieutenant Cheadle explained, codes are the replacement of words, numbers and symbols with a word, number or other symbol, often from a secret code book. He gave the example of Nelson's famous signal at the Battle of Trafalgar. The code number for the first word of the message, 'England', was, he said, 253. So, the first set of three flags raised was for the numbers two, five and three; 'Expects', he said, was code number 269 and so on. Alternatively, he explained, a cipher is the replacement of a unit of language, a letter or symbol, by another unit of the language. A cipher uses a secret set of rules either by substitution or by transposition; so using the 'England Expects' example again he said, the 'E' of 'England' could be replaced by say the letter 'T', the second letter 'N' by say the letter 'B', and so on according to a secret relationship or key.

Lieutenant Cheadle introduced a few notable figures to the group; Vigenère—whose name was given to a very early cipher; Kasiski—who, 300 years later, devised an attack on the Vigenère cipher; and the legendary American codebreaker, William F Friedman—who developed, about 20 years ago, the mathematically based technique called *The Index of Coincidence*.

The Lieutenant also spent some time describing some of the attributes of a code or cipher, some of the trade-offs between security and ease of use, between a system used for tactical, short-term battlefield orders and the need for a more secure system for strategic, high grade material.

Bill was intrigued by the next piece in the Lieutenant's introduction. He talked about how modern warfare, conducted over ever greater distances, had led to the growing use of telegraph and radio waves for transmitting secret messages. Because such transmissions could be intercepted or picked up by someone other than the intended recipient, more and more sophisticated codes and ciphers were needed. And ever since codes and ciphers were invented, Lieutenant Cheadle explained, there have been those bent on breaking them, discovering their secrets.

"And now that includes you," he concluded.

A short discussion ensued. One of the students had quite a lot to say for himself but Bill preferred to listen rather than to take part.

"Now to the course itself," said the Lieutenant moving on.

He outlined there would be sections on Substitution, Simple Transposition and Double Transposition, Playfair, Complex Substitution and some work on Machine ciphers.

"You will work largely on your own from explanatory texts and a variety of exercises based mostly on experience gained in The Great War. We have a few copies of this," he said holding up a book entitled, *'The American Black Chamber'*. *How very odd*, thought Bill intent in getting his hands on a copy. "You can use it as a textbook cum reference book, but please don't hog it, though, as we haven't enough copies for everyone. Some of you will, undoubtedly, work at a faster pace than others. But speed is not important— thorough understanding is. I will be around to help when needed, so don't hesitate to ask me. Some of you will go on to do a short additional language section." He paused to make sure he had everyone's attention.

"Here, I have to set out a very important and invariable rule. You must not take any papers, books, notes or anything else out of this room or to discuss anything about the course outside this room, not even in this hotel, not back at your unit or accommodation, nor the pub round the corner. The Official Secret Act applies to everything here. I hope I make myself clear."

"What can we say when people ask what we do?" chirped a voice at the back.

"Those who are good liars say they work at a weather station," said the Lieutenant in all seriousness. "Those who are poor liars say they just work for the Foreign Office. But those poor liars among you, you must not say anything more than that. Absolutely no clues whatsoever," he emphasised. "Oh, and by the way, please be sparing in your use of paper, it's always in short supply."

Bill and the other students began the course, reading the explanatory notes and attempting the first exercises which introduced them to the important and powerful technique of frequency counts of letters in the code or cipher that can give a strong indication to the letters of the underlying message, the clear text. The notes also pointed out that frequency counts can indicate the language of the underlying message too. Bill learned that simple substitution could come in numerous forms including the use of numbers representing a letter or a short word. One early exercise Bill attacked was a string of 135 numbers divided into 27 groups of five with the clue that the first word was 'possession'. The two 'ss' bigrams in 'possession' gave him entry into the 'unit of substitution' which turned out to be groups of three numbers. To his quiet satisfaction, he eventually worked out the full message, 'Possession is usually nine points of the law', where the number group '000' represented the space between words.

The notes for this exercise explained the clue word 'possession' was called a 'crib', a word known or expected to be found in the plain text. Considerable significance was attributed to cribs as an important tool of cryptography. The notes described how a crib could be guessed from the source and the possible content of the message and from experience of previously deciphered messages.

There was something at the back of his mind that told him he had come across ciphers before. Eventually, it came to him. There was a favourite book he regularly borrowed from the school library called *Mathematical Recreations and Essays*. He recalled it had a chapter on ciphers to which he had not paid much attention. At that time, he was far more interested in other topics in the book, having a particular fascination for prime numbers. In the end, he could not now remember anything useful from the chapter about ciphers.

At the end of the first week, Lieutenant Cheadle introduced an important visitor, Colonel Tiltman who, the group was told, was Head of the Military Section of the Government Code and Cipher School and who had devised the course. The Colonel was a tall, distinguished looking man who spoke quietly in an engaging manner. He had a military bearing but was not in uniform. He gave a short speech of encouragement saying he had set up this basic cryptography course to introduce recruits to the fundamentals of the trade. At one point, he referred to *The American Dark Chamber* written, he said, by an American cryptographer called Yardley who described in it his experiences dealing with codes and ciphers in the Department of State.

"Read it, it's good," he said, adding enigmatically, "but it should never have been written!"

He concluded by saying he did not believe that training could go beyond enhancing skills that had to be innately present. All training could do was stimulate intelligence and imagination. In his view, cryptanalysts were born, not made.

"Work hard and good luck," he ended.

As soon as the Colonel had left, a somewhat awestruck Lieutenant Cheadle turned to the group and said almost reverentially, "Colonel Tiltman is probably the greatest cryptographer Britain has ever produced!"

At the weekend, Bill wrote a couple of letters, the first to his parents to reassure them all was well and that he was very comfortable, indeed, at Mrs Briggs's digs. He could not say much else as he had signed the Official Secrets Act; all he could say was that he was, thankfully, not in the military and that he was doing something for the Foreign Office that should prove interesting. He knew how his mother worried and hoped the letter would allay her concerns; his father would just be quietly impressed by the reference to the Foreign Office.

The other letter was to Cedric. Before Bill left Trinity, he and his mathematician friend had made a pact to write regularly. Cedric had pressed him to say what this 'war work' was, saying there were romantic notions going around that some of the others who had left were involved in spying and secret messages. The letter was to let Cedric know he was fine, where he was staying and that he would go to prison if he told him anything of what he was doing. In the letter, he also told Cedric, tongue in cheek, it was against the law even to ask him about his 'new job' and in any case, it was nothing quixotic.

One evening, Bill asked his landlady if there was a library nearby; he had nearly finished the only book he had room to bring with him.

"There's a public library at the top of Ealing Green, in the Pitzhanger Manor House. The library there has just been rebuilt," she said with a touch of local pride. "You'll need to catch the bus; but there are a couple of subscription libraries along Northfield Avenue and one on the South Ealing Road you could walk to."

The following Saturday, a half day, Bill found a letter for him on the hall table when he arrived back. He recognised Cedric's handwriting. The letter's content was typical Cedric joshing. He wrote that Bill was mistaken, there was no law preventing him asking as often as he liked whether Bill was taking pretty German spies around the night clubs of London, spiking their drinks and getting their invasion plans. Cedric's letter also had some college news and recounted his efforts to find some decent maths books at the local bookshops. Moreover, he thought they should sort out some money matters between them. Bill owed him 1/6d on this term's account plus some more for inks and other things. He hadn't forgotten he owed Bill ten shillings for a book. He would let Bill know the net sum when he had more time. He ended by relating amusing events surrounding a chaotic fire alert one night and hoped Bill was having quiet nights in Ealing. Bill was surprised how much the letter cheered him up. Later, he caught the bus to Ealing Green and was pleased to find two Sherlock Holmes mysteries on the library shelves. He was glad to have some good reading to help pass the long dark, black-out nights.

Whilst he could not take any coursework back to his digs, some days, he purposely memorised a problem to muse over in the evening. He avoided socialising with his course colleagues or with Mr Mitchell who often went out in the evening with his General Post Office engineer colleagues when they too stayed with Mrs Briggs. Early on, he had asked Bill to come out with them one evening but Bill declined. He had not asked again, mainly because his work colleagues thought Bill a bit odd. Rather, Bill preferred passing the time in his room reading, writing letters and making notes for his thesis. When the weather relented, he would go for a walk. At the evening meal, Mr Mitchell sometimes asked Bill if he had a message for his mother which he could pass on through his wife when they spoke on the telephone. The Mitchells were good like that.

One evening before supper, there was an urgent rapping on his bedroom door.

"Bill, Bill. Are you there? It's Mr Mitchell. I've some news from home."

Bill opened the door and invited Mr Mitchell in. He seemed unusually agitated.

"I spoke on the telephone to my wife before I left work," he said breathlessly. "She told me there had been a dreadful air raid in the middle of Newmarket, on market day. It seems a lone raider decided to have a go at the town for some reason, in broad daylight can you believe, machine gunning the High Street and dropping loads of bombs."

"Newmarket?" said Bill astounded that the town should be attacked when there were plenty of obvious military targets in the area.

"There were loads of people killed, my wife said, and hundreds injured. Lots of shops have been destroyed; the Post Office, Boots, Gilberts the Ironmongers, even the Memorial Hall and the cinema next door. It's terrible she says. And there's more. Your mother told my wife that the people from Elms Farm, where your father works, were caught up in it. Mrs Taylor is lucky to be alive, your mother says. Mr Taylor was in the bank when one bomb exploded not far from where Mrs Taylor was waiting in their car. The car was badly damaged by shrapnel which luckily missed Mrs Taylor but she suffered from lots of flying glass. It's terrible. Everyone's in shock and the High Street is cordoned off until they can make it safe. Would you believe it—in Newmarket! Bastards!"

"How dreadful," said Bill. "Poor Mrs Taylor. I hope she will be all right. They have been so good to Dad. Thank you for telling me."

"I said I'd let you know. Anyway, your mother says you are to take great care and heed the air raid warnings. I'll find out more when I go home at the weekend. Are you coming down for supper?"

"I'll be down in a moment. I'd better write home tonight."

By the middle of the following week, Bill had settled into the course, the nature of which suited him ideally being able to progress at his own pace. He always worked slowly and methodically and he soon recognised that the smallest mistake could ruin the deciphering process, leading to a great deal of reworking. He hated wasting time. Not all the students seemed to be progressing so well. There were two in particular that Bill noticed. One was often sighing and scratching his head, furiously rubbing something out or scrunching up his working papers in frustration. The other one was the one who had a lot to say for himself on the first day. He was quite dissentious, arguing with Lieutenant Cheadle that his own methods were much better. Both were obviously some way behind where Bill had reached and he was unsurprised when both of them did not reappear after the third week of the course. They were replaced by two Oxford University linguists.

Another letter from Cedric arrived, this time written in red ink enclosing some reprints of their published paper on rectangles. The main news was that he had been to visit Leonard and his family in Hull. The visit had been interrupted by an air raid which Cedric described in typical fashion as being lively enough and more fun than the dismal alerts at Cambridge. On the train coming home, he said that passengers from further north had the most appalling stories to tell of the snow with no trains running for three days. That night, Cedric wrote, just when he needed a good night's sleep, the Germans thought otherwise dropping flares and high explosive bombs all around. Bill thought it a good thing he was familiar with Cedric's quirky, amusing style otherwise he could easily be misunderstood.

In London, the war certainly intruded much more than in Cambridge. Often the sirens would sound soon after it became dark and regularly, the rumble and dull thud of bombs and anti-aircraft guns could be heard over to the east. Some nights, the all-clear was sounded quite quickly as the German bombers headed north or west sparing London for once. It was easy to become a bit complacent that West London was not a target. That illusion was shattered one night when a surprise attack came very close and Bill and Mr Mitchell dived under a table when they heard the whistle of falling bombs.

"Not much protection from a direct hit," said Mr Mitchell stating the obvious as they crouched fearfully under the protection of the table. "But a near miss could bring down the ceiling!"

They stayed there trembling until the all-clear sounded. Mrs Briggs appeared from under the stairs still shaking. That bomb landed harmlessly on some nearby waste ground but the experience shook Bill up and afterwards made him more nervous each time the sirens went off. He was thankful, at least, there were no daytime bombardments over London at that time, the Luftwaffe bombers preferring the cover of night.

Since everyone on the course worked more or less on their own, the dynamics of the group only became obvious during breaks. Those in the military formed one grouping and within that group, each service tended towards their own sub-group. Almost exclusively, their chatter and banter was about the war and the military. Bill attached himself to the smaller sub-group of academics but only peripherally. In contrast, this group talked of universities and academia. There was a Trinity undergraduate called Stephen Freer who was reading Classics. To Bill, Stephen was the epitome of a Classics student. He was tall and gangly with a shock of brown hair, a high forehead, dark round spectacles and a strikingly intelligent face. In character, he was not unlike Bill himself which is why the two got on together. The newest students were Bernard Willson who was very friendly and Colin Thompson who had already served 14 months in the army.

The course exercises became more complex and difficult. Bill was particularly pleased to decipher one with a long string of 280 numbers. Some analysis was already set out which showed the 'unit of substitution' this time was a number pair, so the message had 140 letters. This analysis also showed the pairs of numbers in the range 01 to 44. Further given analysis indicated the method of encipherment was probably on a period of seven leading Bill to write out the first seven pairs in a row, then the next seven pairs in a second row underneath and so on, 20 rows in all. A frequency analysis of each column was inconclusive because there were only 20 units, too few to give any indication of the underlying letters. Further analysis was, therefore, required. This time, the exercise called for a 'rebasing' of the columns, sliding each column back to a common base. Bill calculated he needed to re-write column one after sliding it back two places, in effect deducting two from each number, similarly for column two by deducting 20, column three by deducting 18, column four by 19, column five needed no adjustment, column six needed a deduction of 17 and column seven by deducting three. Bill now had each number representing its normal place in the alphabet, 01 representing A and 02 representing B, and so on to 26 representing Z. He then wrote out the seven columns replacing the resulting numbers by the letters they represented. Column one started T, P, E, N; column two started H, E, C, S; column three, E, R, A, T. Once that had been completed, he was able to read across the first row which began THE. It took him a little while to make out the clear text but eventually, he could see it read to his amusement:

THE SKIPPER OF THE CALIBAN
STOOD WHISTLING FOR A BREEZE
AND OH HE WAS AN UGLY MAN
AND BANDY AT THE KNEES
AND THE HAIR THAT OVER HIS SHOULDERS RAN
WAS RED AS GLOUCESTER CHEESE

Bill caught Lieutenant Cheadle's eye and pointed out his result.
"A children's poem about a pirate," he said with a wry smile. "What you have just done is actually based on Kasiski's work. You seem to be getting the hang of things, Bill. I suggest you move on to the next section, Simple Transposition."
Bill did not enjoy transposition much because it appeared to require a greater degree of language skills than of logic. Because the letters of the message were not changed, just jumbled up in a pre-ordained way, it needed a bent for anagrams to unlock the clear text. He got the basics but was relieved to move on to the next section of the course, intriguingly called Playfair.
The Playfair cipher, Bill learned, was a classical English method devised in the latter half of the 19th Century and named after Lord Playfair. It was principally used in The Great War for tactical secret messages in combat. By the time it would take an enemy to break the cipher, the information it contained would no longer be of use to them. Bill quite liked Playfair. It was based on a square of 25 letters of the alphabet omitting the seldom-used letter 'J' and using a memorable keyword. Bill found that there was a set of rules for setting up the square and for enciphering pairs of letters. It reminded him rather of the rules of chess, the different moves each piece could make. He cracked one exercise of a long section of ciphertext into a lyrical piece of prose that was unfamiliar to him and which began:

THE VOICES BLEND AND FUSE IN CLOUDED SILENCE

He passed it over to Stephen Freer who took one look and said, "Ulysses, James Joyce."

Bill worked diligently, if slowly but his ready grasp of the various topics coupled with his very accurate workings meant he was actually making more progress than the other students. Working on his own, at his own tempo, paid dividends. As each solution appeared, he felt a real sense of satisfaction.

At lunch break, he would often read a chapter or two of *The American Black Chamber* and study some of the detailed decipherment examples. Bill found that the author took the reader through his thought processes in tackling the problem as well as setting out fully each step. It was an amusing and eye-opening read of espionage and spies, invisible ink and stolen code books. One chapter was about a dangerous German spy Pablo Waberski, real name Lather Witcke, who was arrested as he crossed the Mexican border into the USA in February 1918. Not only was it a fascinating real-life tale but it was also interesting because it included a complete cryptanalysis of what appeared to be a ciphertext of over 400 letters found hidden in Pablo Waberski's jacket sleeve. Unless the message could be revealed, the authorities would have had to release him as he was travelling on a Russian passport. The complicated transposition system which was used to encipher the message was broken by Yardley and his team leading to Pablo Waberski's conviction for spying.

But sometimes, Bill would go out for some fresh air during lunchtime. Occasionally, he walked across the road to Christ Church, a large 19th century church with a tall, elegant spire. It was cold inside but he did not mind. He would sit right at the back. He did not come to pray; it was a convenient place to disappear to if the weather was inclement, a haven to escape from the group.

His upbringing, both at home and at school, had been in the Church of England. And although from a young age, he had taken an interest in the Scriptures, as his education widened, he became sensitive to perceived contradictions between the Bible's teachings and other subjects like history where he learned the Greeks had many Gods and Goddesses. He struggled with the notion of the Kingdom of Heaven and in places, he even found the Scriptures quite boring. Later, he studied the Theory of Evolution and liked it. He recognised the incompatibilities between Darwin's theory and Genesis but did not come down on either side; he was receptive to both. But he kept any intellectual arguments to himself, disinclined to question his teachers. Yet, he maintained his interest in religion through into college, at one point taking a course of religious instruction there. But that course quite quickly crystallised his thinking about the tensions between science and the Bible. It was the science in him that prevailed as he found it hard to see the point of having faith in something that might not be true. And there, he let the matter rest.

For Bill, therefore, a visit to Christ Church was not for worship as it was for others. For him, it became a regular place of seclusion and welcome solitude.

The next part of the course was Complex Substitution and introduced the concept of additive ciphers where a key was added to the plain text to produce the ciphertext. Such ciphers were vulnerable to 'depths', that is where two or more messages are enciphered using the same key. Depths, the notes emphasised, were invaluable to the cryptanalyst. Additive ciphers often used a keyword coupled with a 26 times 26 square table of alphabet letters set out in a certain arrangement. This table was called a Vigenère cipher. Bill's eye lit up when he read part of the introductory text which stated, '…this sort of analysis may perhaps be best understood when treated algebraically'.

"This looks more up my street," he said to himself.

The addition of letters employed 'modulo 26', a mathematical notion of which Bill was aware. For the uninitiated, the note explained one would use modulo 12 to convert the 24-hour clock to the 12-hour clock, which for the afternoon time is the remainder after deducting 12 hours from the 24-hour clock, that is to say 14.00 hours becomes 2 o'clock in the afternoon. The usual techniques of frequency analysis, rebasing and setting out rows on a discovered period all applied.

Great emphasis was placed on setting out the ciphertext in rows. The length of a row was called the 'periodicity' and the process called 'in depth'—not to be confused with 'a depth', being two or more messages encoded with the same key. None of the exercises proved insoluble for Bill, even though the solutions got longer and required significant periods of intense concentration. Even so, Bill found that at times his mind would wander but the nature of the exercises meant he was easily able to re-engage with the problem where he left off.

One night, in the middle of April, brought the war closer to him than at any other time. The capital was suffering one of the most severe bombardments of the war so far. It went on for practically the whole night, mostly to the east but the nearby anti-aircraft guns were, from time to time, quite deafening. Bill got no sleep, expecting at any time to have to head for the local bomb shelter. His previous experience under the table had been alarming enough, but this was a long, long night of high anxiety with no let up. When the dawn came up, he looked out of his window to see a lurid glow over the capital against which the barrage balloons stood out clearly. It was with some trepidation, he headed to the course. Fortunately, the Piccadilly Line was somehow still operating. His fellow passengers were subdued. As he stepped out of St James's Park Underground Station, he could not avoid the activity further down Broadway. There were damaged buildings, fire engines, a tangle of hoses, firemen and air raid wardens working purposefully. As he drew nearer, the sanctuary of Christ Church came into view and what Bill saw made him stop. It was blackened, the roof gone and as he moved on to the corner of Caxton Street, the full extent of the damage became clear. He stood gazing in silence at the scene of utter devastation. The entire church roof had collapsed. Those walls that were still standing had had their windows shattered. It was obvious a fierce fire had raged and wisps of smoke still drifted up from the smouldering, burned-out shell. Acrid fumes permeated the air. The spire had somehow survived as had the rectory. Workmen were trying to clear the road blocked by debris and badly damaged vehicles including a fire engine with its ladders broken. Water spurted from a burst main. Small groups of people had gathered and Bill overheard talk of a shower of incendiary bombs falling in the early hours. Most were put out, he heard, but fire took hold in the roof and soon the church began to burn out of control. One man was telling the group that a fireman was killed and others injured when a bomb hit them as they tackled the fire. The scene was grim; the atmosphere sombre.

Bill had read of the blitz and seen the newsreels but he had never witnessed close up anything like this before. The sight, the smell and the noise were impossible to avoid. He stood staring for a short while. It was an unexpected, charged and confusing scene for him to take in, to work out how he should react. He did not approach anyone because he did not know what to say. It was clear, though, he would have to find another lunchtime haven.

The mood on the course was down. Everyone had a tale to tell of the night's ordeal. Everyone was moved by the tragedy right outside the hotel. That night Bill wrote a letter home to assure his parents he was safe but did not mention the destruction of Christ Church.

The April Bank Holiday was a welcome break. Bill went home on the Friday evening to be met with a barrage of questions from his mother, most of which he could not answer. He had felt obliged to visit them but had arranged to go on to Cambridge on the Sunday to meet Leonard and Cedric. Everything was just the same at home. His parents were well and the children came over to see their Uncle Bill. He was glad he had made the effort but was keen to see his mathematician friends.

It was amongst his close university friends that Bill was most content. He was almost a different Bill, animated and engaged especially when talking mathematics which they did endlessly. They batted complex theories around, discussed some of the topics Bill and Cedric had exchanged letters about, in particular linear vector functions and cubical networks, and proposed ideas for their next joint paper. Cedric could not help pulling Bill's leg about an assertion he had made in one letter concerning a perfect square that had turned out to be entirely wrong. It was a most enjoyable weekend.

When Bill returned on Sunday evening, he was just in time to listen with Mrs Briggs to Prime Minister Churchill's latest broadcast. The Prime Minister started by praising the splendid spirit of those in the areas recently suffering heavy bombing, specifically mentioning 'the streets and wharves of London'. Bill thought it another wonderful speech, not hiding the truth of the still desperate situation whilst pointing to the significant aid the United States of America were now providing to sustain Britain in its struggle. As before, Bill was totally engaged by the speech and went to bed full of admiration for Mr Churchill.

On Monday morning, Lieutenant Cheadle had some important news; for safety reasons, the course would soon be moving out of London. Premises had been secured above the Gas Showrooms in Bedford and suitable accommodation for everyone was being arranged. Generally, the news was well received principally because they were getting out from underneath the German bombardment.

Early May saw Bill in new digs in St Andrews Road, Bedford. The move to Bedford had been less stressful than he had first imagined, indeed, Bedford in springtime turned out to be very agreeable. He had been allocated a room with a retired couple who, Bill sensed, had reluctantly agreed to take a lodger but they were kindly enough, the husband having been a lecturer at the local teacher training college. All in all, his new digs were even a slight improvement on South Ealing and he could walk into the town centre heading for a door at the back of the Gas Showrooms leading to the course rooms above. One further benefit was the very pleasant surroundings of which Bill took full advantage, taking long walks in the evenings and weekends along the embankment of the Great Ouse. That the German bombers seemed to ignore Bedford was a great relief not only to Bill and the others but to Bill's mother too.

Bill felt he was getting to a point where the course was not testing him. He discussed this with Lieutenant Cheadle who suggested he move on to the section headed Machine ciphers. Bill was surprised this section was rather brief. It did little other than introduce the principle behind the few machines that had been independently developed post The Great War most of which had not been commercially successful. All were based on a rotor system, generally with an alphabet around the rim of each rotor. The rotors were usually in a series and turned in some designated order or sequence changing the substitution alphabet for every letter of the message. The techniques already learned on the course were applicable to such ciphers, he read. It surprised Bill that cipher machines were commercially available and therefore, their inner workings were known. But apparently, used properly, they were intrinsically strong cryptographically and very difficult to break even though their structure was known. A few fairly easy exercises followed demonstrating some of the designs.

When Bill indicated to Lieutenant Cheadle that he had finished the Machine section, the Lieutenant suggested he attack some of the supplementary exercises.

It was about this time, towards the end of April, that the course had another visitor. But this time, the visitor was not introduced to the group but taken immediately by Lieutenant Cheadle to the anteroom.

This visitor was Captain Gerry Morgan. He had just been appointed Head of the newly established Research Section at Bletchley Park and Colonel Tiltman had told him he could have, by the middle of May, three or four of the best students from the course. He had come to see who might be suitable.

The Lieutenant and the Captain went through the list of students. Two stood out for the Captain, Stephen Freer and Bill. When the Captain said he wanted one immediately and preferred a mathematician, the choice appeared obvious.

"Let me have a chat with both of them. This Bill Tutte first," said the Captain.

Bill was introduced to Gerry Morgan who just said he was from the Government Code and Cipher School. He wanted to know a little more about Bill's background and what he thought of the course. They discussed the exercise Bill was presently working on, an interesting problem supposedly based on some secret papers found in the Pas de Calais only last year. The Captain asked Bill to send him his solution. Bill was rather puzzled about this unexpected meeting the purpose of which was unclear. Stephen Freer was called in next. Later, Bill and Stephen compared notes about this Captain Morgan. Was there more to the interviews than just a chat about the course, they wondered?

A few days later, the Lieutenant called Bill out and ushered him to his side room.

"Bill, I have been asked to give you this letter that arrived this morning," said the Lieutenant handing Bill an envelope. "You can open it."

It was from the Government Code and Cipher School, Bletchley Park. Bill read:

I am pleased to appoint you to the position of Temporary Junior Assistant Officer with the Government Code and Cipher School, Research Section, Bletchley Park with effect from 1 June 1941.

Please report to Captain Morgan, Head of the Research Section on Monday, 16 June 1941 at 10:00 A.M.

You will receive a salary of £350 per annum paid monthly. Accommodation will be arranged for you but will be at your own expense.

I will be on hand to assist with any administrative matters.

I wish you well in your new position.

Yours faithfully,

A Bradshaw

Chief Administration Officer, GC&CS

"Congratulations!" said the Lieutenant who obviously knew the content of the letter. "Good man, Gerry Morgan. He told me he is setting up a special team to tackle the more difficult codes and ciphers. Should be interesting work!"

Chapter 3
Research Section, Bletchley Park

"Good to see you again, Bill" said Gerry Morgan. "Welcome to the Research Section. Now, let me explain. The Section has just been formed to look at codes and ciphers that are either new to us or ones that other units are having problems with and simply do not have the resources to tackle. The idea is that we turn them around for the others to run with as routine. We've several already on our books including the Hagelin Machine, a Japanese Military Attaché cipher, Floradora and other diplomatic stuff, and three types of high grade Vichy French diplomatic codes. I'll introduce you around in a minute. Clifford and Michel, Michel is a French Naval Officer by the way, have already started on the Hagelin and I want you to help them. It's probably the most urgent. Patricia Bartley is working on the Floradora. There is also Daphne Bradshaw whose husband, Alan, is the Chief Administration Office, a useful chap to know. She and Norman Sainsbury are looking at some of the others. I'm hoping to get more staff in as soon as possible, some from the course.

"Settle in quickly, there's a lot to do. Let me know any problems. Later on, you can go over to Alan Bradshaw to sort out accommodation and such like. Let's go and meet the others."

Everyone appeared very welcoming, interested to meet the new recruit, the first from Colonel Tiltman's course. Most worked in a large room upstairs at the back of the Main Building but Gerry Morgan said that space was at a premium and people were always being shuffled around.

"Here's the Italian Hagelin file," said Gerry back in his office. "Any interesting bits and pieces we get on the Hagelin we keep in here. The version of the machine we have is in the cupboard over there but we don't let it out of this room as it's the only one we have at the moment. The Italians are using a slightly different model to ours. The Swedish inventor, Boris Hagelin, has improved its security over time and since his machines have been commercially available for a number of years, we know pretty much all about them. Have a poke around and see if you can get your head round it and we'll have a chat later on tomorrow. Park yourself in the corner." Bill took the file but before he got up, Gerry delivered a stern warning.

"Remember, Bill! No papers, no notes, no nothing is to be taken out of the Park site. People are tempted sometimes to do a bit of extra work in the evenings or at weekends. Under no circumstances, though; it's strictly forbidden! Secrecy is paramount. Nothing is to be said of this place or what we do here now, not even after this war is over." Gerry fixed his eyes on Bill. "Understood?"

"Understood," said Bill nodding his acknowledgement.

Bill leafed through the file and came across an Operating Instructions booklet in English and started with that. It did not take him long to come to the conclusion that the instructions were poorly written and not easy to follow. He studied the several photographs of the machine which had various parts labelled and gradually, he began to understand its inner workings. He examined the machine itself and was impressed with its engineering. It was purely mechanical, operated by hand and it fitted inside a small robust carrying case. Some sections of the instructions seemed less relevant and he skipped these, returning to the section covering aspects of the system's security which he felt he needed to comprehend as well as the mechanism. There was a lot to take in. After a while, he began to see the machine's mechanical operation in purely mathematical terms and once he felt he had a grasp of the principles of enciphering and deciphering a message, he translated these principles into mathematical notations and equations which he wrote down for his own reference.

It had been an intense day. Daphne Bradshaw came in later on to remind Bill to catch the bus to his digs. She had taken a motherly interest in this fresh-faced young man. The transport turned out not to be a bus but a shooting brake. He had been allocated temporary digs in Woburn Sands, a small village some 6 miles or so to the east of Bletchley. He had been told permanent digs were being found and Mrs Andrews there could only have him that week while her normal Bletchley Park paying guest was away. This was all very disruptive for Bill but there was nothing he could do. Fortunately, Mrs Andrews was obviously used to having lodgers and went out of her way to make Bill feel at home. Bill had promised his parents and Cedric he would write as soon as he arrived at his 'new job' and spent the first evening penning letters, being careful to give nothing away.

He had received a letter from Cedric a couple of days before he left Bedford. Interestingly, Cedric seemed to have his ear very close to the ground when it came to more Cambridge mathematicians arriving at Bletchley Park. He had heard that Jack Good had already left and that Rolf Noskwith would soon follow, both of whom he knew but not well. Cedric reported he had had tea with Rolf Noskwith and found him a very nice chap.

Bill was quite taken with the ingenuity of the Hagelin machine. He learned that once the machines of both sender and receiver were set up exactly the same, the process for enciphering and deciphering a message was the same; the only change when switching from enciphering to deciphering was to turn a small knob at the side from 'C' to 'D' and vice versa. He was also intrigued by the logical and mathematical character of the three elements—plaintext, ciphertext and key—that given any two elements, the third may be found. The machine generated a variable ciphertext letter for each plaintext letter, the variation changing from one letter to the next with each turn of the handle.

One feature Bill studied was the set of six wheels at the front of the machine, each with alphabet letters engraved around their rims. He read that, although each wheel was the same size, they had differing numbers of starting positions from 26 on the left-hand wheel reducing to 17 on the right-hand wheel. For fun, he worked out the number of possible position combinations for just this one part of the operation to give a scale of how difficult it would be to work out a coded message. Looking at the result of his calculations, he raised his eyebrows. "That is some number of combinations!" he said to himself.

One note in the file really surprised him. He had read in the Operating Instructions that a 'Z' should be inserted between words to indicate a space. But the note stated that for the Italian navy codes, the letter used to indicate a space was 'K' because the letter 'K' was not used in the Italian alphabet. "News to me," he again mumbled to himself.

Gerry Morgan came over. "How have you got on?" he enquired.

"I think I have an idea of how it works," Bill replied, "but I still need to understand more how the wheels at the front link with the lug cage at the back."

"That's an excellent start," said Gerry encouragingly. "What we want you to do is to work on the starting positions of those front wheels, or the settings as we call them.

As each of the six wheels can be rotated independently to a new starting position, there are only 100 million or so combinations, so it shouldn't be too difficult!" he suggested with a grin.

Bill looked down at his notes. '101,405,850 to be exact!' he nearly said, but refrained.

"Clifford and Michel will show you what we are doing to discover the internal patterns which our Italian Navy friends, helpfully, don't change too often; possibly for weeks would you believe! Clifford thinks there is a way into the wheel starting positions which he will show you. So, if we can learn the internal patterns which stay the same for weeks, we will have many messages where we only need to discover the wheel starting positions in order to read the messages." He paused.

"I'll give you a bit of background here. When Italy joined the Axis powers in June last year, the Italian Navy was using a variety of hand ciphers which we could not break. We were, however, aware the Italians were looking at a cipher machine and we have known for a few months now this was a version of the Hagelin. The Germans provided them with a type of Enigma which they used for encoding radio communications between Rome and the Dodecanese Islands. A few months ago, a team here broke those Enigma messages which helped Admiral Cunningham defeat the Italian Navy at Cape Matapan which you will have heard about. Some other divisions of the Italian Navy were recently given the Hagelin and last month, we were asked to look at it. From a fortuitous depth earlier this month, we were able to decode a message which led us to believe they are using it for the supply convoys to Rommel's troops in North Africa. Our troops out there have been having a tough time lately so disrupting Rommel's supply lines is vital. Hopefully, we can tell our Air Force and Navy boys the whereabouts of these convoys from successful decodes. But we need to read the messages almost immediately or the convoys will have arrived and unloaded before they can be attacked. That's where we are just now. Let's see what Clifford and Michel are up to."

Bill was incredulous at what Gerry Morgan had just said. Some questions he had had on his mind were totally overtaken by the significance of what he was being asked to do. He could hardly believe he was to be given such a responsible role in a chain leading directly to action in the Mediterranean. And this on only his second day! He had absolutely no idea the 'secret war work' he had embarked on only a few months ago would turn out to be so important. But that thought led to self-doubt, uncertain whether he was up to the role, particularly with such little preparation, added to which he spoke no Italian. Bill's head was still swimming somewhat when they went over to join Clifford Brooke and Michel Moreau.

Clifford and Michel looked up. "Sorry to interrupt you, chaps," said Gerry. "I have brought Bill over to see what you're up to. He has made a good start on the Hagelin file and it's probably a good idea he moves over with you to work on the wheel settings. I'll leave him with you so you can fill him in with progress."

Bill tried to clear his head as he sat down at a large table strewn with papers, in the middle of which was a pot with a forest of sharpened pencils sticking out.

"We've hardly started ourselves really, Bill, so we're still feeling our way around it," started Clifford. "At the moment, we are learning the way the Italians use the machine and the nature of the traffic which appears to be the administration of the supply convoys to Axis ports in North Africa. We're investigating some of Gerry's theories of working out the internal patterns without necessarily relying on a depth. You know depths…when two messages are sent using the same key, that is when the machine has exactly the same set-up for both messages?"

Bill nodded; he recalled from the course how significant depths were.

"Fortunately for us, a few weeks ago, this Italian cipher clerk was very lax and sent the same message twice using the same key with only one letter different. Gerry spotted this depth from the indicator group which tells the recipient how to set up his machine. You will have read the indicator group of letters is sent at the beginning and end of each message. A depth of this sort is manna from heaven for a clever cryptographer like Gerry and he was able to decode the message without too much difficulty. He has asked us to study this nice gift and to look at other messages received around the same time as we suspect the Italians might use the same internal pattern for several weeks which appears to be the case. We also have been able to confirm the machine operates on modulo 26. Now, did they show you modulo 26 on the course where letters of the alphabet are given numbers zero to 25 so they can be added and subtracted in a particular way?"

"Yes, but I will need to refresh my memory," said Bill paying close attention.

"Don't worry. There is a lot to learn," said Clifford understandingly. "Let's press on and look at the internal pattern; it will help your understanding."

Clifford took him through how each of the front wheels had a set of pins which could be moved so they became either active or inactive. The number of pins on each wheel was the same as the number of positions the wheel could be turned to, adding up to 131 pins around all six wheels. Across the back of the machine was the lug cage, which reminded Bill of a squirrel cage. This horizontal cage had 27 bars, each of which had a moveable projection called a lug that could be set opposite any of the wheels or in a neutral position. The countless combinations of patterns and settings, Clifford pointed out, meant a 'brute force' attack was totally impractical, that is to test each and every possible combination. Bill was just about keeping up.

"Now," said Clifford, "when the handle is turned after the message letter is selected in the little dial at the side, the cage does a full rotation, at the end of which all the front wheels move on one position and the ciphertext letter is printed on a paper tape. So, as the cage moves round, when there is a lug, a sort of clip, opposite a wheel with its pin in the active position, the bar on the cage is nudged. The number of nudges, or kicks we call them, is a function of the number of wheels with an active pin for that turn of the lug cage and the number of lugs opposite those wheels. No active pin on a wheel, no kick generated from that wheel. No lug opposite a wheel, no kick from that wheel even if it has an active pin. With me so far?"

"So far, I think," replied Bill. "If every bar had a lug opposite an active pin, the kicks would total 27. Is that right? And if there was no active pin on any of the wheels the kick total would be zero."

"Correct," said Clifford. "You will have seen sample set-up patterns in the Operating Instructions. The patterns are designed to produce a pseudo random key stream; that is to say an irregular pattern of kicks per turn of the handle. There is a further feature on the machine that the Italians seem to use, called a 'slide'. This adds an extra fixed number to the key generated by the wheels and lugs—up to a maximum of 25. As I said, we think the Italians change the internal pattern every few weeks but they appear to change the slide every few days. Of course, for each new message, they should change the wheel settings, that is the starting position for each of the six wheels."

Bill followed closely as Clifford took him through their embryonic process for estimating the slide of a message. It was complex and employed the statistical analysis of as many key numbers as they could garner from messages on days which possibly had the same slide. The theory appeared sound if there were long enough messages, Clifford explained, but the analysis needed more work and was not an absolute guarantee of success.

Whilst Bill could follow the logic of each step as they came to it, he knew it would take him some time to become sufficiently familiar with it all before he could make any sort of contribution.

It had been an intensive day. Clifford looked at his watch and said that if Bill did not hurry, he would miss his lift. Bill wanted to carry on but reluctantly collected his things and made his way down to the waiting line of busses and shooting brakes.

Captain Bradshaw called Bill to see him about moving to his permanent digs. Bill had been at Woburn Sands only three nights and now, he was to move to the Post Office in Adstock, the last move for some time Bill hoped.

"Accommodation is getting a huge problem and we have to go further and further out," the Captain said. "Adstock is some ten miles away towards Buckingham. In fact, we are establishing an outstation there for some of our machinery so you've no need to worry about transport; you will still be able to get to and fro. No doubt," he went on, "the locals will think you are something to do with it. Curiosity may well get the better of them and they could ask you what is going on there. Rest assured, it has nothing to do with you; you will not be involved at all. So, you can truthfully say you don't know. Lastly, I believe the lady has room for two in which case you may find a colleague joining you there. Let me know if you have any problems."

A letter from Cedric was waiting for him when he arrived at the Woburn Sands address for his final night. In his usual jocular manner, Cedric said he had had a letter from Jack Good which he thought, from the writing on the envelope, was from Bill. Then the next day, he had a letter he thought was from Jack Good but was in fact from him. For some reason, he mentioned again that Rolf Noskwith would be arriving at Bletchley, adding he was naturalised British but German by birth and with well-to-do parents. Cedric was turning out to be a very regular and very welcome correspondent. There was plenty of mathematical content too which kept Bill engrossed until he had to stop to pack his suitcase for the morning.

The following evening on his way to Adstock, Bill took stock of his 'new job'. His task, as far as he understood it, looked daunting. There was so much to absorb but he judged nothing he had seen so far was actually beyond him. The sort of calculations and tabulations he had covered that afternoon whilst needing both accuracy and patience were, in mathematical terms, very simplistic. But it was neither the introduction to the Hagelin nor his understanding of the specific task he had been given that caused his reflective mood. Rather, it was the abrupt realisation he was no longer a bystander, an observer, of the war—he was about to become part of it. He had supposed he might find himself doing this 'secret war work' in some scientific backwater. But it was immediately obvious that Bletchley Park was no backwater. People in the main house and in the growing number of surrounding huts did not bear arms: nevertheless, if they were all engaged in similar codebreaking activities, they were nonetheless directly involved in the conflict.

The driver dropped Bill off at the crossroads in the centre of the village and said the Post Office was just on the right at the back of the first house. Bill looked around. The village reminded him of Cheveley. There was a row of thatched cottages, small houses of mellow brick or whitewash, trees and grass verges. The whole character of the place was in marked contrast to London. In the early evening summer light, it was a scene of rural peace and tranquillity.

"Mrs Clarke?" asked Bill to the lady who answered the door.

"You must be Mr Tutte. Come along in."

He followed her into a hallway. On the left was a door marked 'Post Office'. In front were some stairs and she led him through the door on the right into a front room.

"Here we are. This is Miss Jones. She helps me in the Post Office and has supper with me. The kitchen is out the back and I'll show you your room upstairs."

Both Mrs Clarke and Miss Jones were about the age of his parents, if not a little older, and it soon became obvious that Mrs Clarke was the stronger character and was firmly in charge. They busied themselves getting the evening meal which was eaten in a somewhat awkward atmosphere.

That evening as Bill took a stroll through the pastoral surroundings of the village, his mind turned over and over the events of the last few days, recognising his world had fundamentally changed, suddenly, seriously and in an unexpected direction. The whole situation unsettled him, probably because so much had happened. Some of it he put down to being new to Bletchley Park, reminiscent of his first term at Trinity College when he felt completely overawed by the academic world there. But more importantly, he sensed he had been catapulted into a position he certainly had not anticipated, a position that appeared to carry considerable responsibility. In the past, he had been pretty much self-reliant, confidently working mostly by himself towards his own academic goals. Bletchley Park presented a very different prospect. At first glance, the work itself looked interesting from an intellectual point of view, if mathematically unchallenging. The people he had met seemed friendly enough and the informal atmosphere in the Main Building had rather surprised him. Not knowing what to expect, he was relieved to find the place was not run on military lines and in some respects, there was an academic feel resonant of Trinity College. The weight of secrecy that initially seemed onerous was one aspect he felt he could bear. Added to the mix, was the novelty of a job with a salary and a supervisor. Yet, he could not shake off the feeling that he had been thrust, perhaps prematurely, into the 'front line' and it was probably this more than anything that made him uncomfortable.

As for Adstock, Bill was a bit disappointed the accommodation was not up to the standard of his previous three digs. There was no electricity, no running water upstairs and the toilet was in an outhouse at the back. It was no great matter to him since it was just like at home and not much different from his rooms at Trinity; curious though, there were two single beds in his room. It did not take Bill long to gain the distinct impression Mrs Clarke had not taken paying guests before; conversely, he himself was becoming quite the professional guest. Nevertheless, it was all clean and tidy. In the morning, however, he did have to ask for some hot water to shave and a pail to pour away the water after washing. *Maybe it was a while since Mrs Clarke had had a man in the house*, he thought. Stepping outside the front door on his way to the crossroads where the car would pick him up, he posted two letters in the post box on the wall of the house. Posting letters was going to be very convenient. They were letters to his parents and to Cedric advising yet another change of address.

There was one aspect of routine at Bletchley Park that had already begun to irk him and that was he had to leave the Park when the shooting brake set off on its rounds of the more remote villages. By choice, he would rather work on than have spare time in the evenings.

Gerry Morgan was already at his desk when Bill arrived the next morning.

"Everything all right at the new digs?" he asked.

"Fine, thank you," answered Bill. He was not one to make a fuss and anyway, he thought it would be impolite to voice so soon his disappointment that his permanent accommodation was so far away and rather less comfortable than Woburn Sands.

By now, Bill had moved over to work on the main table. He preferred working on his own but recognised the benefit of their working closely together. Up till then, he had said little but took an opportunity to ask some questions that had been on his mind.

"The other day, Mr Morgan mentioned Enigma. What is that?"

"It's another rotor-type encoding machine used by the Germans," said Clifford. "It is very complicated with wiring and plugs. You will get to see it no doubt."

"What about the version of the Hagelin the Italians are using? Do we get to see one of those?"

"Soon, I hope," said Clifford. "Gerry is trying to get hold of one—by surreptitious means no doubt. But the principle is the same. It's only the drum cage and lugs that are different, and possibly the slide."

"And do I have to learn Italian? I have some French and a few German words but I have not learned any Italian."

"No, no, Michel has all the Italian we need. He was brought up bilingual. His English is not too bad, either!"

Michel began explaining in detail the plan of attack they wanted Bill to follow, which to Bill mimicked the sort of mathematical puzzles he and his Trinity colleagues used to tackle. As such, he quickly became engrossed, shutting out any lingering uncertainties.

He learned that the plan relied on the use of a crib, a word or words the Italians regularly used in their naval messages. Michel explained the Italians had a habit of starting messages with the name of the transmitting unit or with a message number or such like. Michel would give him a list. Trying a crib alongside the first letters of the ciphertext would give a string of probable key numbers. There was a special chart with which Bill needed to familiarise himself that tabulated the relationship between the message letter, the ciphertext letter and the relative key number.

"Look," he had said pointing to a copy of the special chart. "If the message letter is say, 'C', and the machine makes a key of '17', then the ciphertext letter the machine prints out will be the letter 'P'. Again, if the message letter is 'T' and the ciphertext letter printed is 'D', we know the machine has made a key of '22'. We remember the key number represents the number of letters the print wheel has go along the alphabet—that is the total number of kicks made by the wheels and lug cage plus the 'slide'." Michel paused and looked to judge how much Bill had absorbed.

"Do not worry," he assured Bill. "There is much to take in. Perhaps the machine is conceived to make decoding very difficult, is it not?"

Bill studied the method outlined by Michel. As a test example, he worked on the message previously decoded by Gerry Morgan where the positions of the pins and lugs and also the slide were all known. First of all, he considered the lug positions. Each bar had one moveable lug and it was possible to set out how many lugs per turn of the cage were opposite each of the six wheels. He wrote them out. He also wrote out the patterns of the pins on each wheel—signifying against each position letter whether that pin was active or inactive. He then wrote out the string of key numbers having deducted the slide. Next, he studied the string of key numbers, each individual number of which was the product of the number of lugs opposite wheels that had an active pin on that turn of the handle.

The method now was an iterative process of logic and deduction to analyse which lugs opposite a wheel most likely contributed to a particular key number and which lugs certainly did not, indicating an active or inactive pin respectively. High and low key numbers were good points to start, Michel had said, bearing in mind a key number which was a genuine zero meant all wheels had inactive pins. He reminded Bill that if the kicks total 26 then the key is also zero because the print wheel makes a full turn. Similarly, if the kick is the maximum 27 it is equivalent to a key of one. Michel suggested Bill consider first the sixth wheel which had the fewest positions, not forgetting its pattern of active and inactive pins would repeat after every 17 turns of the handle.

Steadily and persistently, Bill ploughed his way through eventually matching up the pattern of the sixth wheel against a run of key numbers indicating the start point for that wheel. Once he had three wheels determined, the rest fell out easily.

He showed Clifford and Michel his analysis to which they gave a thumbs up.

"Try this message from the end of May," said Michel. "We think it will have the same internal pattern as the one you have just done and a slide of three. I have written down some good cribs for you." He pushed a sheet of paper over to Bill pointing to the top word. "Here, this word, Supermarina, is the Chief of Naval General Staff at Naval Headquarters. It is in Rome. This one, Marina Taranto, is the major naval base at Taranto in southern Italy. Some bases you see on my list are on the coast of North Africa. We think all these naval bases have a secret list of internal patterns and message settings. If you can steal one of these secret lists, that would be good!"

"Thank you," said Bill taking the list and smiling at Michel's attempt at humour.

He looked down the list. Some place names he knew, others he vaguely recognised from war reports in newspapers. Some words on the list were not places. Michel pointed some of them out. "This one 'alt' means stop, for full stop; and this, 'e' means 'and', and here 'per' is 'for'. These are obvious, 'messaggio'—message; 'numero'—number and 'Ammiraglio'—Admiral."

Bill started on the new message using the crib SUPERMARINAK to produce a string of key numbers, remembering to insert a 'K' for the word space. After a while, his analysis produced what he thought was an impossibility and he asked Michel for help.

"Try putting a K at the beginning to see if that helps."

That too drew a blank. Next on the list was Marina Taranto, so he tried that as he already had initial workings for seven letters. Taranto also proved incorrect. But at that late point in the afternoon, there was no time to start another crib before he had to leave for Adstock and so, frustrated because he was perfectly capable of continuing, Bill headed off.

His annoyance at having to stop work was tempered later when he took his now usual evening walk through the village and along the network of country footpaths and bridleways. It was a perfect summer's evening and as an antidote to the war and the bombing of London, he felt such a place could not be improved upon. He could easily imagine himself at home on a ramble through the footpaths around Cheveley. He switched off the part of his mind that had been turning over the day's events and simply took in the joys of his walk in the soft evening air, stopping now and again to take a closer look at the wild flowers by the hedgerows, to listen to the birdsong or to see what crops were growing in the fields. As he strolled along, the trees cast their dappled shade across the lanes as the sun went down.

The following morning, Bill tackled the unfinished message from the previous evening. MARINAKBENGASIK proved to be the correct crib but it took him until the next day to work out the wheel starting positions. Disappointingly, the message proved to be a routine test and so not important.

That lunchtime, Bill was walking alone on the path by the lake deep in thought when he felt a tap on the shoulder.

"Hello, old chap," said a voice behind him. Bill turned. It was Jack Good, instantly recognisable with his Jewish features, shock of black hair, prominent moustache and round spectacles.

"Jack!" said Bill a little startled but pleased to see a friendly face. "How are you? I imagined we'd bump into each other before too long. Congratulations on your doctorate, by the way. How are you finding it here?"

"Well, it's all very strange; a far cry from Cambridge," he confided. "There is a lot to learn but from what I've seen so far what they do here is just amazing. I hope I can be useful. What about you? I heard you had gone on a course. What was that all about?"

"It covered the fundamentals of cryptography," said Bill. "There were a lot of exercises on various codes. It was pretty intensive. I've only just started here myself, helping to break into one of the newer codes."

They strolled on towards the Main Building in the warm sunshine.

"It's rather odd," said Jack, "that you were sent on a course but I was sent straight here. I believe Noskwith is coming straight here too. Why is that, do you think?" he inquired.

"I did wonder that myself," said Bill. "I suppose it's because I'm not a statistician and a chess champion like you. I've only, maybe, a bit of a reputation for solving mathematical puzzles."

"It sounds to me as though you were specifically recruited for code breaking," Jack surmised, "whereas, I think I've been brought along merely to apply statistical techniques to codes they already know how to break. At least that's what I think I'm doing."

He paused for a moment.

"Have you met Mr Turing, my section chief? The other night on a late shift, I felt tired and took a nap on the floor and got into fearful trouble. Mr Turing found me and thought I was ill. When I told him I'd just taken a nap, he was very cross and wouldn't talk to me for days. I thought I'd get the sack. Fortunately for me, I came up with an improvement which dramatically reduced the time taken for one of his procedures and I think I'm safe. Do you know Mr Turing?"

"Not really," Bill answered. "He interviewed me at the beginning. Other than that, I don't know him."

"He's ex-Trinity, of course. A bit odd but highly respected here, I believe," said Jack. "Anyway, better get back in case I get into more trouble."

As he hurried off, he called over his shoulder, "Look out for Noskwith."

A few days later, Gerry caught Clifford in the corridor and took him aside for a few words, particularly wanting his impressions of Bill.

"Bill? A nice young chap…very quiet. Oddly the expression on his face never seems to change…appears quick on the uptake, though."

Gerry nodded in apparent agreement. "Do you think he's right for the Research Section?"

"Oh, yes. I'd say so. You can see he is very bright. He seems to have the necessary dogged patience and concentration too. In fact, I'd say he was capable of tackling more than the Hagelin."

"Interesting…" mused Gerry. "Thanks for that."

One morning, Gerry Morgan called them all together to discuss progress.

"I think we can be confident now that the internal patterns are changed only once a month and the slide every couple of days," said Gerry summarising the work of the past few weeks. "I'm still looking at the indicators to see if they provide another way in." Turning to Bill he explained, "The indicators are the first two five letter groups transmitted at the beginning and sometimes repeated at the end of each message to tell the recipient how to set up his machine." Bill nodded his understanding.

Clifford spoke. "We're struggling to determine the wheel patterns for June. There hasn't been a depth since the beginning of the month so should we abandon work on depths and near depths altogether do you think? As it is, we're trying to find a long enough length of key to try out your differencing techniques. It's difficult but we're working all out."

"Hmm," pondered Gerry. "I don't think we can rely on the Italians to oblige us with true depths any more. We should still keep an eye out for near depths though, but I'm sure we're going to need a robust and quick system that does not depend on any sort of depth. So, yes press on with those possible key differencing methods. We do not have the luxury of time so don't waste effort on any approach that appears to be going nowhere. If we can devise a workable routine, albeit not perfect, then we need to test it, document it and introduce it quickly. Involve me more should you need."

Clifford continued, "On the wheel settings, we think we have a reliable attack. Bill is working to make this routine now."

Gerry Morgan gave instructions to Bill. "Keep me in touch with progress, please. As soon as Clifford has June's internal pattern, we'll attack the latest traffic. In the meantime, refine your process where you can. Speed in decoding is the essence."

Bill's impression of the meeting was one of resolve, of important matters that needed urgent attention, matters on which the imperative was understood. There was a military-style crispness to the meeting, a brevity which was in marked contrast to some of the meandering meetings he had attended at Trinity College. He came away feeling somewhat privileged to have been involved being such a new recruit.

Bill attacked another late May message that had not been attempted. After several abandoned cribs, he tried Marina Messina. With this as his new crib, he worked his way carefully through the process and as he did so, one piece after another fell into place. Two wheels were solved quite easily. Adding the full period of pin positions for those two wheels to his analysis solved a further wheel. It needed meticulous work; the slightest mistake would ruin the whole analysis. He pressed on. Two more wheels had part patterns that fitted in two separate places. He considered how to solve this conundrum. There appeared to be no shortcuts so he tried all four combinations. Three failed but one was possible. That meant he now had five out of the six start positions looking good. His heart beat a little faster at the prospect of success. But he could not match up the last wheel; there were too many unknowns and it did not seem to fit anywhere. To reach this point, he had based his analysis on the letters of Marina followed by a 'K' for a word space plus the first three letters of Messina, making MARINAKMES. This was because Michel had said only nine or ten letters would normally be required. He tried extending the analysis to all the letters of MESSINA and added at the end the letter 'K' for another word space, making MARINAKMESSINAK. This was still inconclusive, matching in two positions but when he substituted 'ALTK' for the last 'K' this gave him the sixth wheel. He had done it! He turned to Michel.

"Have a look at this. I think I have all six start positions."

"Bien!" exclaimed Michel. "Laisse moi voir." He and Bill had developed a little friendly banter speaking in French.

Using the special chart, Michel produced a short string of message text and proclaimed, "It is good!"

A rare smile emerged on Bill's face. For the first time, he felt he was contributing rather than being a burden.

"Decipher the rest of it, Bill. You know how to use the chart," said Clifford with a sense of urgency.

Bill eagerly set about it, thinking it was a shame he could not use the machine in the cupboard. Letter by letter, he very carefully wrote out the message. Each time a 'K' appeared, he left a space. But he understood nothing of the message in Italian that emerged, only recognising a couple of words. The atmosphere in the room grew tense. Eventually, Bill finished. Michel cast his eye over it then started to write his English translation under Bill's clear Italian text. Bill watched Michel closely. From time to time,

Michel gave a slight nod as though he was satisfied with what he was seeing. The wait was broken when Michel sat back.

"It is from Messina to Benghazi advising a convoy will be passing through the Strait of Messina the next day and giving an escort identity call sign. It does not give details of the convoy though only the convoy number."

"Is it no good, then?" questioned Bill, disappointed.

"Non, non," said Michel, "on the contrary. This is a convoy we did not know. This is important information even if it's too late for it to be attacked." He turned to Clifford. "We'd better check it before it goes to Hut 4 and I'll have a look at the register. There may be a possible connected message, probably from Rome or Naples with the convoy's manifest."

"Splendid work, Bill!" said Clifford clearly pleased.

Outwardly, Bill showed little reaction to Clifford's compliment. Inwardly, though, he was very satisfied with his efforts; in particular that he had made no mistakes. Whilst he appreciated the compliment, nevertheless, it was meeting his own exacting standards that gave him most satisfaction.

Over the course of the following days, Bill began to feel more at ease with his colleagues, particularly with Gerry Morgan whose temperament was similar to his own and who was only six or so years older. Over lunch one day, Norman Sainsbury had told Bill some interesting information about Gerry. Apparently, he was a Trinity PhD mathematician and also a recently commissioned officer in the Intelligence Corps. Thankfully for Bill, Gerry ran the team on purely civilian lines but undoubtedly, he had many officer-like qualities. Instinctively, though, Bill deferred to Gerry as head of the section and he knew the Hagelin assignment was only one of a number of important projects he was managing.

Because of its role, the Research Section necessarily had a central position in the structure of Bletchley Park and Gerry was close to most of what was going on. Bill was beginning to understand that being in the Research Section placed him in a relatively privileged position, in contrast to almost everyone else who did not necessarily know what work was carried out in the next room or hut let alone elsewhere on the site. But not only that, Bill noticed everyone abided by the unwritten rule that you did not even ask. Occasionally, some argued that sharing information would help efficiency but the need for such tight security generally went unquestioned.

So, when Gerry suggested Bill went over to the Cottage across the stable yard to see someone from the Enigma Research team, Bill welcomed the idea.

"They use a rodding technique which just might be of interest. I'll check with Dilly Knox first," said Gerry. "Dilly guards his girls closely. I think they use their method to find Enigma wheel starting positions. I don't know if it will help, but go and have a look."

The suggestion had come during a discussion on the latest situation regarding wheel settings. Bill had described the somewhat tedious and time-consuming iterative process he followed to find the wheel settings using pencil and paper. His powers of total concentration for extended periods served him well and he had become adept at manipulating the numbers, patterns and wheel periods in order to tease out the wheel settings for a message. But Gerry felt Bill was taking too long on each message. It was imperative, he said, the process be speeded up; hence his suggestion.

The next day, Bill crossed the yard to the Cottage and asked for Claire Harding who was in charge of Dilly Knox's team of girls there. As it happened late last night, Clifford had at last broken the internal patterns for June and Michel was working on the slide of a suitably lengthy message.

Bill was pleasantly surprised to be welcomed to the Cottage by an attractive and very confident, young lady; younger than Bill himself which surprised him. How could such a young lady be involved in codebreaking?

"I'm Jill. Claire's not around but we're expecting you. Come in and I will show you how we use rodding."

He followed Jill to a table in the middle of the room on which, intriguingly, there were three loose piles of flat wooden rods. The rods of each pile were of a different colour, green, red and blue. Lots of eyes followed him for there were a number of other girls in the room curious of Jill's young gentleman visitor. When Bill told her he did not know what the Enigma was, Jill said to wait a moment and disappeared. Sensing he was under scrutiny, Bill waited awkwardly. At one point, he was unable to avoid eye contact with one of the group. He smiled nervously.

"Dilly said I can show you our Enigma," Jill said as she breezed back into the room. "You're lucky, Dilly isn't usually as amenable to people from other sections. Over here," she beckoned him.

She opened up a wooden box to reveal an Enigma machine, a basic model she explained, adding there were other more complicated versions but not saying more. Bill was fascinated by the machine with its keyboard, lamps and three interchangeable wheel rotors, each one differently wired inside, he was told. But it was difficult to take in everything. Jill explained about its complex encoding system. She went on to describe how their rodding technique attacked the wheel order and wheel settings using the three sets of coloured rods, one for each of the three Enigma wheels. It required a crib first, she explained, quoting as an example 'PERK' at which Bill nodded his recognition of the word 'for' plus a word space. Jill then showed him how two rods would be selected from one of the coloured piles and laid lengthways against each other flat on the table. Bill could see that each rod had a different, jumbled stream of alphabet letters along it. The team, Jill said, would be looking for pairs of letters to match with pairs from the crib and ciphertext streams. Delightful as she was, Jill delivered her brief tutorial at such a rapid pace that to Bill, the whole process seemed like a magician's trick; and a trick that appeared to rely heavily on linguistic skills. At that point, Bill could not see how it would help him and he became worried he would leave empty-handed.

Whilst looking closely at the pair of rods, he accidentally nudged the bottom one along changing the sequence of pairs of letters. Suddenly, his clumsy action led to a brain wave. It came to him in a flash how he could adapt the rods for his own purpose. He left as quickly as he could, politely thanking Jill who appeared a little perplexed at his hurried departure.

"Quick, I need some cardboard and scissors!" announced Bill to no one in particular as he rushed into the Research Section. A startled Clifford had never seen him so animated. "Ah, this will do!" said Bill finding what he wanted. A bleary-eyed Clifford asked what all the fuss was about but Bill was already immersed in bringing his idea to life.

"I'll tell you later," came the distracted reply.

Bill cut seven long thin strips of cardboard and marked them with small, equal spaces. On the first strip, he wrote in the spaces the key numbers from a broken May message. Then on each of the other six cardboard rods he wrote the kick or no kick pattern for the different wheels, and also marked off the period end for each wheel.

Every now and again, Clifford looked up curious to learn what Bill was up to. Seeing Bill was so immersed, he did not interrupt.

Bill first picked up the cardboard rod representing the 17-period wheel which also happened to have the largest kick. Carefully, he moved it back and forwards like a slide-rule above the cardboard rod representing the key numbers. His spirits rose when he found it surprisingly easy to spot where the wheel's pattern certainly did not fit with the key stream and, using his experience, where there was a potential fit. Applying logic and trial and error, he slid the other rods backwards and forwards above each other until the number of kicks in each column of spaces added up to the key number on the bottom rod. Holding his breath, he carefully checked that the position of each rod above the first key number indicated correctly the starting point of the wheel it represented. It worked! Not only did it work but the process was much, much faster. He demonstrated it to an inquisitive Clifford who was suitably impressed. By then, Michel had a probable slide for this morning's message.

"Try it on this," said Clifford pushing across this morning's message. "What's the slide, Michel?"

"Five."

The atmosphere suddenly changed. Often, there was little conversation in the room, as though there had been some unresolved argument or quarrel. Now, though, the silence was laden with expectation.

Bill made some new rods on the new numbers. He worked methodically. He had to abandon two cribs as incorrect. He tried Naples next. The 17-wheel rod fitted. Sliding the other rods back and forth, they gradually fitted into place. Holding his breath, he checked the result. It looked good.

Clifford and Michel knew not to disturb Bill when he was in the middle of something but could not help looking over anxiously as Bill started decoding the message.

"Have a look at this," said Bill eventually passing his workings across for Michel to translate. His words were impassive but inside, he was unusually nervous. Seldom had the tension of the moment held him in such a grip.

After writing for only a few moments and not stopping to look up, Michel ordered, "Get Gerry!"

When Gerry arrived, they all gathered round Michel reading the message over this shoulder as the translation emerged. It was about a convoy of four large liners, troop ships due to leave Naples today for Tripoli with a heavy escort.

"Check it and get it across to Hut 4 as soon as possible," said Gerry in his usual crisp manner. "Looks as though we're in business!"

That night, Bill went to bed tired after the day's events but woke up suddenly to a commotion downstairs. He stayed where he was trying to make out what was happening, what time it was. Someone was coming up stairs! Not knowing what to do, he half hid under the blankets. The door opened. A flickering candle lit up the shadowy figure of a man.

"Who is it? What's going on?" squeaked Bill.

"Regret to disturb you. I guess it's bit late," came the heavily accented reply. Bill could now make out the man's face and was staggered to recognise the intruder as someone he knew by sight at Trinity.

"You're Noskwith, aren't you?"

"Yes, who are you?"

"Tutte"

"Tutte from Trinity? Terribly sorry it's bit late. It appears I am billeted with you."

"What on earth time is it, Noskwith? What are you doing out so late?"

"Today is my first day and mistakenly, it seems, I sat out evening shift. I apologise. I didn't realise it inconveniences everyone." He turned to Mrs Clarke who was standing at the top of the stairs in a copious dressing gown looking extremely displeased and at the same time puzzled at these exchanges. "It's OK. We know each other. Apologies again to be late."

There was a clatter as Rolf bumped into the other bed and dropped his suitcase. Bill did not quite catch some expletive. The apologetic Rolf Noskwith eventually settled down and extinguished the candle.

"Let us catch up in the morning. Sorry to disturb. Night, Tutte." Then a moment later, "By the way, Tutte, it's my birthday. Twenty two years. Well, yesterday now, I suppose."

"Happy birthday for yesterday and good night," mumbled Bill with a touch of exasperation, turning over and trying to get back to sleep.

In the morning on the way into Bletchley, Rolf started asking all sorts of questions about Bletchley Park and what Bill was doing there. Bill had to slow down the over-enthusiastic Rolf, reminding him the utmost secrecy was needed.

"Yes, sorry. Of course. Love the old shooting brake though. Papa's got one. Goes everywhere in it. Great fun."

After a short silence, he was off again. "How long have you been at Adstock? Digs not very comfortable. Is that the best they have?"

"Accommodation is very difficult round here," said Bill. "Mrs Clarke is kind enough but I think she is not used to having paying guests and she has to run the Post Office too. This time of year, it's not so bad and it's only a guinea per week. It's certainly a lot safer than living in London."

"Not sure I get used to living in countryside; it's bit isolated out there."

"I like the countryside," said Bill, "but it is rather far out."

"Amusing to meet you here. We must have a beer or something, catch up."

Rolf had quite a serious look about him with intensely enquiring eyes. For the rest of the journey, though, he was chat, chat, chat, obviously trying to be friendly. He appeared very keen to have joined Bletchley Park at long last having been turned down more than once on security grounds.

Oh, dear, thought Bill, *I seem to have been lumbered with the over-enthusiastic Noskwith.* But fortunately, a couple of days later, Rolf told him he had found far more suitable digs in Newport Pagnell. It was treble the cost but Rolf's papa apparently provided a generous allowance. Bill was, thankfully, on his own again.

The following Saturday morning, Gerry came into the room and dropped a copy of The Times on the table and tapped a front page article. Clifford, Michel and Bill came around to look. The headlines read: 'Axis Convoy Attacked', 'Three 20,000-Ton Ships Hit', 'Air Success in the Mediterranean'. The article briefly described the RAF's evening attack off the south coast of Italy against ships possibly carrying reinforcements to the Axis armies in Libya. At least two ships were hit by torpedoes and a third by a heavy bomb, it said, but further results were not observed owing to darkness.

Suddenly, for Bill the war seemed very different; no longer was he just cowering from the Luftwaffe—he was now, albeit tangentially, part of the counteroffensive.

Within a few days, the papers were full of reports of the German invasion of Russia. Allied leaders were reported to say it was a heartening development, with the hope Russia would offer maximum resistance, diverting enemy forces and materials and so helping us in other theatres of war. Bill listened as this significant escalation of the war was discussed around the table, with speculation there could even be implications for their own workload.

Towards the end of June, changes at the Research Section began to happen quite quickly. Stephen Freer had joined them, glad to see a familiar face in Bill. Stephen was attached to Clifford and Michel in preparation for the attack on the new wheel patterns taking effect on 1 July. Regular success against the Italian Naval Hagelin in July led to a review that decided the day-to-day responsibility for this traffic should be passed to the Naval Intelligence unit in Hut 4. Someone from Hut 4 would join the Research Section temporarily specifically to learn as much as possible about the Hagelin in order to smooth the handover. That someone turned out to be a colleague from the cryptography course, Bernard Willson. In a further measure to support Hut 4, Bill was asked to spend nights in an adjoining room so he could be consulted if need be over some particularly awkward message. If Bernard was on the late shift, he would pop in occasionally for a chat to break the monotony. He was very easy to get on with and they would generally talk about Cambridge rather than work. Bill felt quite important, being now regarded an expert on wheel settings. During the long evenings, Bill reviewed the draft of a paper Gerry Morgan had written on the cryptanalysis of the Hagelin, a sort of handbook for Hut 4 and for others. Clifford and Michel, who had contributed to the paper, had returned to their military sections by then. Bill was pleased to see his small section on rodding was included. Gerry had asked Bill to thoroughly check the whole document of about 22 pages before it was released, a task Bill really enjoyed as it enabled him to study the techniques used for finding the wheel patterns and slides. It also allowed him to work quietly on his own, another bonus.

Summer had really arrived with temperatures soaring, lifting spirits after an unseasonably cool spring. People relaxed outside during their lunchbreaks, sitting by the lake or watching a game of rounders on the lawn at the front of the Main Building. The hot spell continued long into July making working conditions almost unbearable especially in the huts by both day and by night. The often raucous games of rounders were not for Bill who took to walking round the perimeter paths. He had a favourite spot in the far south west corner of the estate which backed on to the grounds of St Mary's Church and where there was a garden seat in the shade. He enjoyed a few minutes of quiet solitude there listening to the birds and the rustle of leaves, disturbed only by the occasional whistle from a train about to leave the nearby station.

One evening, at the end of July, Bill was working on Gerry's document in a small room next to Hut 4 when a young lady came in.

"Oh, I wasn't expecting anyone to be in here. Is it all right if I do some work; I won't disturb you? I'm Helen Dennis by the way."

"By all means," said Bill. "I'm Bill Tutte. I'm on standby in case Hut 4 wants a bit of help."

The young lady sat down opposite Bill and laid out some paperwork on the table. Bill returned to Gerry's paper and silence ensued. Occasionally, Helen looked up from her work at Bill whose concentration appeared total. After a while, she thought to exchange a few pleasantries just to lighten the atmosphere but held back for fear of disturbing him. Several times, she nearly broke the silence but refrained. But after nearly three hours, the tension was too much for Helen.

"For God's sake, say something!" she exclaimed, exasperated by his diffidence.

Bill was taken aback by this sudden outburst. Embarrassed, he defaulted to defence mode.

"Sorry. Sorry, I was concentrating. I tend to get rather involved. Sorry, I didn't mean to be rude."

Bill's sheepish apology melted somewhat Helen's frustration. They chatted briefly before resuming their separate tasks and ended the night parting on just about cordial terms.

Gerry asked Bill to lend Patricia Bartley a hand until some help for her could be recruited. She had been working on a German diplomatic code that was proving very difficult. He had to go along to the room she was sharing with Nigel de Grey, one of the senior people at Bletchley Park.

Patricia proved not only intelligent but also a most charming young lady. She explained that the code which was called Floradora was based on a plain text code book of five-digit groups of numbers, each group representing a word, phrase, number, date, etcetera. Each word group was doubly enciphered with two 5 digit number codes selected by a bigram table from a secret additive book. The selection of the double encipherment was advised to the recipient by a special indicator system that combined a key for the day. The British knew how the encipherment process worked because this had been described to them by a French spy who had seen it carried out. The task, she explained, was to recreate the additive book of which they had only a scrap saved from a raid on the German Consulate in Iceland as the staff were burning their secret papers. She gave Bill a copy of the plain text code book, a copy of the bigram table and some daily keys for this year. All these, she explained, had been fished out of the Panama Canal at the end of last year by the Americans after they were thrown overboard from a Japanese steamer by an under-surveillance German courier. Bill could hardly believe what he was hearing; it sounded like a tall tale straight out of *The American Black Chamber*. He was also taken aback by the revelation that an American Intelligence officer had been to Bletchley Park earlier in the year and had brought all this material with him.

They worked together at a table by the window overlooking the lake teasing out a few more groups of additive code using cribs which then led to a few more groups. Patricia suspected the additive book may contain many tens of thousands of such groups. To Bill, it appeared to be a herculean task. Whilst the surroundings were pleasant, Bill found the work laboriously slow and tedious. He thought about taking a brief holiday.

He had a day's leave due and decided to go home for a long weekend as his mother was worried about his father's health. In her letters, she told of calling the doctor on a couple of occasions because of his breathlessness. Bill was relieved to see his father was recovering quite well and more irritated by the all fuss than anything else. Yet, it was apparent his father had slowed down and he looked noticeably older. Bill also spent a couple of days at Trinity College with Cedric who had written that his hearing at the local Tribunal for Conscientious Objectors was coming up. They discussed what might happen to him, but mostly talked mathematics. Bill took the opportunity to have a bath in the communal bathroom as a bath did not seem to be on offer at the Post Office.

One Saturday morning, soon after Bill's return, there were unusual comings and goings. Something was afoot. The mystery was solved later on when a procession of official cars swept up the drive and drew up in front of the Main Building. What Bill and Patricia then saw from their vantage point took their breath away. Stepping out from one of the cars was none other than the unmistakable figure of the Prime Minister, Winston Churchill. They looked at each other excitedly.

"Look who's here," Patricia exclaimed, beckoning Nigel de Grey.

"Oh, he's arrived has he," said Nigel getting up and making for the door. "I'd better go; I'm part of the welcome party. Keep it quiet for the moment. People will have a chance to see him when he leaves."

They could barely believe what they had just seen. The Prime Minister. Here! Unable to concentrate, Bill and Patricia kept a watch for any movement outside. After what seemed an endless wait, Winston Churchill and his entourage emerged and made their way over to Hut 8. Bill and Patricia dashed downstairs and hurried over near to the hut hoping to catch a glimpse. Others began to gather as the word got around. The official party moved to the adjacent Hut 6. Bill, Patricia and the others waited impatiently.

When the Prime Minister finally reappeared, he was greeted with an enthusiastic reception by the small crowd. He surprised everybody, including his entourage, by stepping on to some higher ground and began addressing the group.

"To look at you, one would not think you knew anything secret," he said, reflecting on the eclectic mix of people he had met on his visit. This brought a ripple of laughter.

"I have only words of gratitude to every one of you for the work you do here and you can have the utmost confidence it carries great importance in our efforts against our foes. Your tireless work around the clock, to lift the stones on our enemies' secrets, brings priceless intelligence not only to our High Command but also to the very heart of the War Cabinet. You are the geese that lay my golden eggs," he said with a glint in his eye, referring to the intercepted messages sent to him daily. To him, they were precious, pure gold. He continued, "Foreknowledge of the intentions of our adversaries, be it far across the oceans or close to our own shores, grants us significant expedience in the dangers we face and in the protection of the lives of our servicemen, indeed, in the defence of our realm. You have a grave responsibility and I know you will discharge it with all the strength and diligence you can muster. I leave you now, encouraged in the knowledge that we have a potent weapon in the minds and resourcefulness of you all here at Bletchley Park."

It was all delivered with a genuine emotion that affected all those present.

Up close, Winston Churchill was rather smaller than Bill had expected, rather bent and older-looking, his complexion pallid. The voice and the oratory, however, had Bill tingling.

But it was over in a moment and the important visitors made their way through the crowd towards their waiting cars. Bill had half turned to watch them when his eye caught the gaze of a young lady opposite. She smiled. Bill nervously smiled back. She had an open, friendly face. Maybe he had seen her before. Most of the girls were in groups chattering excitedly but Bill noticed this young lady stood apart and appeared more poised. He turned just in time to see Winston Churchill raise his hat to the gathering crowds before disappearing into his car.

As the motorcade headed off down the drive, loud cheers rang as more and more people rushed to hail their Prime Minister. When Bill looked back, the young lady had gone which left him somewhat confused. He was a little disappointed she was no longer there but had no idea what he would have done had she remained. Thoughts of the young lady receded as the whole place was abuzz and little work was done for the rest of the day.

Bill knew that had his mother known of the day's important visitor, she would have been so thrilled she would have told everyone she met for days afterwards. As it was, his next letter home made no mention.

Chapter 4
The File

"See what you can do with this," said Gerry Morgan handing Bill a thick file. Bill looked at him quizzically.

"Some of the others have been working on this unknown cipher for a few months now but they have not made any progress lately. Maybe a fresh eye is needed."

Bill looked at the cover. On it was written 'Hellschreiber' and underneath the name Col Tiltman.

"Colonel Tiltman has been working on this?" queried Bill somewhat incredulously.

"He and couple of colleagues, but it's worth another look."

Bill's initial reaction was to hand back the file as he could not contemplate the prospect of adding anything to a piece of work the renowned Colonel Tiltman had abandoned. Gerry sensed his hesitation.

"The Germans have been up to something, Bill; experimenting with a new cipher, using non-Morse transmissions. John Tiltman managed to get out a long length of key from a depth but has not managed to discover what produced the key and he is now needed on something else. As you know, we have full working models of the Enigma and the Hagelin machines whose ciphers are transmitted by Morse code but we still have very few clues as to what sort of encryption method is behind these non-Morse transmissions. Originally, they were transmitted using the Hellschreiber method but the more recent transmissions were sent using teleprinter equipment. Signs are, if these transmissions continue, they may carry high grade material. That is why it must be worth pursuing."

Gerry could see Bill was still wavering.

"This is what the Research Section was set up to do, to look at new ciphers without operational pressures. At the last meeting of the Directing Committee, John considered the Hellschreiber was a most important commitment for the section. Read up on what we know so far, Bill, and see what you can make of that length of key."

Bill hesitated further but only briefly. Although nothing Gerry had said relieved his initial concerns, he relented, deferring to Gerry's position.

"What is a Hellschreiber?" Bill asked signalling, albeit reluctantly, his acceptance of what was effectively an instruction.

"It is a method of transmitting an image of a letter using a mosaic of dots, but don't waste any time on that. The file was called Hellschreiber because that is how it started. Concentrate on the teleprinter transmission and the key."

Back in the main room, Bill set down the file on the table then, without saying anything to the others, walked out. The day was dry but fresher than of late with the wind from the northeast; but Bill did not stop to put on his coat, he was too preoccupied.

It was not in Bill's nature to display his emotions, underneath, though, he was disconcerted at suddenly having to change tack. The self-doubt he had felt back in June crept back. He went for a walk to be away from the others while he thought through this latest turn of events. He needed to look at the issue objectively, not for it to be clouded by the spectre of John Tiltman. He needed to rationalise Gerry Morgan's instructions. The fact that Gerry had chosen him for this responsibility rather than anyone else carried, for the moment, no weight.

He took the perimeter path, walking slowly deep in thought. One obvious choice he had was to hand back the file. He would need to have a cogent reason and the consequences of doing so were difficult to discern. He was averse to any waste of his time and at first glance, there was potential for a great deal of wasted effort, either because of his own limited experience or because the task was innately impossible. On the other hand, the assignment did appear to have a familiar puzzle-type ring to it, the sort of mental amusement he enjoyed. He reflected on these aspects, concluding nothing could be decided without a detached assessment of the situation. Maybe it could be approached like an academic research project.

His mind began to clear and he felt a little less unsettled so he turned around and headed back to the Main Building. Stage one, he said to himself, was to investigate the problem. Setting aside and ignoring what the master cryptographer himself, John Tiltman, had already done would not be easy but somehow, he must try and maintain total objectivity.

"Are you all right?" asked Stephen who had been worried having witnessed Bill's sudden and silent departure. Stephen found Bill difficult to make out. Despite many efforts to engender a friendship given the many common bonds between them, Stephen felt Bill never really responded, never opened up. He appeared distant, almost as though he was on a different plane and not just with Stephen, with the others too. Stephen found it rather disconcerting but still kept a kindly look out for Bill.

"Err, yes, yes I'm fine," Bill replied as if not quite comprehending why the question had been asked and so not offering an explanation for his absence.

Bill opened the file and working from the bottom up, began to acquaint himself with the events that had brought the Hellschreiber to the attention of Bletchley Park. The beginnings reminded him of the Waberski affair from *The American Dark Chamber* when absolutely nothing was known about the ciphertext found on Pablo Waberski when he was arrested, neither the encipherment method nor the message language. This was almost the situation when the first Hellschreiber messages were picked up in June on a radio directional link between Vienna and Athens. For two reasons it was pretty obvious the message language would be German, the first being un-enciphered German first names appearing at the beginning of the transmissions and secondly, the transmissions themselves were between cities under German control, Greece having recently fallen to German occupation.

Bill was quite keen to learn more about the Hellschreiber method of transmission, not having heard of it before. There were many messages in the file on pasted strips like a telegram, only the printing was of poor quality and at a slant. Nevertheless, the names of Gustav, Ludwig, Otto, Konrad and the like were clearly visible at the beginning of the messages, such names preceding the ciphertext. Bill resisted the temptation to look into the Hellschreiber text transmission remembering Gerry's instructions to concentrate on teleprinter transmission. There was a note in the file that, in May, some transmissions, possibly practice transmissions, had been sent in a five unit code which led to the suspicion a teleprinter was being used. He was aware the teleprinter was in common use as a mode of message transmission usually by cable but he knew nothing of the technical side. He made a note and also wrote a second note that the use of names must have some significance.

The next set of papers in the file convinced Bill he needed to acquire an understanding of teleprinter equipment before going any further. These papers were an analysis of a series of messages sent on 22 July. The conclusion of Colonel Tiltman's team from this analysis was that the standard international teleprinter system was being used. If he was to question this conclusion, he needed to study independently the whole teleprinter structure.

As it was a Saturday and he had the afternoon off, he caught the train to Cambridge and headed for the Central Library where he found what he wanted in the Reference section.

He read that a teleprinter had a typewriter-type keyboard and when a key was depressed, the machine converted the letter, number or punctuation mark into a signal of five consecutive electrical impulses which were sent down a wire. The receiving teleprinter then converted the signal back into the letter, number or punctuation mark which it typed out. It was also possible, in a separate mode, to create a perforated tape which when run improved speed and accuracy particularly for long messages.

Bill paid particular attention to the system of impulses which had been laid down by an international convention. Each impulse was characterised either as a 'mark' or as a 'space' and because each signal was made up of five impulses, there was a range of 32 possible different signals, 26 letters for the letters of the alphabet plus six control characters. Bill made copious notes. He also carefully copied out the table of 26 letters and six control characters, indicating a 'mark' with a 'cross' and a 'space' with a 'dot' as he had seen in the file. He wrote 'A' equals x x • • • through to 'Z' equals x • • • x plus the six control characters two of which particularly interested him. One was • • x • • the signal for a word space or separator which on a printout showed as a '9'. Bill thought that character would occur very regularly. The other was • • • • • which, apparently, had no meaning and was used as an idle code for when no messages were being sent; it showed on a printout as a '/'.

He studied his notes on the return journey and again on Sunday so when Monday came, he felt more equipped to tackle the file.

First, he set out the analysis of the series of messages sent on 22 July. Strangely, only 16 different letters and control characters appeared in these messages and the analysis showed all these had a dot as the first impulse. Bill checked a sample and agreed with the conclusion they all correlated to the international convention and that probably a machine fault had resulted in all first impulses being sent as a dot.

Bill looked at the second part of the analysis which examined the German names that appeared at the beginning of the messages. Again, Bill followed some samples, H/INTRICH, TH/O3OR and GI9T4V. The first was quite obviously Heinrich where the convention for the first impulse of all the letters apart from 'E' was a 'dot'. Bill checked that if, as suspected, the first impulse was corrupted then the 'E', for which the convention was x • • • •, would be corrupted to • • • • • and print as '/' which it did. It was the same case for the 'E' in what was probably Theodor, where the 'D', x • • x •, was also corrupted to • • • x •, the control character '3'. Following the same principle, Bill converted GI9T4V to Gustav. The separator '9' character often appeared doubled to '99' when printed between the names, the character not being affected by the corruption.

Bill worked slowly through the papers, on his own as he preferred, making notes as he went but could not fault any of the analysis and agreed with the conclusions that the 26 alphabet letters and the six control characters correlated to the international convention. But he was less convinced with the file note which stated that the names clearly represented a 12-letter indicator. Whilst Bill agreed the method of transmission had been established, the Germans having developed a means of remitting the enciphered messages over the air rather than by cable, so far there was nothing to reveal the system of encipherment itself, no mention yet of Colonel Tiltman's long length of key. But there was plenty of other material in the file to work through.

Bill's eyes lit up at the next discovery Colonel Tiltman and his team had made. In a note written by Colonel Tiltman headed *Letter Subtractor Cipher,* he had summarised the analysis of several, more recent, pairs of consecutive messages 'in depth'. The analysis was based on two assumptions that the initial letters of the same group of German names at the beginnings of the messages provided a common 12-letter indicator and secondly that the arithmetic was Vernam modulo 2.

"This appears to be Hagelin territory," Bill said to himself.

His confidence was not misplaced as he was able to check each step of the analysis, recalling from Gerry Morgan's paper that with a letter subtractor cipher like the Hagelin, adding the two ciphertexts together eliminated the key and produced a stream of letters representing the addition of the two plaintexts. The trick then was to unpick this combined stream into its two separate streams of plaintext for which a successful crib was necessary to get started. But that alone was not enough because it was not possible to say which of the two plaintexts the crib belonged to, and so usually, more independent evidence was needed to make progress.

Had Colonel Tiltman read Gerry's Letter Subtractor paper, Bill wondered? Probably, but maybe he already knew the theory anyway.

But first, Bill needed to understand the arithmetic, the 'Vernam modulo 2' assumed for the analysis. He understood the mathematical principal of modulo 2 but needed to follow its application here and to appreciate what Vernam meant. In the end, it was very simple and was written out in the file note using dots and crosses;

$$\bullet + \bullet = \bullet$$
$$\bullet + x = x$$
$$x + \bullet = x$$
$$x + x = \bullet$$

It checked out as modulo 2 when Bill substituted '0' for a dot and a '1' for a cross. He also noticed it had the curious feature that addition was the same as subtraction.

What further impressed Bill was that Colonel Tiltman had spotted a group of seven letters that appeared a number of times in earlier plaintext messages and decided to use this group as a possible crib on one pair of messages. The result was extraordinary. It produced for the other plaintext message the string SPRUCHN and the Colonel had written underneath 'spruchnummer – serial number' and a triumphant 'Da bist du ja!' By adding SPRUCHN to the relevant seven ciphertext letters, he calculated a short stream of key letters. But despite much effort, no further progress appeared to have been made on that pair of messages or on other messages where a brief start had been made.

It all checked out and Bill could not shift any of the results. However, for Bill these results were useful confirmation of a number of further findings. Firstly, the 12-letter indicator system which he had doubted now appeared valid. Secondly, the method of encipherment was clearly of the letter subtractor type. And possibly of equal importance, a form of modulo 2 had been established as the method of addition and subtraction of letters. Somehow, Bill felt the discovery of the arithmetic of letters was of major significance as it appeared to link directly the system of encipherment with the method of transmission, something he had not seen before. He continued to make his own notes.

Nevertheless, Bill reflected, whilst considerable advances had been made so far from a Pablo Waberski-type beginning, when nothing was known, the additive key still remained a mystery, still no clue. All in all though, his regard for Colonel Tiltman had risen considerably. He closed the file. He had the whole weekend off and Cedric was coming over to stay.

In the morning, Bill walked the couple of miles from Adstock to Winslow Railway Station. He was surprised by how busy it was. The train from Bletchley was on time and he and Cedric walked back to Adstock in the warm early October sunshine. Bill introduced Cedric to Mrs Clarke who was busy behind the Post Office counter. Mrs Clarke had come to like the quiet young Mr Tutte whom she suspected was very intelligent and well read. Any friend of his from Cambridge was likely to be of a similar disposition and she had readily agreed to Cedric staying; she would make up the other bed in Bill's room.

"Pleased to meet you, Mr Smith," she smiled then addressed both of them. "I have made you up some sandwiches. They're in the kitchen. Don't forget, though, I have to balance up after we close this evening so tonight, you'll have to get your supper at The Olde Thatched Inn. Enjoy your stay Mr Smith."

"I will," said Cedric. "I've really been looking forward to meeting you and exploring your lovely village. Bill has told me so much about it."

They dumped Cedric's small case in their room, collected the wrapped sandwiches and made their way round to the postman's house where he said he would leave two bicycles they could borrow. Tucking their trousers into their socks, they headed north towards the village of Thornborough. The going was easy, the weather perfect and the traffic non-existent. They enjoyed the exercise, the wind on their cheeks and the peaceful rural scenery. Beyond Thornborough, they stopped at the bridge over the Great Ouse and picnicked on the river bank.

"Aren't we lucky with the weather? It's just like I remember when we went Youth Hostelling to North Wales last summer," said Cedric as they opened their sandwiches. "Thankfully, the terrain is a lot flatter. Some of those hills in North Wales were killers."

"At least you are more proficient at cycling than you were then. I don't know how you made it there and back in one piece!"

"You should get a bike," said Cedric. "You would have a lot of fun cycling around here."

"It's been on my mind. I could ask Mrs Clarke if I can put a wanted notice in the Post Office. Bikes are difficult to get hold of round here, though."

They chatted as they ate in the sunshine, talking about their families, the latest news from Trinity College and heavily censored bits and pieces from Bletchley Park. Cedric was keen to hear of Jack Good and Rolf Noskwith and whatever Bill could tell him of his work but Cedric learned nothing more than it was, 'interesting'. Over a meal at the inn, they talked mathematics to the bemusement of the locals who were curious who these two gobbledegook-speaking young men might be.

They discussed mathematics all morning while Mrs Clarke was at church and while a joint of beef was roasting in the oven, a special treat for her special guest, she said. Mrs Clarke had found Cedric most amusing, although she was not always sure of his quirky humour. They enjoyed their special Sunday lunch after which Bill and Cedric set off to walk back to Winslow Station.

"What are you doing about your call-up?" asked Bill on the way, knowing his friend had voiced his objections to any kind of military involvement.

"I have applied to register as a Conscientious Objector. I had to go and fill in a form at the Labour Exchange. Needless to say, there were whisperings and murmurings from those around me. But I am totally convinced in my belief and some caustic comments are not going to unnerve me. I have already been subjected to a few purposely loud comments around Cambridge that I am not in uniform. I shall have to wait now to be summoned to a tribunal. My father is coming down soon for a visit and just to be purely perverse, I bet they call me then."

"I know what it's like when people say you should be in uniform. What does your father say?" Bill wanted to know.

"I think he may be disappointed but doesn't say so. All he says is that I'm his son and he will support me in whatever I do. I suppose your brother is still having a go at you for not joining the military. I've said before, I think it's jealousy. I know you can't tell him what you are doing now which must be pretty galling."

"What will happen at this tribunal, do you think?"

"The Peace Pledge Union advise you to take one of their people along to represent you but I think I can do it myself. I may take someone from the Friends to vouch for me, to say I didn't join last week! I'm hoping to go to the Quaker training place at Cullompton in Devon which should help my cause. I rather think, though, that they will not let me off completely. I expect I will be ordered to do some menial civilian work. If they refuse my application altogether and say I have to go into the military, even in a non-combatant role, I shall refuse to serve and will end up in prison. You will come and visit me, won't you?"

"Oh, Cedric," sighed Bill. "This really is serious. I know you are totally committed. In a way, I envy you. I'm not really committed to anything. Well, except maths! I don't know what I would have done had this job not come up. I could never have survived in National Service. I just would not have fitted in. It would have been like I was back at school where I was picked on by the other boys and ridiculed because I was clever and didn't fight back. I couldn't survive. But if I had registered like you, I think the tribunal would have dismissed my application. Then where would I be? If I had to do something, I guess what I am doing is useful employment, although I know you won't agree on principle. I might have mentioned the work is even interesting. Bletchley Park is a bit like university where intellect is respected so I guess I'm lucky. If you think about it, you and I differ, yet we are the same. You have a faith; I have none. You shun conflict; I shy away from it."

"I'm glad you have found a niche that suits your talents," said Cedric. "I'm not worried what happens to me. I will accept whatever punishment is metered out. This whole thing, though, has made me think I'd really be interested in taking up some sort of peace studies, some form of conflict resolution. Not Mrs Jones chasing her husband with a rolling pin when he's late home from the pub! No, international conflict. At a level that can make the world a better place. That interests me."

"A laudable aim, Cedric but I'm afraid after the tribunal, you may have plenty of time to think about it," Bill said with pointed wit.

"You are a true friend, Bill, not judging me like most people. But don't be upset when I write poking fun at those prosecuting this stupid war, it's just my way."

"Keep writing, Cedric. Your letters always cheer me up, especially when you get the maths wrong!"

"Enough of this morbid stuff! Let's talk about something more uplifting like my latest idea, a functional matrix."

The pair strolled along, happy in each other's company. Cedric could never understand people who said Bill was so quiet and reserved. With him, well, they were just like any other close friends.

Monday morning saw Bill re-immerse himself in the Hellschreiber file. The next section was Colonel Tiltman's work leading to the long string of key that Gerry Morgan had mentioned. After Bill had followed the Colonel's workings and sampled a number of his calculations, he was utterly amazed at what the Colonel had achieved.

Two messages of about 4,000 letters had been picked up on 30 August 1941, both from the same source, both with the same indicators and both with the same first seven letters of ciphertext. It was obvious that Colonel Tiltman had deduced the same key had been used for both messages and had, as earlier, added one stream of ciphertext to the other to eliminate the key. What Bill saw next, he found staggering as the Colonel, bit by bit and zig-zagging back and forward, had unpicked the stream of the combined plaintext messages for the whole of the slightly shorter of the two messages. Bill could see how the Colonel had used a crib to find a partial word in the second message and then having guessed the full word, extended the crib. At one point, the Colonel had written a note to the effect that he thought both messages were essentially the same with arrows pointing to very similar groups of letters in both plaintext streams. But Bill could see in the second, shorter message these groups were not in the same position but were slightly earlier in the stream and that the Colonel had used this divergence to his advantage. Bill followed some examples of confirmed letters in the longer stream being predicted by the Colonel to appear at a certain earlier position in the shorter stream. By going backwards and forwards and up and down between the two plaintext streams and the combined stream, the Colonel succeeded in recovering the letters of the shorter plaintext message. He had then added this plaintext stream to the shorter ciphertext stream to reconstruct the length of key and had ringed the number 3,976 which Bill presumed was the number of letters in the length of key. The Colonel had also made a short test of adding the key to the longer ciphertext to prove the two plaintext messages were the same apart from some abbreviations and short cuts that the operator had made when presumably re-sending the first message.

Bill came across a translation of the message which was a report for the personal information of the German Military Attaché in Athens on the situation on the Russian front after the first few weeks of the invasion. It was interesting but well out of date as the British newspapers were now full of the German onslaught against Moscow.

So, Bill reflected, this is the long length of key that Gerry wanted him to investigate. How, Bill wondered, after this tour de force by Colonel Tiltman had the Colonel not been able to progress any further? There were various workings in the file, lengthy attempts at breaking the key on wheel periods comparable to the Hagelin. All these attempts petered out which surprised Bill as everything else was a demonstration of the Colonel's cryptographical brilliance.

There was one last investigation in the file, several pages analysing the frequency of the indicator letters. Bill was unsure of the purpose of this analysis as he had not seen anything of this nature before. Nevertheless, he studied the results in case there was something interesting. The conclusions noted were brief. Only 25 letters of the German alphabet were used, excluding 'J', ä, ö, ü and ß. The first 11 positions of the 12 indicators utilised all the remaining 25 letters. The twelfth position, however, only ever utilised 23 letters, the pairs omitted differing from month to month. The middle letters of the alphabet had a greater frequency than letters nearer the beginning or the end of the alphabet. Beyond that, the writer had not drawn any inferences from the analysis. Bill suspected the twelfth position with only 23 letters may have some significance but the analysis gave him no hint.

Bill closed the file.

"What now?" he said to himself. It had taken him nearly a month to get this far and he was at a loss what to do, where even to start. Since the Colonel had abandoned various attempts based on a particular hypothesis, there was probably little point in going down that route again. He could not imagine the Colonel had not thought of and rejected other hypotheses which left Bill at a complete loss of what to do.

He pushed the bulky file into the lockable cupboard and fetched his coat. It was cold outside, with a brisk northerly wind and rain in the air. He pondered the problem on the way to Adstock but was soon distracted when Mrs Clarke said there was a letter for him. It was from Cedric. Bill wondered if there would be news of his application for Conscientious Objector status.

After supper, Bill retired to his room as usual. He smiled as he unfolded the letter to see Cedric had started to write it while waiting in a train at Paddington Station on his way to the Spiceland Quaker Training Centre at Cullompton.

He had attended a tribunal and he could report the outcome was as expected. It had agreed he could go to Cullompton and afterwards work for the Friends Relief Service. He asked if Bill would be prepared to certify he was a fit and respectable person to do Friends Relief Service work in support of his application. But of course, Cedric added, it will depend on whether the Friends Relief Service has any money to employ him! Otherwise, he was ordered to report to the Head Porter at Addenbrooke's Hospital. He had asked for time to publish his PhD thesis but his request had been turned down which was a shame. He wrote that most people had been very sympathetic saying what a pity it was that the tribunal always puts people into jobs for which they aren't suited. Even non-pacifists at the college were complimentary about the Friends Relief Service. The rest of the letter was written over several days and Bill was pleased to see he was his usual amusing self, talking of being a general duster, sweeper and dead rat remover at Cullompton. But there were also some net theory ideas which kept Bill's mind off the Hellschreiber question.

The following morning, though, the problem faced him again. Bill was only too aware of Gerry's words that Colonel Tiltman had told the hierarchy this was a most important piece of work for the Research Section. He abstractly opened the file without real purpose. Where should he start? He had no point of attack. He got up and moved over to the window where, for some time, he just stared in contemplation into the distance, twiddling his pencil. He put his pencil down on the window sill and unconsciously cupped his chin with his right hand whilst supporting his right elbow with his left hand, a pose he sometimes unwittingly adopted when totally absorbed.

This odd stance caught the attention of Jerry Roberts, a recent linguist recruit, who whispered rhetorically to Stephen Freer.

"What is he doing? He's been there ages."

But Bill's mind did finally alight on one small detail which he had vaguely noticed a number of times but had passed over as being of no consequence. All the Hellschreiber messages were very long compared to the much shorter Hagelin messages. Maybe the Germans were using longer periodicities than other systems and that was why the Colonel's approach using typically short periodicities did not work. He remembered from his coursework that writing out a key on a period sometimes produced patterns which could be useful. But what periodicity? The only numbers in the file were those relating to the supposed indicators, 25 letters for most of the indicators and 23 for one indicator. Maybe he should use one of these; but which one? Perhaps, he could look for patterns for both at the same time by writing out the key on the multiple of 25 times 23. It seemed pretty unlikely the Germans would use such a long period but Bill decided on this in the absence of anything else. Since the key was nearly 4,000 letters long, he would get seven rows to look at for patterns.

Eventually, he became aware of noises in the room and thought he ought to look busy and sat down taking up a pencil and paper. He wrote out the multiplication of 25 times 23. The product, 575, certainly looked an improbably long periodicity. Colonel Tiltman's key was a string of teleprinter characters and Bill thought any patterns might be difficult to spot. Since each character was made up of five impulses, maybe he could write up the individual impulses. Just possibly, the part might be cryptographically simpler that the whole. Bill decided on writing up all five individual impulses, starting with the first.

He had no real confidence in this method but he had to start somewhere. But there was insufficient room on the table he shared with the others so he gathered up a handful of sheets of squared paper, a pot of glue, a couple of pencils, a rubber, tucked the file under his arm and traipsed out.

"What's Bill up to now? Where's he going?" asked Jerry Roberts puzzled again by Bill's antics. The questions were directed at no one in particular. A shrug of the shoulders was the general response. The others were used to Bill's long periods deep in thought and his occasional odd behaviour.

Bill was looking for somewhere with a big enough space for his 575 lengths of the first impulse. Fortunately, just down the corridor there was a room that was temporarily vacant. He took up residence and set about carefully sticking together his sheets of squared paper into a long enough length. The only furniture in the room was a small table and soon, his length of paper was hanging over both ends. He was about to start filling in the squares when he realised he was hungry. He looked at his watch. No wonder he was hungry, the second lunch sitting was nearly over. He dashed down to the canteen just in time before the shutters came down and gobbled his meal, anxious that someone might claim rights to the room in his absence.

There was no chair so he had to crouch over the table as he very carefully began to fill in his long sheet with pencilled dots and crosses in the squares that represented the first impulse. Whilst his expectations of any sort of outcome were low, he knew he had to proceed with total accuracy otherwise the exercise could be made useless.

He had not realised how stiff he had become until he pulled himself upright after the last mark. With both ends of the paper overhanging the table, it was not that easy to scan it for patterns and so he laid it out carefully on the floor. It was beginning to get dark. He put the light on and at the same time looked at his watch. It was nearly time to go. In the dim light of the single bulb, Bill started to look for repeated patterns of five or more dots and crosses occupying the same position in the seven rows but saw nothing noteworthy. Luckily, there was a key in the door so he locked the room and pocketed the key before grabbing his coat from the other room and hurrying to his transport to Adstock.

All evening, Cedric's letter again provided a distraction. In the morning, he half expected some sort of telling off for locking the vacant room as space was at such a premium in the Main Building. But his luck held and he managed to 'borrow' a spare chair from a nearby room.

He spent hours on his hands and knees looking unsuccessfully for patterns of possible statistical significance. He gave up and sat back, his disappointment not altogether unexpected.

Then all of a sudden, being a little further away from the grid of dots and crosses and at a slight angle to it, he began to pick out some patters on the diagonals. He got back on his hands and knees. Yes, there were definitely patterns on a number of diagonals, sufficient enough in length and in number to be of some significance. His heart began to race. What should he do? Call some of the others? Such impulsiveness was not in his nature. He got up and turned away moving to the other side of the room to ponder this development.

Slow down, he told himself; haste could lead you up the wrong path. Patterns repeated on the diagonal did not fit with the training exercises he had completed on the course; they needed to be in the same position in the rows, in line vertically with each other in the grid. The answer came to him. He needed to write out the key again but this time, on a period of 574 not 575. That would bring the patterns he had seen into line vertically. But that needed another long slog of carefully writing out the 4,000 dots and crosses again but it had to be done to enable the proper analysis of the patterns. He decided to keep his discovery to himself, for the time being, until such time as he had greater proof that here was something of real significance going on within the key. But he did not have enough sheets of paper and had to go back to the main room to get some. Inevitably, faces looked up as he entered the room. Everyone was curious at Bill's absence and silence.

"What are you up to?" Jerry Roberts called out pointedly, never shy in coming forward.

"Just trying something," Bill replied vaguely as he helped himself to some more sheets of paper.

"Any chance we may be allowed into the secret?" persisted Jerry.

"Later, maybe," said Bill distractedly as he hurried out.

Jerry threw up his hands in exasperation. The others smiled wryly being more used to Bill's rather taciturn manner.

Laboriously, Bill wrote out the key on a period of 574. As he did so, the diagonal patterns he had spotted before became readily apparent, but now in line vertically. They practically leapt out of the grid at him, as he progressed. He could feel his heartbeat as he recorded the results which he then studied. There were definitely enough repeated patterns to be of significance, repeated patterns that could not be the consequence of a random key, that must be the product of some mechanical operation, probably of a rotor type. Nevertheless, 574 as a period was surely far too long to be likely. So what other possibilities were there? He contemplated the number 574. In his head, he quickly factorised it giving him the prime numbers two, seven and 41. Seven was too small a prime number to be applicable but 41 looked probable. It was also a much larger number than the Colonel had been working on earlier. He decided to write out the key yet again, this time on a period of 41 which would give him nearly 100 rows. Fortunately, he had earlier grabbed enough paper for this rewrite.

The results were remarkable; the grid was replete with repeats of patterns of five or more in length; a few were even over 20 dots and crosses long. Short reversed patterns too were common above and below each other in adjoining rows. In his mind, there was no doubt he was on to something very significant, potentially a wheel with 41 active or inactive pins, or something similar, producing with each full turn a repeating pattern of dots and crosses. But it had been quite obvious from early on as he wrote out the grid on the period of 41 that he had only a partial answer. If there was only one rotor of period 41 in operation, every row of the grid would have been the same; but they were not. Something else was affecting the key, something that caused the pattern repeats but otherwise produced a grid that appeared random. His initial satisfaction at alighting on the period of 41 was tempered by the 'something else' yet to be solved but he was encouraged it was solvable.

But should he tell Gerry Morgan what he had so far? No, there was much more to do. He wanted to see if he could prove his current thinking that there was a first wheel of period 41 and possibly, a second wheel of an unknown period or of unknown action. He wanted to tease out both components, comparable in his mind to Colonel Tiltman teasing out the two messages from the August depth, before involving anyone else.

The weather over the weekend had been foul with torrential rain which had kept Bill indoors. He spent his time thinking about some graph theory topics for his thesis. He could not know when he might return to Cambridge but the subject was always on his mind.

Monday morning dawned brighter and he was expecting the usually cheery driver to make a remark about the change in the weather but he was taken by surprise.

"Have you seen the news?" said the driver obviously referring to something major.

"No," said Bill. "What's happened?"

"The Japs have bombed Pearl Harbour, you know the US fleet in the Pacific. We're now at war with Japan with the Americans!"

"Is that true?" exclaimed Bill. The news was a total shock.

"Oh yes. The papers are full of it, calling it a World War. I don't know what to make of it, me, but it sounds serious. What will it mean, do you think?"

"I don't know," answered Bill at a loss. There had been talk of deteriorating relations between the United States and Japan but Bill had not taken a great deal of notice of it.

On the way, the driver repeated some of what he had heard on the radio. The surprise and deadly attack had caused considerable damage and loss of life; the full extent of which was not yet clear but the ramifications for America and for Britain were immense. The course of the war had taken a sudden and dramatic turn.

When Bill arrived in the Research Section room, everyone was huddled over the day's newspapers, the atmosphere sombre with disbelief.

"See this," said Jerry Roberts reading from one newspaper. "Germany and Japan now stand arrayed together against all the liberties and sanctities they have outraged, and the flames they have kindled unite into a conflagration that encircles the globe."

Someone else pointed to a headline, 'Japan's Infamy'.

Speculation of what this might mean was bandied about. Those from the military focussed on the fact that Britain now had a mighty ally committed to the fight. Others quoted further from the newspapers that it would take time for America to mobilise fully its forces and to turn its industry to maximise military production. One article said America's attention would be on the Pacific which might mean less help for Britain, that our immediate predicament may not improve and we must prepare to do more for ourselves. Someone reckoned it would not be long before we saw US Intelligence people at Bletchley Park. Everyone was dismayed at the news which had come right on top of the headlines from only two days before that furious German attacks on Moscow had been beaten off. In the days that followed, the seriousness of the situation became more and more apparent as formal declarations of war were made.

Bill turned his attention back to the Hellschreiber and over the next few weeks made many attempts to analyse the 41-period grid. There was no discernible fixed period second wheel that he could find by conventional methods. One possible deduction was that the regular patterns he had found were actually sections of the 41-wheel unchanged by the secondary component. But that could only be caused by strings of dots or of crosses in the secondary component much longer than might be expected. He recalled from the Hagelin manual that long stretches of active or inactive pins was cryptologically unsound and he could not believe the Germans would be that lax.

Gerry Morgan, who had been away, called in on Bill for an update.

"Ah. Still here on your own, Bill! Are you all right tucked away here? What progress on the Hellschreiber?"

"I think I might have a foot in the door," said Bill modestly. "It's not certain yet but I believe I may have the periodicity of one wheel. I'm still trying to prove it. But I'm pretty certain the key is made up of two wheels, or maybe even more; one of fixed periodicity and something aperiodic. If I can separate out the fixed periodicity from the key, I will be able to attack the aperiodic element."

"That sounds promising," said Gerry encouraged at the news. "Do you want any help?"

"Not at the moment, Gerry. I'd rather plough on by myself."

"Mmm. Keep me in touch though. This work is still seen as very important and if we have a breakthrough we should not waste time if more hands to the pump are needed." Gerry turned to leave not absolutely sure he had made the right decision to let Bill carry on alone. "Oh," he added. "Are you going home for Christmas? You haven't put in a request yet. Oh, and another thing, if this room is needed, you know you'll have to give it up."

"I know," said Bill returning to his papers, glad to have been allowed to press on with solving his own personal enigma.

"Christmas!" he said to himself. "I'd forgotten about Christmas." He remembered Cedric had said in his last letter that he was going home for Christmas. "I suppose I had better go home too," he said to himself unenthusiastically. He glanced out of the window. The thick fog that had persisted for several days still blanked out the view and he hoped it would soon clear otherwise travel over Christmas would be difficult. He made a mental note to fill in the leave request chitty.

The trains were extra busy on Christmas Eve but Bill got home in time for a warm welcome from his mother and father, some supper and Churchill's broadcast to the world from America. It was short and encouraged everyone to enjoy the celebrations, albeit short, with their families. Churchill ended:

"Let the children have their night of fun and laughter. Let the gifts of Father Christmas delight their play. Let us grown-ups share to the full in their unstinted pleasures before we turn again to the stern task and the formidable years that lie before us, resolved that, by our sacrifice and daring, these same children shall not be robbed of their inheritance or denied their right to live in a free and decent world. And so, in God's mercy, a Happy Christmas to you all."

Again, Bill was enthralled by Churchill's oratory.

"We ought to drink to that," said Bill's father. "It's Christmas after all. Shall we get the bottle of sherry out, Mother?"

"Only a thimbleful for me though," said Bill's mother with a little tee-hee. "You know it goes to my knees!"

The rest of the evening was like the Spanish Inquisition with Bill's mother wanting to know everything. There was a lot he could tell her and a lot he could not.

"As long as you are all right," she kept saying seeking reassurances which Bill gave regularly. Yes, Mrs Clarke looked after him all right. Yes, he had enough to eat. Yes, he didn't have to work too hard. Yes, the people were nice. And more.

Christmas Day saw Brother Joe, Lola, young Joey and Jeanne come over for a traditional dinner and presents. Bill had managed to get some sweets for the children, a real treat, and he played games with them by the fire. For once, Joe held his criticisms. It was all too brief though and Boxing Day saw Bill head back to Bletchley Park with his mother's plea not to leave it so long next time.

Back in his solitary confinement, Bill resumed his attack on the Hellschreiber. One analytical attempt produced useful results. By conducting a frequency analysis of patterns found in sets of five columns, he found they could be brought into close alignment by adding a constant sequence of dots and crosses, and that the constant sequences could be fitted together to form a periodic sequence of 41. It looked promising. He set about adding that sequence to the length of key using modulo 2, a process he knew would cancel out the fixed period of 41 revealing a sequence of nearly 4,000 dots and crosses that represented the other element.

After another long session of concentration, he gave a deep sigh and leant back. Pausing for a moment, he thought it would be useful to identify each stream by giving it a name. Being a mathematician, the Greek for X and Y came into his head. He decided to call the 41-period wheel Chi and the other element Psi.

"Now, what are the non-random properties of psi?" he asked himself, setting out on the hypothesis that there was a set period but that it was being masked in some way.

Bill studied the psi stream. He noted down what he called local peculiarities, sequences he would not have expected to find. An examination showed a dot was more likely to be followed by a dot and a cross by a cross. This equality was evident in about three quarters of the stream. Oddly, sequences he would expect to find, like dot, cross, dot and its reverse cross, dot, cross were almost non-existent. He puzzled over the effects of these peculiarities. It occurred to him that if proportionately there were many more double dots and double crosses than changes from one character to the other, then equally many of the changes from dot to cross from one column to its adjacent column in the grid must be due to a change in the 41-period chi sequence. He tried out this theory with spectacular results. When he analysed the number of dot/cross and cross/dot pairs in adjacent columns, the totals produced a definite split between those counts that were well above half the total number of pairs in the columns and the counts that were well below half. He concluded a high count must mean the wheel had made a change when it moved on to its next state and a low count meant there was no change. He very quickly reproduced the chi sequence using this method which had a very remarkable alignment to his earlier findings. The very definitive differences between the two sets of counts convinced him this 'pairs' method was the more accurate method. He was satisfied he had the final proof of the chi wheel.

He returned to his attack on the psi stream with renewed confidence. But a week passed with no progress. At one point, he stood in a corner of the room sighing deeply in frustration and disappointment that his latest efforts turned out to be wasted.

The weather turned very cold at the weekend. Bill was reduced to sitting in his room at his digs, wrapped up in his coat and scarf passing the time on one of Cedric's theorems they had discussed at New Year when Cedric had visited him. They had gone along to The Olde Thatched Inn to get warm rather than to have a drink, making a glass of cider each last as they talked earnestly about Cedric's latest idea to the bemusement of the locals. Something Cedric said then about an irregularity of distributions problem came to mind that made him stop. It came to him that in relation to the psi problem perhaps, the psi wheel sometimes moved on with each letter of text and sometimes it stood still. This stuttering, as he called it, could explain the unusually long sequences of dots or of crosses in the psi stream; and if this stuttering was irregular that could explain why a second fixed period had not emerged.

On Monday morning, Bill returned to Bletchley Park through the fog that had returned accompanied by bitter temperatures. He was, however, full of excitement at testing his new hypothesis for the psi wheel. After much experimentation reducing the strings of all dots and all crosses to produce a much more cryptologically acceptable wheel pattern, he eventually arrived at a period of 43 which appeared to produce statistically valid results.

Without doubt, he had reached a pivotal moment and he drew back in his chair, stood up and paced slowly round the room, not sure how he felt. It was not exactly elation, more a deep satisfaction. This was not the end of it; he had not mastered his adversary the Hellschreiber, far from it. But he had gained just a soupçon of confidence to think to himself that mastery may be possible one day. He had not just a foot in the door but he had pushed the door ajar sufficient to see there was a machine behind Colonel Tiltman's key, a machine which in all probability had five pairs of wheels, each pair of wheels operating on one of the five teleprinter impulses. He was confident he had discovered one set of wheels; a chi wheel, as he called it, with a period of 41 and the corresponding psi wheel with a period of 43. Although he had looked briefly at the stuttering of the psi wheel, he had not come to any conclusions about the law governing its action. But it was time to acquaint Gerry Morgan with his findings.

"Any chance of a word?" Bill enquired nervously having poked his head around Gerry's door.

"A bit later on, Bill, I've got a meeting in a minute. Come and see me after lunch. Good news, I hope!" he said.

"I think so," said Bill a little piqued at the rebuff, at having to contain the news of his crucial discovery for a little longer.

Bill went along to Gerry's room soon after the lunch break.

"Now what have you got," Gerry invited.

"I have the period of the two wheels that operate on the first impulse," Bill blurted out with rare enthusiasm.

"You have what! Why didn't you tell me before? Show me!" exclaimed Gerry, suddenly all attention.

He followed Bill's step-by-step, truncated account of the past few months, listening closely. He remained silent throughout, only nodding his agreement now and again. He saw no need to question Bill's methods and was anxious to learn his conclusions.

Bill finished, "To identify the two different streams I've used Greek letters: the periodic stream I've called 'Chi' and the aperiodic stream 'Psi'."

There was a slight pause as Gerry absorbed the very significant import of Bill's findings.

"I should get John along," he said picking up the phone.

A minute or two later, Colonel Tiltman came into the room, his demeanour brisker than usual.

"What have you got, Gerry?" he demanded, obviously keen for news.

"Bill will show you," said Gerry gesturing to Bill to go ahead.

Bill repeated his account condensing it even further, confident in front of 'the master' having had Gerry's tacit endorsement. He could see from the Colonel's eyes, he was completely absorbed, following every word. Indeed, the Colonel's mind was soon working ahead.

"A breakthrough at long last! Impressive stuff, Bill. I suggest you get everyone on this, Gerry. See if we can't get out the rest of this machine quickly. Good stuff, indeed; Kasiski to the rescue again. Let me know how you get on or if you need more resources. This could be very important."

After the Colonel's departure, Gerry called in the rest of the Research Section. Bill felt all eyes on him as Gerry explained developments. The others all knew Bill had locked himself away looking at the Hellschreiber, wondering if he had made any progress yet suspecting he had not as enquiries had received the usual Bill reticence. But the mood in the room quickly became buoyant, the excitement palpable and the team eager to get stuck in. Gerry divided up the task, giving three of the other four impulses to the rest of the team to work on, leaving himself and Bill to work on the fifth impulse.

Gerry gave the team directions.

"I suggest you book repeated patterns of seven in the first 500 characters and factorise the intervals in true Kasiski style. We're looking for relatively large prime numbers. Go carefully as mistakes writing out the stream of dots and crosses can lead to much wasted effort. Take your time. Come and see us if you have any problems." The chatter was all animated as the others left the room to work on their allotted impulse streams.

Matters had certainly moved much more quickly than Bill had expected and the look Gerry gave him as the others departed indicated their relationship had changed, changed to a closer and more mutually respectful one.

"Let's attack that fifth impulse," he said with a sparkle. This was the type of moment a seasoned codebreaker like Gerry Morgan dreamed of.

The fifth chi wheel was cracked by Bill and Gerry well before the others reported success, largely because of Bill's practiced eye at spotting patterns.

"Ah!" said Bill when it emerged the fifth chi wheel had a period of 23. "I thought that indicator with only 23 letters, the odd one out, must have significance. Now we know."

By the end of the next day, they had all five chi wheel periods. Bill, Gerry and the rest of the Research Section then tackled the remaining psi periods, unravelling them with increasing proficiency. It soon became obvious all the psi streams suffered the same sort of stuttering that Bill had found in the first one.

"Let's see what we've got," said Gerry reviewing the situation. "The chi wheels look like 41, 31, 29, 26 and 23, mostly prime with decreasing periods. The psi wheels 43, 47, 51, 53 and 59, again mostly prime but with increasing periods. That's 403 active/inactive pins compared to the Hagelin with 131. And we have still to work out the law governing the psi movement. This machine is some monster!"

It took another couple of days of mathematical analysis of the blocks of dots and crosses in the psi streams to work out the stuttering. Gerry thought there was another key acting on the psi streams and called it the Motor Key; Bill labelled it 'Mu' after the Greek letter 'M'. Since Bill had identified the fifth chi wheel with the indicator limited to 23 letters, the assumption was made that the first five of the 12 indicators related to the psi wheels and the last five to the chi wheels. That left the two middle indicators which they deduced controlled the Motor Key. Several hypotheses were tried without success until Bill noticed the key was nearly periodic and finally, they discovered there were two linked mu wheels. The first mu wheel they found had a period of 61 and moved on with each text letter like the chi wheels. The second mu wheel, however, only moved on when the first mu wheel showed a cross. That second wheel proved to have a period 37 and it moved all the psi wheels together only when it too showed a cross. The final piece of the puzzle, the stuttering of the psi stream, was now settled. A great sense of satisfaction pervaded the Research Section tempered by the knowledge that understanding how the machine worked was just the beginning.

"This afternoon," announced Gerry, "we'll make a mock-up of the machine as we know it."

At lunchtime, Jack Good saw Bill in the canteen sitting on his own and seeing a potential new recruit to the Chess Club went over and sat down.

"Bill, how are you? I've been meaning to catch you to see if you want to join the Chess Club. We could do with a few more members."

"Hello, Jack. I had heard there was a chess club but wasn't sure about joining."

"Come along. There are not that many of us at the moment but they are a good crowd, all abilities so everyone can have a decent game. Our next meeting is Tuesday evening in the Main Building, 7:00 P.M. I can introduce you around. Do you have a set?"

"Yes, I do. Cedric sent my set on to me when he had to move out of Trinity."

"Good, bring it along, we're short of boards. I'll see you there. Must go."

Knowing Jack would be there, he decided he would go along. He had been a member of Cambridge University's chess club but unlike Jack, who played competitively to a high standard, he played for enjoyment only.

Later that day, Colonel Tiltman paid an unannounced visit and was taken aback by what he saw as he entered the room.

"What the deuce is going on here!" demanded the Colonel. Bill and Gerry Morgan, both on their hands and knees on the floor, looked up at him somewhat startled at the outburst. As they scrambled to their feet, Gerry Morgan composed himself and began explaining.

"Look," he said pointing to some cardboard cut-outs and lengths of string on the floor, "we have mocked up what we think the Hellschreiber machine might look like. We cracked the last two wheels just this morning. The bits of string represent the impulses." He knelt down and Colonel Tiltman came around and crouched by him. "The first impulse comes along this bit of string here and is encoded by the first chi wheel represented by this cardboard cut-out wheel with 41 bits sticking out depicting its pins. It then goes along this piece of string to the first psi wheel here with 43 pins and is encoded by that wheel. But that wheel may or may not have moved after the last text letter, unlike the chi wheels which all move on one pin position each time, like this." He moved all the five cardboard chi wheels on one pin position. "This is because of these two linked wheels which we have called the Motor Key. They combine to determine whether the psi wheels move or not. This Motor Key wheel has 61 pins and moves on one position with each text letter. This second one has 37 pins and moves on only when the 61 wheel has an active pin, a cross in our notation. Only when the 37 wheel has a cross does it move on all the psi wheels together one position. This first impulse, then, having been encoded a second time by the 43-psi wheel, comes out here and is sent with the other four impulses to the teleprinter transmitter.

"The machine, John, encodes not only once, through the chi wheels, it encodes again through the psi wheels, and effectively a third time by the operation of the Motor Key wheels." Gerry adjusted a piece of string which was not quite correctly aligned and stood up as did a thoughtful Colonel. Everyone waited for the Colonel to say something.

"What about the rest of the periods?" asked the Colonel.

"Oh, we have all 12 of them," answered Gerry and he listed the two series and the two Motor wheels.

"My!" said the Colonel. "An excellent effort everyone. This has the potential to be a very significant breakthrough. But we need to push on to the next stage. We need to find out how the Germans use this machine. Most of you will know the Enigma has a set of interchangeable wheels which are set for each message according to a protocol. We need to find out what changes the Germans make to this Hellschreiber machine between the encipherment of different messages. Do they swap around these 12 wheels in some way, for instance? What do you think, Gerry? Maybe look at some messages around the date of 30 August? That's probably a good start point." He looked pointedly at Gerry Morgan. "We should give this priority. Can you let me have a one-page note please to take to Commander Denniston."

They all set to work again. But their efforts failed. Bill thought they may have more success attacking an earlier depth of 3 July knowing now some of the plain language to expect because of the experience gained from Colonel Tiltman's breakthrough. Excitement grew as they teased out two relatively long passages of plain text and so obtained two streams of useful key. Step by step, the analysis showed that the psi wheel patterns of the 3 July message were the same as the 30 August message but the other patterns were different. It was progress.

Bill found another depth that he thought might help, this one dated 21 July. The analysis of this depth provided vital information as all the wheel patterns were the same as 3 July depths except for the two motor wheels. Deductions from all these analyses enabled them to be pretty certain they now understood the basic operational procedures the Germans were following.

Gerry Morgan called all the Research Section together.

"Gather round everyone, I have some important news."

A buzz of anticipation rippled around the room.

"I think we have cracked the Hellschreiber! In little over six months since the very first breakthrough, we have a pretty good idea of the machine that produces these teleprinter encipherments. And unlike the Hagelin and Enigma, we have not had the machine in our hands to take apart.

"Bill and I are going to see Commander Denniston later today to tell him about your tremendous achievement. You should be proud of what you have accomplished, a real team effort. Doubtless, it is a further validation for having a dedicated Research Section. I will let you know what happens next after our meeting; meanwhile, I think you should pick up your other assignments where you left off."

Commander Denniston, the elderly, distinguished-looking head of Bletchley Park, sat at his large desk with Bill, Gerry Morgan and Colonel Tiltman in an arc in front of him. Colonel Tiltman knew Commander Denniston well and had great respect for him but it was rumoured that the Commander was about to be side-lined and his deputy, Commander Edward Travis would take over. Commander Denniston's lack of influence in Whitehall had been seen as a hindrance to the rapid expansion necessary at Bletchley Park and several months earlier, Alan Turing, Hugh Alexander and two other senior codebreakers had written directly to Churchill, bypassing Commander Denniston in a completely unprecedented fashion, complaining they were not being given the resources they needed. In their letter, they reminded Churchill of his recent visit to Bletchley Park. Without hesitation, Churchill responded that they should be given all they wanted on 'extreme priority'. Despite the rumoured changes at the top of the organisation, Colonel Tiltman felt that as Commander Denniston had backed his idea for a Research Section, the Commander should be presented with the Section's recent and most significant achievement.

Bill was never comfortable in such situations. He had not met the Commander before, having seen him only rarely at a distance, and was nervous in the presence of such exalted company. However, the Commander had smiled kindly when the Colonel had introduced him.

Gerry Morgan did most of the talking, praising Bill for his breakthrough and subsequent efforts but also acknowledging the contribution of the whole team. He explained how the 12 wheels had been revealed and ran through the conclusions of their most recent efforts.

"So, we know the wheel periods," said Gerry, "and we now believe the order of the wheels is fixed. We suspect the Germans leave the psi wheel patterns unchanged for periods exceeding one month but change the chi patterns more regularly. By comparison, though, the patterns for the motor wheels are changed quite frequently, maybe daily. That is where we are now, sir."

"Thank you for the update, Gerry. I did read your recent note. Impressive progress indeed," said the Commander. "Bill, a bit of luck you happened on your 574 period."

"Had I continued as I had planned, sir, to apply that period to all five impulses, my method would have found the many repeats on the fifth impulse. So yes, I saved myself a lot of work," was Bill's reserved yet pointed response.

"Well, well done again. Now though, gentlemen, we must press home our attack on this machine to see what intelligence we can glean from more current messages. I suspect it will be of great importance."

Bill left the meeting in quite a good mood, such that he looked forward to going along to the chess club that evening. He hoped Jack would already be there as he was always uneasy at entering a room full of unfamiliar faces.

Later, Bill looked inside the doorway and was relieved to see Jack already there.

"Bill, glad you could make it," he said. "This is Mac Chamberlain, Club Secretary. Mac, this is Bill Tutte."

"Welcome, Bill. What standard are you? Just so we can get you started."

"A bit above beginner, perhaps," said Bill with his usual understatement.

"You're too modest, Bill," chided Jack. "You used to win plenty of games at Cambridge. Put him with John Phillips."

Mac Chamberlain consulted his list.

"That would work," he said and called out, "John, come and meet Bill Tutte, your opponent for tonight." He then addressed them both. "Just a friendly to start with to see how you get on."

They shook hands and made their way over to a table. Bill set up his board.

"Much of a player?" enquired John.

"Not really," said Bill. "Just a few games at university."

"Me too. I wasn't sure about joining. I thought I'd be way out of my depth. Several internationals belong you know, Hugh Alexander, Stuart Milner-Barry, Tony Perkins and more. Not all of them come regularly; work, I suppose."

Bill took a white pawn and a black pawn and swapped them around behind his back. John chose white. His first move was pawn to king four. Bill followed; pawn to king four. John moved knight to king's bishop three. Again, Bill followed; knight to queen's bishop three. John paused then moved his bishop to queen's bishop four. Bill considered these opening moves and then developed his bishop to queen's bishop four, testing John to see if he was aware of the Evans Gambit, one of the few recognised openings he knew and often used himself. If John was familiar with the Evans Gambit, his next move would be pawn to queen's knight four. That was his next move from which Bill inferred John was no novice.

Bill now had to decide to accept the gambit or not. He deliberated for a few moments and decided to accept by taking the pawn, expecting white's pawn to queen's bishop three. John duly obliged. In consequence, Bill retreated his bishop to queen's rook four. The game then moved at a slow pace as Bill took his time over each move much to the increasing annoyance of John. But John eventually prevailed.

"Well done," said Bill. "I'm afraid I'm a bit rusty."

"Thanks," said John. "I enjoyed that." He was polite enough not to criticise Bill's slowness of play. "Let's see what the others are up to."

Bill sat behind Jack watching the endgame, impressed as Jack, having an extra pawn, faultlessly forced checkmate.

Afterwards, they sat for a while. Jack with his usual brevity explained his endgame tactics using his pawn advantage. Bill blamed losing on not having played for a while, rueing his failure to gain control of the centre of the board. Despite their different results, they both agreed it had been an enjoyable evening and with Jack's encouragement, Bill agreed he would come to next month's meeting.

The next day, Gerry Morgan told the team about the meeting with Commander Denniston and that the direction was now to attack current traffic. Initially, Bill and Jerry Roberts would tackle this next phase.

In effect, Jerry looked to Bill as his knowledge was greatest. They knew the wheel patterns for July but in order to decode a message not in depth, they needed to find the wheel settings. Bill called on his experience with the Hagelin, trying a probable crib. They had a couple of possibilities, S P R U C H 9 + + and S P R U C H N U M M E R 9 + +. Adding this clear language to the ciphertext would give a short string of key which could, with considerable and tedious analyses of the individual chi and psi streams, be unravelled and the settings found.

For a long time, they had no success but then one morning in early March, Jerry Roberts suddenly announced that he had something. Gradually, letter by letter, a recognisable message emerged. Gerry Morgan and the others quickly gathered round. A discernible excitement began to fill the room. Everyone recognised the huge significance of the moment. The first single message had just been successfully set and the plain language text was coming into view like the growing light of a dawn sun on a mountain top, as Jerry put it.

When Jerry Roberts sat back indicating the last letter was done, spontaneous applause rang around the room. Broad smiles were everywhere. Bill embarrassingly found himself the centre of attention; his face, for once, giving away a hint of satisfaction.

The Research Section was abuzz for several days and efforts to decode several more July messages were renewed with vigour and led to more success. Word came back from the intelligence hut that translations of the messages made interesting reading and confirmed the importance of their content but the information was stale and more up to date messages would be welcomed, please.

For Bill, however, the content was of far less consequence than the challenge the machine still posed. He had worried that since last August few signals were being picked up and there were no two or more messages encoded with the same key, no depths to work on. That is until February when traffic started to increase and depths began to appear again. The Germans had, apparently, ceased the Hellschreiber transmissions and were using tone transmissions but the basic teleprinter system remained the same. Bill was keen to attack these and asked Gerry for permission. His initial results were encouraging as the messages seemed to follow the same stereotyped forms as those from last July. He managed to read nearly three hundred letters of one February depth but his success ended there as he could not break into the wheel patterns and frustratingly had to abandon his efforts. Then anticipation rose when a depth of three came through towards the end of March and all attention was diverted to it. All three messages were read for about 1,000 letters but all attempts at finding the wheel patterns failed. Bill gave Gerry his conclusions.

"I reckon the Germans have changed the motor key so that we do not get the long stretches of dots and crosses which last year allowed us in. I'm afraid we are at an impasse," he said rather forlornly.

"Bit of a roller-coaster this one," said Gerry. "What now then?"

"Let me think about it."

Chapter 5
The Days of the Indicator

"Ah, there you are," said Daphne Bradshaw. "I thought you would like to know that there are a few digs in Bletchley that will become vacant when the Diplomatic and Commercial people move back to London. Would you be interested? I could put a word in for you with my husband if you like."

"Well, I would," said Bill. "But I wouldn't like to jump any queue."

"I think it would be justified because of the work you do. It's not like shift work where someone comes along and takes over at the end of a shift. I know how frustrating it can be to have to stop what you're doing simply to catch the transport home. Shall I ask my husband what might be available?"

"Well, yes please," said Bill.

The weather had been bitterly cold these couple of months, so much so that at night he had taken up a hot water bottle, had every blanket available on his bed, had worn a jumper over his pyjamas and some nights had even lain his overcoat on top of the eiderdown. Trying to do anything after supper in his room had become almost impossible it was so cold. The only source of heat in the house was from the range in the kitchen cum living room, occupied in the evenings by Mrs Clarke who hardly ever went out. Sharing with her was hardly conducive to thinking about Cedric's theories and puzzles. Bill had taken to reading a book by the warm glow of a gently hissing Tilly lamp before retiring early. Mrs Clarke was kindly enough and really quite astute but her conversation beyond the village and postal matters was somewhat limited. Unsurprisingly, Mrs Clarke had a great deal of interest in and knowledge of the village, always well versed in the latest gossip yet discreet when necessary. Bill, of course, could not talk about Bletchley Park and it was abundantly clear Mrs Clarke had no clue about the higher mathematics that interested Bill. Bill, however, paid her due respect, she could add up a long column of figures quickly and accurately and her mental arithmetic was spot on. The idea of somewhere more comfortable, nevertheless, was very appealing.

A few days later, Dorothy said her husband had somewhere nearby that Bill might find suitable but warned him it was inevitably more money. He called on Captain Bradshaw.

"Mrs Batchelor has a room in her place on Buckingham Road near the Methodist Church. It's within walking distance which would be handy. I've had good reports of her, especially her cooking! It's £3 a week. Can you afford that? It will be available on Sunday," said the Captain.

"I don't spend much, so I could afford it," said Bill. "It would be much more convenient."

"I will arrange it then and confirm you can move in on Sunday. No more early starts!"

"What about Mrs Clarke? Do I have to give her notice?"

"No. I'll write to her today to tell her. I have someone lined up to take the room there, someone on shifts at the nearby outstation."

The following day, Stephen Freer came over to Bill to have a word.

"I don't know if you have heard but Commander Denniston is heading up the Diplomatic Section which is moving back to Broadway. I'm going with them, leaving at the end of the week."

"Oh, dear," said Bill. "That's a shame, to have to move again so soon."

"Well, I don't have a choice really. Bletchley Park is not that bad. I quite like it here in the Research Section. But there's a war on so I suppose I have to go. I leave at the end of the week. At least you and I have found something useful to do in this ghastly war, Bill. What you have done here has been terrific. Hopefully, we will bump into each other again, if not soon then at Trinity after the war is over."

Stephen still felt awkward with Bill. He had expected the passage of time would naturally see Bill more communicative and friendly and he was rather bewildered and not a little frustrated that their relationship, as far as he was concerned, had not really improved that much. Even so, he hoped they could stay in touch if nothing more than as Trinity colleagues.

"Good luck, I'm sorry you are going," said Bill being polite, then he added enigmatically, "but I guess I am not sorry at the same time."

With a wry smile he explained, "On Sunday, I am moving to new digs five minutes' walk away, into a room being vacated by one of your people. It means I have an extra half hour in bed in the morning."

Stephen could see Bill was obviously pleased at his good fortune. "Jammy devil!" he declared, glad to have elicited a good-natured response at last. Maybe all was not lost with Bill.

There was a letter from Cedric at the Post Office when Bill arrived for his last night at Adstock and he spent the evening writing a reply. How typical of Cedric to convey a most important piece of news by a brief post script written vertically in the margin at the end of the last page of the letter, 'P.S. I'm a PhD.' Bill was so thrilled for his friend that he had to write a glowing congratulatory letter straight away. And to emphasise Cedric's achievement, he purposely addressed the envelope to Dr C A B Smith in recognition of his new official title. Cedric's letter, however, was not all good news. He seemed very upset. He had gone home to pack ready to take up a job with the Friends Relief Service only to hear they had suffered a financial setback and were unsure of anything. He was expecting the worst that the position would be cut altogether for lack of funds. Bill offered his commiserations, knowing how much Cedric wanted to be involved in this valuable community work.

When Bill arrived at Mrs Batchelor's house, suitcase in hand, she weighed up the shy, well presented, quiet young man and decided she liked the look of him. She knew not to enquire too much of people from the Park. She thought he would be a good replacement for the gentleman that just left for London.

Mrs Batchelor was a widow, a small, rotund lady who looked as though she took no nonsense. The large semi-detached house was immaculate. His room was twice the size of his Adstock room, had a hand wash basin with hot and cold water, electric light and an electric fire on a meter. There was a desk and a chair and the window overlooked gardens and trees. The communal bathroom was along the landing. Worth every penny of the extra rent, Bill judged. He learned there were two other let rooms in the house regularly occupied by visiting railway engineers. The place reminded him of South Ealing.

It quickly became obvious that Mrs Batchelor was house proud and she made it clear it was her house and her home and that she expected residents to be respectful and to abide by a few house rules. Nevertheless, she appeared kind-hearted and made Bill feel very welcome. He was pleased that while Mrs Batchelor announced the evening meal would be ready about six o'clock she also said she knew it was not always possible to get away on time and that she would keep the meal in the oven if he was late. It turned out she had the very welcome knack of keeping a meal hot without spoiling it. For Bill, life outside the Park had taken a distinct turn for the better.

Whilst all the changes at Bletchley Park had been going on, Colonel Tiltman had been in Washington. He had gone there specifically to discuss the avoidance of duplicated cryptographic effort between the Americans and the British. On his return, he called Gerry Morgan to see him to update him and find out the latest on the Hellschreiber. He told Gerry it had been agreed the British would concentrate on Axis codes, although some work would continue at Bletchley Park on Japanese codes. The Colonel did not expect, however, that Gerry would need to be much involved in any Japanese stuff as the Americans were taking the lead and sharing their cryptanalysis. One concern at Bletchley Park, the Colonel said, was the lack of Japanese speakers, a problem he was looking into, jokingly asking if Gerry fancied learning the language. They discussed the worsening news from the Far East; the fall of Singapore was still bitterly painful. Eventually, the conversation turned to the Hellschreiber.

"As you know," said Gerry, "we have been doing a lot of analysis on the July and August depths as few new depths were coming through. We have gained much useful data but no further breakthroughs. However, with the new tone transmissions replacing the Hellschreiber-style transmissions, depths are coming through again and so we turned our attention to current traffic."

"About the tone transmissions, Gerry," interrupted the Colonel, "I am in discussions with the wireless intercept people and I've put forward serious proposals for a dedicated listening station just for this important non-Morse stuff, but it is early days yet. They have some ingenious machines that pick up the very fast tone transmissions the German's are now using. The signals are then manually converted onto punched tape. We discussed the quality of the output they send to us and the need to give depths priority. They're new at it but they are developing processes to improve turnaround times and accuracy. They know what we want. And I am pretty sure we will see the quality we need."

"Let's hope so; some tapes have arrived corrupted which is very frustrating. One depth last month looked very promising but in the end, we failed to break it and we spent a great deal of effort on a recent depth of three without success. We were worried the Germans had closed the door on us. However, Bill Tutte has come up with another remarkable discovery. He had noticed one or two what he calls 'near depths' whose indicators agree in all but one or two of the 12 letters. By now, we are fairly confident we know how the 12 indicator letters represent the start positions of the 12 wheels of the machine. Incidentally, we think the indicator letters are not in alphabetic order round the wheels."

"Go on," said the Colonel, intrigued.

"Bill reckoned that when, say, a near depth of two had only one chi wheel indicator different then, having obtained the key for each message, the difference between the two keys would represent the modulo 2 sum of the two versions of the chi wheel directly corresponding to the two different wheel settings. He also reckoned the difference would have a period of that wheel. Adding that difference to one of the messages would turn the near depth into a true depth."

"Does it work?" asked the Colonel following the hypothesis intently.

"There was a near depth of 3 March which he attacked and got out nearly 300 letters of decode. So yes, it works. Not only that, he went on to analyse the resulting data on the chi wheel. That led, eventually, to his breaking that wheel which in turn led to breaking all the other wheels."

"Really! That is impressive!" said the Colonel, obviously pleased at the progress in his absence. "So, you have the wheel patterns for March?"

"Yes, and we were able to set, successfully, the abandoned depth of three, although the motor wheels were different. We were able to set more messages and as we did so, our understanding of the indicators grew and that knowledge became a more and more powerful tool."

Gerry could see a question forming in the Colonel's mind.

"This Bill Tutte of yours. He seems to be pretty involved in this. What's he like? I thought he was a chemist?"

"I'd say he's immersed himself totally in the Hellschreiber work. Actually, he's one hundred per cent a theoretical mathematician these days. I asked him the other day what he did with his spare time and it seems he and a Trinity friend of his bat back and fore some arcane mathematical theories for fun. He showed me some and they were, indeed, extremely esoteric."

"He's not divulging anything he shouldn't?" asked Colonel Tiltman with concern.

"No, no. I don't suspect anything like that. I know how the minds of some of these more abstracted mathematicians work, having come across a few in my time. He's a deep thinker, very deliberate. He understands the vital nature of the work here and the significance of the output but in my opinion, he is fixated on the theory of the Hellschreiber itself rather than its intelligence value. I may be wrong; he doesn't give much away." Gerry gave a small chuckle. "Except when we were discussing his friend's letter. Then he was unusually animated, quite voluble actually."

"Is he another Turing?"

Gerry wondered where John Tiltman's line of thinking was leading. Was he looking to set up a Hellschreiber hut, separate from the Research Section? With Bill as its Head?

"Mmm," mused Gerry. "I hadn't thought about him in those terms. Overall, I guess not, but I suppose there are some similarities. He is a young academic, still only 24. He is really quite reserved and at times appears distracted, even naïve. Has he what it takes to do what the Prof has done with Enigma? In terms of sheer mathematical analysis, very probably. In terms of leading a team, most probably not; certainly not now."

"How can you best use him, then?"

"He's definitely better suited to the research, analytical side of things. That's his forte, I'd say, not the practical, production side which is why I gather the Prof originally turned him down for the Enigma team. It's propitious he came to the Research Section otherwise, we may not have made such progress against the Hellschreiber. Who knows? There's a long way to go yet on this machine and I'd keep Bill on it in a primary research role. He's full time on it right now. That's how I see it."

The Colonel nodded in agreement.

"Look John," said Gerry. "With all this progress on the month's patterns and message settings, we would be much quicker at decoding the plain text if we had a machine that mimicked the German machine. We could simply set it up and crank the handle. It's probably not wise to pinch one as the Germans would undoubtedly abandon the system; in fact, we were worried for a while they had switched to another system altogether when our efforts on March's depths failed. But now, we are pretty confident we know the construct of the machine and the indicator method, couldn't we get an imitation machine built, perhaps by those people who are building Turing's bombes?"

"I agree, we should," said the Colonel. "It's justified now. I'll take it forward. But don't hold your breath, Gerry. Materials will inevitably be in short supply even though we have the necessary priority. I will push for it though and let you know."

For some time now, Bill had dreamt of working out a way of decoding a message which has been encoded with a machine setting not used for any subsequent messages, a message not in depth. Depths, and now near depths, could, with considerable effort, reveal the wheel patterns which in the case of the chi and psi wheels stayed the same for many weeks. He knew though, that just like the Hagelin, to decode a message not in depth both the wheel patterns and the start position of each wheel were needed. Yet, how to find the start positions for a message not in depth but for which the patterns were known?

Bill began returning to the Main Building after supper to think about this problem in the quiet of the evening. After discarding some ideas, he began to think about the information they were building up on the indicators. Could they provide a way in? What if the indicator of a chi wheel whose pattern was known from a broken depth also appeared in a message that was not in depth but was from the same period? Would it be reasonable to assume that that chi wheel had the same start position in both messages? He considered it would and started to find examples in the many messages for February and March. To his surprise, there were plentiful examples both of chi and psi wheels. Obviously, the German operators were lazy and only changed a few chi and psi start positions between messages but followed the rules to change the two motor key wheel positions every time. Encouraged, Bill pursued his theory.

Several days later, again working on his own in the evening, he was plodding on in his usual very deliberate manner with what looked like a promising message when Gerry Morgan came into the room. He had just left a late meeting and, seeing there was a light on in the room, entered to switch it off. Both men stopped and looked at each other in surprise. Gerry was the first to speak.

"What are you doing here, Bill, so late?"

"I had an idea and thought I would test it in the evening when it's quieter and I can concentrate," said Bill feeling rather like a schoolboy caught doing something he should not. "I am hoping my idea will open up messages not in depth."

"I'll leave you to it, then," said Gerry deciding to give Bill his head. "But don't stay too late." As he was leaving, he turned and said, "By the way, at the meeting I've been to this evening, it was decided we can have a machine built to function like the Hellschreiber. We may need your input into its design. Tell you more tomorrow. Good night."

In his quiet way, Bill was delighted at this heartening news. He got up and walked around the room contemplating what such a machine might look like and how it might compare with the real thing. He worked on, completely forgetting Gerry's instruction not to stay too late, and had to creep very quietly up Mrs Batchelor's stairs to bed.

"What's this idea of yours, Bill?" asked Gerry the following morning.

Bill explained his thinking that knowing the wheel patterns and one chi wheel start position, from its indicator letter, it may be possible to unlock the psi stream. That in turn could then reveal the settings of the other chi wheels. It should then be possible to set the psi wheels and decode the message in the usual way.

"I've checked; there are plenty of duplicated indicators in a period. I'm nearly there with one message and if I'm right then the more progress you make, the more indicators for that period will become known and so more messages can be attacked."

A smile came across Gerry's face, a smile of acknowledgement that again, Bill appeared to have prised open a chink in the Hellschreiber, a very important chink that should enable them to attack messages from current traffic.

"Stop whatever else you are doing and concentrate on your idea. Let's see how this message you're working on comes out. If it's good, we can switch our resources to this month's messages."

Even Gerry was excited at this vital development which would, no doubt, please the intelligence people who, at long last, could have many messages of current traffic to get their teeth into.

The mood in the section positively improved when Gerry announced all hands were to be diverted to March messages after Bill's latest idea proved successful. A new recruit, Sergeant Johnny Rylands, was assigned to Bill to relieve him of the tedious task of dragging the crib one letter at a time until it fitted. Johnny had an infectious Cockney character, the opposite to Bill, yet somehow, they got on well together; Bill even responding occasionally with some dry quips of his own. Bill once teased Johnny that he could tell his children when they asked him what he did in the war he could answer that he dragged a crib around. Together with the others, they began to turn out increasingly more and more decoded messages. Bill was not that interested in the content, unlike Gerry and the intelligence people who urged the section for more of this highly important material. At one point, Gerry went across to the intelligence hut to see for himself what happened to the decoded messages his section were producing. He was told that unlike other ciphers whose messages tended to be brief and of a tactical or routine nature, the much longer Hellschreiber messages between high level Army Commanders contained text covering topics such as strategic objectives, situation assessments, planning and troop strengths and readiness. The intelligence bods were clearly very excited by what they were seeing and were greedy for more.

March passed into April. Work continued apace on March messages but a suitable April depth was now needed to attack April messages. Each morning as Bill came into the section room, he asked if a good enough depth had come in overnight but days went by with nothing useful appearing. Meanwhile, he involved himself in March messages but became more and more exasperated at the holdup. At last, after three weeks of waiting, two messages came in, the second of which differed in the fifth chi indicator; two other chi indicators in the second message were corrupted and unreadable. It was successfully attacked, the wheel patterns obtained and also all the settings; the two corrupted indicators in the second message turned out not to be the same as the first message. From then, on many April messages were attacked with Bill's method. Almost all the section was involved including Johnny Rylands who cheerfully set about his dragging with pencil, paper and rubber. Everyone quietly worked away diligently deciphering message after message. The atmosphere was intense; everyone was absorbed knowing they were now engaged in the essence of what they were there to do.

"Come in, Bill. Take a seat," said Gerry Morgan who had sent a message for Bill to join him. "I want you to meet someone."

Bill looked across to Gerry's guest, a confident looking chap in civilian dress, possibly in his middle forties.

"This is Frank Morrell from the General Post Office Research Station at Dollis Hill in North London. He is going to design our decoding machine. It has been decided, for security reasons, to build an electrical machine as too many people would need to be involved in building a mechanical version. Frank has the necessary clearance and has been given an outline concept. Since you know more than anyone about this, you are the best person to help Frank with his design."

"Hello, Bill," said Frank. "What we propose is to build it from available telephone exchange electro-mechanical equipment such as relays and uniselectors replicating the functions of the German machine. What I need from you is a thorough understanding of how all the elements interrelate and the inter-dependencies. Once we have a robust design, I don't expect it will be too difficult to build."

Bill was pleasantly surprised at this unexpected turn of events. The idea of an electrical approach to the project appealed to him. "What do I need to do?" he asked.

"Come over to Dollis Hill, tomorrow afternoon if you can and we can make a start," said Frank.

"What do I need to take?" asked Bill, addressing the question to both Gerry and Frank, concerned he had been told never to take any material out of the Park.

"Nothing," answered Gerry. "The basic data has been wired over a secure line to Dollis Hill already."

"Good," said Frank. "I'll see you tomorrow, say two o'clock. Your admin people will give you a travel warrant and will tell you how to get there. Just ask for me at the main reception."

Bill was about to leave with Frank when Gerry asked him to stay on.

"You should read this," he said pushing a memo across his desk.

It was from Commander Travis addressed to Colonel Tiltman. Bill read it. It stated the Hellschreiber cipher was now to be known as 'Tunny' and that Colonel Tiltman was to deal with all Tunny matters inside Bletchley Park including the construction of a new decoding machine to be known as 'Mr Heil's machine'.

"Who is Mr Heil?" asked Bill.

"I'm told he is the Senior GPO representative, responsible for provision and maintenance of all telecommunications equipment here," said Gerry with a smile which Bill interpreted as meaning Gerry had had to ask the same question. Anticipating Bill's next question, he went on, "They have given this cipher a fish name. They seem to like fish names. Don't ask me why. Hence, 'Tunny'."

Bill was not keen on having to travel to Dollis Hill. Normally, he avoided unfamiliar places but with all the upheaval in the past 18 months, he was less anxious these days than he used to be, yet he still preferred a settled routine. As he walked across Gladstone Park from Dollis Hill's Underground Station, he could see commanding the skyline the long, three story brick-built office block with a tall cupola crowning the central roof he had been told to aim for. Frank Morrell met him at the main entrance and took him along endless corridors to a locked room where some electrical circuits Frank had already sketched out were laid on a large table. They got on well and made rapid progress. Frank was impressed that Bill was familiar with electrical circuitry, although typically, Bill did not expand on how he had gained such knowledge. Equally, Bill was impressed with Frank's grasp of the requirement and found little to correct or to add. Nevertheless, Frank said how pleased he was to have confirmation of his design before he went any further. Despite his misgivings at having to make the visit, once down to work, Bill found it a surprisingly interesting afternoon's interlude.

Everyone was deeply involved in the decoding of April's messages. Spirits rose as message after message was decoded, translated and passed on. The process was slow, needing concentration and it became obvious how a machine could substantially increase their pencil and paper based output. From time to time, Bill was called over to help other members of the team when they came across a particularly difficult problem. Often, with his greater understanding of the process, he was able to point the way forward, but not always in which case the message had to be abandoned.

Jerry Roberts was in the thick of things, his decoding skills and his knowledge of the German language meant he was fully occupied. In a rare interval, he posed a question to Bill.

"I find it odd that since it is a sin to send two messages on the same key, the Germans of all people, masters of discipline, keep sending them; even more so with these significantly important messages. Surely, they have trained their people on this new machine. You would expect they would monitor outgoing messages for such cardinal errors. We have made such progress but I worry they will tighten their procedures. What happens then?"

"I am convinced one day we will find a way of breaking messages without a depth or near depth. These indicators may offer a gateway. I'm thinking about it but there is not much spare time at the moment," said Bill.

"The rest of us can crack on with these messages. Why don't you ask Gerry to take you off to work on your idea?"

Bill had come to respect Jerry whose practical and energetic approach had quickly made him an integral member of the team. Encouraged by his remarks, Bill asked to see Gerry Morgan.

"What have you got for me this time?" asked Gerry light-heartedly. He was in a good mood with all the current success.

"We can't be sure of getting depths," stated Bill earnestly. "If the Germans tighten their procedures, all our work could be for nothing. We need a method independent of depths."

"Yes..." Gerry agreed, wondering what was coming.

"I have been thinking. Because we know so much more about the indicators and have a significant volume of them now, maybe a method could be developed by their study. Possibly tabulate against them the constant of the first few letters of messages which typically give us a series of crosses in the fifth impulse. It may be possible, bit by bit, to get the pattern of a single chi wheel at least; and possibly, by going forwards and backwards, all the wheels may fall out."

Gerry appreciated the vulnerability of their position on depths. There had been too much going on lately to set aside time to address the matter. He could see from Bill's demeanour that he had been worrying about it more than anyone including himself.

"How many messages might you need, do you think?" posed Gerry.

"Several hundred; maybe ten days' worth. I need a couple of days to work out an experiment though," said Bill.

Whilst Gerry was not entirely convinced of Bill's hypothesis, he was prepared to give him room to pursue it.

"It is worth an initial investigation, I guess. I suggest you collect the first ten days of this month, Bill. That will also give you a couple of days to prepare. I may have someone who can help you with the volume of data. Captain Wyllie only started the other day so he could be free. I'll arrange it. Keep me in touch with progress."

Bill parked himself in a small room at the end of the corridor to develop his experiment. This is what he preferred, working on his own. The main room, where most of the team were working flat out, inevitably had distractions, comings and goings, people wanting his help, a general low-level murmur as work progressed in groups of three or four.

A head popped round the door.

"James Wyllie. I gather you need a hand."

"Come in," said Bill, his tone not altogether welcoming, rueing that his peace was about to be broken.

"I have brought along ten days' worth of messages, well at least the beginnings of messages as that is what I was told you want," said James in a cultured but distinctly Scottish accent. Bill was at least pleased to see James was not in military uniform.

Bill set them to work on his theory. He had prepared a number of grids on squared paper, each a square of 625 small squares labelled with indicator letters A to Z across the top and down the side. He had omitted J which never appeared as an indicator letter. He explained to James how to populate a grid starting with the fifth impulse of the second ciphertext letter of each message.

"This message here," he demonstrated, "has the second ciphertext letter V. From this table, the fifth impulse for V is a cross. These 12 letters at the beginning are called the indicators. We are interested in the fifth and twelfth indicator letters; in this case P and S, respectively. Next, we find the grid intersection for row P and column S and place a cross in the square at that intersection. I'll explain how it all works later but first we need to get a volume of data. I will follow on after you, plotting the third ciphertext letter. Have a go at the next message."

James attempted the next message and only needed guidance to identify the second ciphertext letter from the stream.

"Go carefully or the data will be useless," cautioned Bill.

Every now and again, Bill checked one of James's plots and was soon happy he had the hang of it. The two settled down to the meticulous and lengthy task of plotting several hundred messages. Silence reigned. Bill quietly worked at his usual moderately slow pace. James too worked quietly, every now and again glancing across at Bill to assess the character of his new colleague but not gaining much.

The silence seemed to suit both men. James too was used to working alone for long periods. Occasionally after a break, Bill would explain a little more of the background to Tunny and what he was trying to achieve from this experiment. James appeared extremely quick to understand. Towards the end of the next day, Bill eventually moved to analysing the grids.

"Ah!" Bill said out loud as he sat back. James looked up at the sudden outburst and saw Bill animated for the first time.

"That is why we had difficulty with the first letter decode!" he said tapping the grid he had been working on. James looked at him quizzically.

"This shows the psi wheels do not operate on the first letter," said Bill with a hint of triumph.

Bill's analyses yielded yet more important information on how the psi wheels operated on the first few letters. He was able to piece together pattern fragments and gradually built up ten possible patterns for the fifth wheel.

He took his findings to Gerry Morgan who was aware of two rather corrupt depths just in. By trial and error, the ten possible patterns were applied to the key from these depths and all the wheel patterns for May were completed before the end of the month. Everyone was very pleased as this had not been done before and it quickly led to May's messages being read.

But Bill's real goal of finding all the wheel patterns by his method proved more elusive. The ambiguities caused by the stuttering of the psi wheels only increased as he made progress until in the end he got bogged down. Bill was still convinced of his hypothesis but it was becoming onerous with diminishing returns. James had become more and more involved in the analysis as his understanding grew and when he could see Bill more and more exasperated at the slow progress, he spoke up.

"Let me take over. I think I see what is needed. This is just the task for a lexicographer!"

Conversation between them had been largely confined to the work at hand but James had opened up a little on his background. Bill learned that before he joined the military and became an officer in the Intelligence Corps, James had been an editor of the Oxford Latin Dictionary. From then on, Bill viewed James in a rather different light.

Bill accepted his offer, deciding his time and his mind were better applied to other ideas he had. They continued to share the room with Bill offering advice when needed. Because James applied himself with almost boundless energy, yet worked meticulously and methodically, piece by piece he gradually added more certain fragments until finally, he had reduced the ten possible patterns to one almost certain pattern. He then continued with the other wheels until all were broken. They both sat back in shared satisfaction; Bill having had his theory proved and James having slogged through a mountain of detail to achieve the result. They apprised Gerry Morgan of their findings who again was moved by Bill's tenacity to dig deeper into the Tunny machine and to come up with solutions. They all agreed, however, the downside of this particular solution was the sheer volume of messages required that most, if not all, of the month would have passed before the results could be useful.

During June, the wait for a depth grew more and more frustrating until, in the end, several of the others from the section were brought in to work through the indicator method which Bill generously called Wyllie's Method.

The daily frustration of not getting a depth was interrupted in the middle of the month by the arrival of the new Tunny machine causing great excitement. In one of the nearby huts, Frank Morrell and an engineer carefully unpacked and assembled what looked like a tall rack resembling a manual telephone exchange board. When it was ready for a test, everyone gathered round, amazed at the sight. There were banks of plug sockets, switches and indicating lamps and an array of connecting leads. To the side was a desk affair with a teleprinter keyboard behind which was a myriad of electrical leads and motors. Bill stood at the back of the group drawn to see the physical embodiment of the design that he and Frank Morrell had agreed upon.

"We set it up like this," said Frank Morrell, explaining how the banks of plugs and switches mimicked the wheel patterns and start positions. His colleague then sat at the keyboard and typed in the ciphertext of a message they had used to test the machine. Gradually, letter by letter, the machine printed out the German clear text which Jerry Roberts translated as it appeared. Broad smiles spread across the faces of those assembled and then a ripple of applause rang around the room at the obvious success. Gerry Morgan felt the occasion needed marking and addressed the group.

"This is a tremendous achievement by everyone to get us this far. Frank Morrell and his team are to be congratulated on designing and building this impressive machine in next to no time. It will have a considerable impact on our ability to decode Tunny messages in volume. I can tell you that approval has been given for several more machines. There will be a training programme set up to operate them and engineering back-up to keep them working. This is another major step forward."

Frank Morrell then spoke.

"As Gerry said, we'll have engineers on site under Mr Heil to maintain these machines and to install the next ones. I have to thank all you people here who have helped us with the design and testing, but particularly Bill Tutte. For us, it has been an interesting project. For you, this machine should help you turn out the plaintext of many more messages than was possible before. Let's hope so. Good luck with it."

Bill looked at the floor in embarrassment when his name was mentioned. Everyone was keen to see more of this fascinating machine which was nothing like they had imagined. The atmosphere remained buoyant for the rest of the day.

It was not until the early part of July that June messages began to be decoded. The wait was on again, this time for a July depth but luck was with them when a good depth yielding several hundred letters of key was received early. The section all joined in to complete the analysis and by the middle of the month, they began processing current traffic for the first time and with the new decoding machine, they were reading messages the Germans had transmitted in some instances only the previous day. The whole place was tingling with excitement. Even Bill felt a remarkable sense of achievement. As Jerry Roberts busily translated the German clear text, others gathered around amazed at the content of the messages, from a lengthy appraisal of the situation in the Balkans to a report on the quantity of German equipment and troop deployments in the Athens area. At one point, Jerry pointed to some text he was translating.

"Look," he exclaimed. "With the German penchant for detail, they are even reporting troop sickness levels!"

Chapter 6
The Testery

The Research Section's accomplishment with Tunny had led Colonel Tiltman to a strategic decision and had asked Gerry Morgan to see him.

"I have decided," said the Colonel, "with the success we are having, to set up a new section to tackle Tunny on an operational basis. Ralph Tester will head it up. I need you to stay with the Research Section. Ralph is not strong on cryptography; he is a German linguist and foremost, a good team leader. He will need a small group to kick off with. I suggest Jerry Roberts from your unit and maybe four others. I leave it to you to liaise with Ralph over the final selection. And it will mean moving to one of the new huts. There is not enough room in the Main Building here for Ralph's section and it's better you are close to him."

"When is all this happening?" queried Gerry, having half expected something like this might come about but not so soon.

"Straight away, as soon as a replacement is found for Ralph on the German military police codes. You can talk to him to sort out arrangements."

"Is Ralph to take over all Tunny work?" asked Gerry thinking about demarcation lines and who would move over to the new section.

"I see Ralph's new section applying the methods of attacking Tunny that your team have developed. I see you providing a sort of Tunny consultancy, still looking at ways to streamline processes or to help with any difficulties."

"Then I would hold on to James Wyllie and Bill Tutte as they are not really operational people," proposed Gerry.

"I remember you saying something like that about Bill Tutte. So, yes, retain those two," agreed the Colonel.

"I'll see to it," said Gerry as if acknowledging an instruction with which he did not wholeheartedly agree.

The Colonel paused before continuing. Telling Gerry about the reorganisation was awkward enough but there was something else on his mind.

"This next bit is a little tricky," he said. "The Prof, Alan Turing, has expressed an interest in Tunny. Obviously, he knows where we are. He has asked me if he can have a look at it; he's quite interested in the teleprinter aspect. I think it is no bad idea to have a fresh eye on it so I've agreed he can join you for a short while, only temporary. Hopefully, he won't be too disruptive. He is pretty au fait with the principle but he may need to talk to Bill, say, to check on some features. He can have one of your small rooms."

The Colonel looked at Gerry for his reaction, knowing this was cutting right across his responsibilities, and coming straight on top of hiving off part of his Section. Gerry's momentary silence spoke volumes. But, of course, it was an order.

Once the details of who would transfer had been agreed with Ralph Tester, Gerry called his team together to make the announcement which was greeted rather halfheartedly as Gerry had expected. There was a general moan when the move to one of the huts was mentioned. Whilst Bill was relieved to hear he was staying at the Research Section, he was dismayed at the consultancy role Gerry described for him, which he immediately saw as the end of pure research into Tunny.

But Bill's heart really sank when he heard that Alan Turing would be joining them to look at Tunny. This was a complete shock, totally unexpected. As the day went on, Bill became more and more anxious at the prospect of Alan Turing's impending presence, albeit temporary as Gerry had emphasised. He knew only too well that around Bletchley Park things that were meant to be temporary had a habit of becoming permanent.

That evening, Bill fretted continuously about the Turing incursion into what he perceived as his own purview. Rightly or wrongly, he had come to believe the cryptanalysis of Tunny to be his personal domain. It was unsaid, unwritten but he knew no one had the depth of understanding that he had; no one had revealed more about the machine and its cipher than he had. And no one appeared to be as immersed in it as he was. He saw himself as the spearhead to prise yet more from Tunny's recesses, eventually to lay it bare to attack with nothing more that the ciphertext alone. The puzzle that was Tunny was only partly unveiled so far. He did not want someone entering his province, to push him aside and take over. That was his fear of Alan Turing, knowing his powerful position within Bletchley Park. He was well aware of the intellectual might of the Prof, as he was known, yet Bill had an inner confidence that given time, opportunity and resources he could completely solve the complexity of Tunny without the Prof's interference.

There was no one in the Research Section with whom he felt able to confide his concerns. He was troubled enough that he decided to write to Cedric. He could talk to Cedric in the abstract without giving anything away; Cedric was much better than he at facing awkward situations. He penned a letter enquiring if Cedric could be free if he came over to Cambridge. Even having written the letter, he did not sleep well.

Cedric was his usual cheery self when they met. His main news was that the Friends Relief Service could not take him and he had been required to take the post of hospital porter at Addenbrooke's Hospital on the Trumpington Road. There were benefits, he explained. He quite enjoyed the physical side of the work and he was helping people in need, which is what he wanted to do. Soon, he was telling the story about a notice he came across a few days ago on his way to the hospital blocking his way on Bridge Street in the middle of Cambridge. 'Danger: Unexploded Bomb' the notice had read. Not his idea of a joke he went on, describing the destruction from a rare air raid on the city. The Union Society building had been badly damaged and one of the Trinity buildings had a fire bomb land on its roof that fortunately went out. Three big bombs failed to explode, hence, the notice. Several people had been reported killed, he said, adding it had been another bad night in this senseless war. On the lighter side, Cedric talked about life and the gossip at the hospital and as always, seemed to have news of their college friends. "Casimir Lewy and Wilfred Corlett have decided to apply for Fellowships this year," said Cedric. "Wilfred will submit his draft thesis, all 200 pages of it, he says. Wish them luck."

Eventually, Bill raised the matter about which he had come.

"There have been some developments at Bletchley which worry me," he started.

Cedric realised this was serious.

"I can't tell you details but it's to do with this project I've been working on for nearly a year. I've made more progress on it than anyone and I probably have a greater understanding of it than anyone else. But they have moved most of it out to a new unit and now, one of the senior people is barging in. I'm not sure what to do. They have said I now have a consultancy role but I'm not sure what that means."

"Oh, dear," said Cedric. "I thought things were going so well. What does your boss say?"

"It's only just happened. I haven't spoken to him."

"Maybe you should. Maybe you need to find out exactly what this new role is. Did you want to go to this new unit then?"

"No, no. They did something similar with another project I was on. We had taken it so far that others needed to take over the day-to-day running. But there is a lot more to do on this project that I want to pursue."

"What about this senior chappie?" asked Cedric. He was curious but knew Bill would not divulge anything he should not about Bletchley Park. Even so, Cedric had a fair idea of what went on there. At the beginning, he had subjected Bill to some jocular probing but thereafter, restrained his inquisitiveness out of respect for his friend.

"He's very senior, can do almost as he likes. I'm afraid he wants to take over now that we have made some progress. My boss says it's only temporary but I'm not so sure."

"Do you trust your boss? Do you get on with him?"

"Do I trust him? Yes. He's a Trinity mathematician but I guess he can't divulge all he knows. Do I get on with him? I think so."

"Maybe he's worried too," suggested Cedric. "You need to talk to him. Need to sort out exactly what he has in mind for you. Is it all military rankings there? I suppose he can't tell this senior chap to get lost!"

"No, it's not run on military lines. But I don't suppose my boss is in any position to block this senior someone pushing in."

"Then you need to have a face-to-face talk with your boss. Find out what's going on. You may be worrying about nothing. I've always said: don't worry about what you can't control."

"Easier said than done for some," said Bill wistfully. He knew Cedric's advice was sound and probably what he wanted to hear in order to do something. He returned to Bletchley in a better frame of mind.

Gerry Morgan gave Bill some reassurances. He still wanted him to work on Tunny along with James Wyllie but now that current traffic was being read the priority was to improve and speed up the processes developed so far. And if Ralph Tester ran into some difficulties, Bill would be needed to help him out. Bill wanted to take the opportunity to argue his conviction that this German 'Tunny' machine could, with some purely academic research, be broken without the additional information that was presently required, but sensed he would not gain support just now so held his counsel.

But Gerry's assurances did not extend to the advent of Alan Turing. He still was not entirely sure what the Prof wanted to do. "However," said Gerry lowering his voice, "I said Alan would be joining us temporarily and I believe this to be so as rumour has it he will be going to the States shortly. He is really only filling in time with us. Keep that under your hat, though."

At this, Bill felt less anxious but his underlying anxieties had not gone away entirely.

The move to one of the new huts and the establishment of Ralph Tester's team was completed by the end of the month. There were grumblings that the hut was too hot, too dimly lit and the furniture was somewhat basic but generally, everyone settled down to get on with the work. Gerry had his own small room in the Research Section hut and there was one other small separate room which Bill had his eye on.

It was in some trepidation that Bill went to see Alan Turing at his request. His concern was not meeting the person per se, but what might be about to happen. Was his position about to be usurped, or worse? Alan Turing was well-known for being impulsive, unconventional and no respecter of hierarchy, no lover of bureaucracy. Was the unpredictable Mr Turing about to take Tunny into his Enigma section? If so, what would that mean for Bill?

Bill need not have worried, at least for the time being. He found Alan Turing in a surprisingly amiable mood. Bill was pleased and relieved that the Prof very plainly knew who he was and even recalled Bill's joint paper, *The Dissection of Rectangles into Squares*. What Alan Turing wanted was to understand Bill's latest discoveries, particularly those relating to the indicators. His intention, apparently after discussions with John Tiltman, was to see if there was an alternative way of finding wheel patterns. He certainly impressed Bill with his grasp of Tunny and its teleprinter transmission. In turn, Alan Turing was openly respectful of Bill's accomplishments on Tunny and listened intently to his answers. 'I see it!' was his usually quick response to Bill's explanations. The Prof's notorious impatience was, thankfully, absent.

Bill came away with markedly mixed feelings. There was the distinct impression he had been in the presence of someone unique, someone with a far greater intellect, yet not some stuffy, aged professor type but someone youthful, intense and energetic, even inspirational. He could understand why Alan Turing was held in such high regard within Bletchley Park. On the other hand, though, he viewed the Prof's declared intention as directly undermining his own position, as cutting right across his own work on Tunny, which only served to revive his anxieties.

It was not long before Ralph Tester called for Bill's help. He and his new team had run into difficulties with August's traffic. The problem turned out to be the Germans had introduced a change to some message beginnings. Arbitrary padding words appeared that disrupted the stereotypical start to messages which had up to now provided regular cribs. Bill took the problem back to the Research Section to work on it with James.

One morning, Bill arrived to find on the desk a folded note with his name on it. He opened it out, all curious. It was a request from someone called Outram Evennett to come over to Hut 5 to meet him. Bill was even more curious. The name rang a vague bell, some Trinity connection perhaps. He walked over to Hut 5 and was introduced to Outram Evennett, a large, commanding figure in his late 40s, who guided him to a small room where they could talk.

"You are no doubt wondering what this is all about. Let me introduce myself. I'm H Outram Evennett, Fellow in History of Trinity College, Cambridge. I've been here since the outset but I remain in close touch with the college; in fact, I am still President of the University Pitt Club. Are you a member?"

"No," said Bill but now recalling the name.

"You should join when this is all over," said Outram with a twinkle in his eye. He appeared very friendly and open but Bill still did not know where this was leading.

"However, I asked you to come over to discuss this year's autumn Fellowship elections at the college. Have you put yourself forward as a candidate?"

"No. Not this year," said Bill. "I did apply last year but had to cancel my application once I came here as I had no time to write a presentable dissertation." He was still unsure what was on Outram Evennett's mind.

"I thought as such," said Outram. "I can, however, tell you the college has, in the present emergency, introduced a measure by which candidates may be assessed on the basis of their war work. Of course, a very high standard is required of all candidates. But from what I know of your work on Tunny, I feel you would be an excellent candidate. I would be prepared to recommend your name go forward should you agree."

There was a silence.

"How can it be possible?" Bill queried. "The work here is top secret."

"There are ways round these things in deserving cases. What do you think? The competition is severe but should you be successful such an award would stand you in good stead once the war is over. I would urge you to consider this seriously." Seeing Bill was not responding immediately, he added, "Think it over if you want and let me know. I do believe you would be a strong candidate."

Bill hesitated further then asked, "What would I have to do?"

"Nothing really, you have already done it! I made some initial enquiries. Because of my position, I can make a submission statement on your behalf, subject to your approval, of course, which the Electors will accept. They may seek an independent report from the senior management here. All you need to do is to sign this application form which I took the trouble to obtain for you. Let me have it back should you decide to apply and I will draw up a statement for you to approve."

Bill's earlier curiosity had turned to embarrassment at such flattering comments. He resorted to prevarication as was usual for him when confronted with a decision.

"Do you really consider my work here worthy?"

"I do. Much tremendous war work is being done by Trinity people such as yourself and it is right the college recognises that alongside purely academic submissions. So yes, I do believe your work can properly stand alongside the more traditional application."

"I am not sure what to say," said Bill. "Thank you for taking so much trouble on my behalf. May I please consider it?"

"Of course! Of course, dear boy! Let me have the form back in the next couple of days if you are happy for it to go forward and we will take it from there."

Bill took the form with him and on the way back, mulled over the quite extraordinary meeting that had just taken place. Although he had not met Outram Evennett before, Bill likened Outram's commanding and open character to that of a college tutor; someone trustworthy, someone whose opinion could be held in high regard. But it was the idea he was still eligible to submit a Fellowship application that had taken him by complete surprise. Very reluctantly, he had had to cancel his application last year because there was simply not the time or the opportunity to complete the necessary research on a suitable mathematics topic and to write it to the required standard. In the circumstances, he had resigned himself to a considerable interval of many years before he would be in a position to re-apply, probably nearing the end of his PhD studies, whenever that might be. The idea was, therefore, appealing yet he had no way of judging if his application would be competitive. Without Outram Evennett's very strong opinion, he would perhaps not have given it serious consideration. Of course, should he be successful, a Fellowship would put him in a good position when—hopefully, it was when—he returned to Trinity. He was, however, heavily reliant on Outram Evennett whom he had only just met. Who could he sound out? There was no time to go over to Cambridge to talk to Patrick Duff or to Cedric but there was Gerry Morgan. He decided to consult Gerry.

"Ah, Outram," sighed Gerry. "He's Trinity through and through like a stick of rock. Be assured he is held in high regard. He mentioned his idea to me and I am happy to back it. I'm pretty sure he is au fait with the standard required for Fellowship elections these days. He wouldn't put his name to an application if he did not feel it stood a high degree of success. My advice, Bill, is to permit your name to go forward. But don't be too concerned if you are not selected, few are first time; it's always good to be seen to apply though. Don't worry about security; that will be covered. Good luck with it."

Bill took Gerry's advice, signed the application form, approved Outram Evennett's statement with a few edits and with everything else that was going on, largely forgot about it.

During August, Bill had had a second meeting with Alan Turing who explained a method he had devised; Gerry was keen to hear Bill's opinion of it.

"It is a bit of a curate's egg," said Bill. "It is a complicated method calling for much intuition and much effort but given suitable messages it can work. Essentially though, it still requires a depth plus a message of at least 500 letters. To my mind, it is more artistic than mathematical."

"Did you tell him that?" exclaimed Gerry somewhat alarmed at what he took to be a rather uncomplimentary remark.

"Oh, no," said Bill. "The method can work and that's what I said."

"Why the reservations then?" Gerry wanted to know.

Bill was still smarting at the Prof's intervention and for once voiced his opinion.

"It requires guesses or assumptions to be made. It calls for choices, some of which have a 50% chance of being correct. And a bit like a maze it means going back if a dead end is reached and taking an alternative route. My grannie used to say that she made choices on what she felt in her bones. I think she would say this method needed very reliable bones."

Gerry raised his eyebrows and looked slightly askance at Bill. Rarely had he seen him so expressive; never so disparaging.

"It will be interesting to see how the Testery gets on with it then," said Gerry.

"I suppose they will become used to it with practice," Bill responded rather dismissively.

Together Bill, James and the Testery diagnosed the German innovation that introduced padding words at the beginning of some messages and together, they were able to find ways around it, though necessitating much more material. The change, however, had considerably slowed down the breaking of August messages until a good depth was received near the end of the month.

The end of August saw the arrival of a new recruit to the Research Section. Bill was very surprised when Gerry came into the main room accompanied by someone he knew slightly, Max Newman a Cambridge lecturer in mathematics who had given talks to the Trinity Mathematical Society. Gerry introduced him to Bill.

"We know each other," Max Newman revealed. Turning to Bill he said, "I hear you have made great strides since you have been here. I'm not surprised, this stuff is right up your street. I'm keen to learn more."

"Max will be attached to The Testery to start with," said Gerry, "but I know you will help him get to grips with Tunny."

The idea of him being teacher to pupil, Max Newman, made Bill chuckle to himself. Mr Newman, as Bill knew him, was an eminent mathematician in his mid-forties, having published many papers, a Fellow of St John's College at Cambridge and a Fellow of the Royal Society. It was an interesting juxtaposition and Bill was uncertain how this reversed relationship would work.

The Testery had subjected an early September depth to Turing's method and the month's wheel patterns had been successfully found, although finding the settings of other messages in the month proved slow. Bill and James had devised some refinements to the indicator method which they introduced to the Testery resulting in current traffic being progressed much more quickly. October brought a near depth which continued the production of highly valuable intelligence. Very nearly, all messages since July had been read. Spirits were high.

Gerry called Bill over one afternoon.

"Take a look at this," he said. "It's a new teleprinter link between Sicily and Libya. But look, it's curious. There are large numbers of passages on the same setting. At the beginning, here, is a short passage in cipher, then comes some operator chat in clear. Then the signal 'Um Um' is transmitted and the cipher message continues, with the machine brought back to its initial setting. This happens again and again resulting in multiple depths. There has been quite a bit of similar traffic for a few weeks now. What do you think?"

"It could be a new Tunny link or they could be testing a new machine. What does 'Um Um' mean?" asked Bill.

"It will be short for 'umschalten', switch over. From Tunny and Enigma decodes we've seen mention of a T52a/b and a T52c machine; perhaps it's something to do with them. I've got Michael Crum coming over from Hut 8 for a spell. I thought I'd give it to him to have a look at. Widen the knowledge. Do you know him, he's an Oxford research mathematician? Perhaps, you could give him a bit of an introduction. With our understanding of teleprinter codes and all those depths, he should be able to make some progress."

Bill was quite put out that the task had not been given to him but said nothing other than, of course, he would help Michael Crum who he knew by name.

Bill found he and Michael Crum got on quite well being of similar character and age. Bill gave him some papers he had written on Tunny, talked him through the initial breaking of the machine and left him to it with the offer of support when needed.

From early evening, Mrs Batchelor had kept a special ear out for the sound of a key in the front door. Earlier in the day, a telegram had arrived for Bill and she wanted to be sure he had it as soon as he returned from work. She was not a nosy landlady but she was curious; telegrams were rare. In her way, she liked to think she made a home from home for her guests without being intrusive. She had a soft spot for Bill who, being much younger than her usual guests, brought out her motherly instincts, although she respected his obvious shyness. She was ready to offer sympathy should the telegram bring sad news.

"A telegram has arrived for you," she announced from the end of the hallway, envelope in hand.

"Oh," said Bill quite taken aback. "Thank you," he said taking it and making his way upstairs to his room, watched by a concerned Mrs Batchelor.

Bill looked at the envelope which gave no clue to the sender or to its contents. He had never had a telegram sent to him before. Telegrams were for older people and contained important stuff. In fact, he could not remember his family ever having received one. With a little trepidation, he opened it. He read:

'I have the great pleasure of advising you that in response to your application, the Electors of Trinity College have awarded you a Title A Fellowship. Further details follow by letter. Heartiest congratulations. Chairman of Electors, Trinity College.'

Bill sat down. He re-read the telegram just to be sure. This was beyond his wildest dreams despite the confidence Outram Evennett had exhibited. He got up and walked around the room, telegram still in hand. He was not sure how he felt. Without doubt, this was by far the most prestigious award of the many academic awards and prizes he had received over the years. It would certainly make a considerable difference to his return to Trinity after the war should this be possible. He was in a daze. He sat down again, his face set with a rare grin. What should he do? He must write to his parents. Cedric should know; perhaps he already knew as this sort of thing was posted on the main notice board at the college and someone may well have told him. Who else was successful, he wondered. Of course, he must see Outram Evennett tomorrow to thank him and Gerry Morgan will want to know. Energised, he got out his pen and notepaper and began a letter to his mother and father.

A little later as he walked into the dining room for supper, the obvious question was all over Mrs Batchelor's face.

"It was good news," he said. "I have been given an award by my university."

Mrs Batchelor smiled broadly. "It must be a very grand award to be sent by telegram," she said fishing for a bit more information. Bill replied with some brief comment that it would help with his post-graduate studies after the war. Not having had such an eminent scholar staying with her before, Mrs Batchelor inwardly basked in the reflected glory of her young and very clever university guest.

Later the following morning, Bill went to see Outram Evennett who had asked to be told the outcome of the Election. He offered his hand in warm congratulation. In his mind, he said, Bill's election was not in doubt. Make sure Gerry Morgan knows, he urged, as his support had been important.

Gerry Morgan was equally effusive in his congratulations but that was not all. Gerry Morgan had further good news.

"I've managed to get you promotion to Temporary Senior Assistant Officer. It's not easy to get promotions these days because money is so tight but in your case, it is well deserved. You will get official confirmation in the next few days. So, it's double congratulations."

Gerry insisted in making an announcement to the whole Section. There followed several hours of extreme embarrassment for Bill as all and sundry came round to congratulate him enthusiastically on his Fellowship and on his promotion, Max Newman being among the first to shake his hand. Bill was glad when all the fuss died down.

It seemed that everyone was more pleased than Bill himself and the news only served to bolster the general buoyant atmosphere already generated by the Tunny successes.

Over the last few days of October, however, concerns in the Testery grew because no messages were received. Urgent checks were made at Knockholt, the newly established listening station in Kent. The operators there assured Colonel Tiltman and Ralph Tester that they were searching the airwaves day and night. The worst scenario was that the Germans, for some reason, had abandoned the Tunny system but with the volume of recent traffic coupled with the improvements to the system the Germans had made in the last few months, the hope was it would come up again. It was an anxious few days waiting for news.

When Bill arrived first thing on Monday morning, he was called immediately into Gerry's room. There was Gerry with Colonel Tiltman and Ralph Tester, all looking despondent. Gerry spoke first.

"Come and join us, Bill. Tunny transmissions have resumed but the Germans have made a significant change. The indicator letters have disappeared. Messages that have come over start with 'QSN' in clear followed by a number. It looks as though the operator sending the message selects the indicator settings by looking up a number in a code book of some sort and sends it prefixed by a special radio Q-code. They must have distributed an indicator code book to everyone."

"Without information on the indictors and if we don't get any depths, we're stymied," said Ralph Tester dejectedly.

"Just when the Germans appear to be expanding the links," added Colonel Tiltman. "Knockholt tell us these latest messages appear on two links, Königsberg to the Ukraine and Berlin to Salonika. Maybe what we've been attacking was an experimental link.

With this latest Q-code enhancement, the Germans must be satisfied enough to roll it out. Yet, in doing so, they have shut us out."

The room fell silent.

Chapter 7
A Way Back In

"What's going on?" asked Max Newman who had come over from the Testery to see what was happening.

"I suspect," said Bill, "that a German cipher expert has taken a look at their Tunny system and told them off for giving us the 12 indicator letters which is wrong in principle. So, now they are sending a number which no doubt refers to a code book of indicator letters. Without the code book, we can't know the wheel settings. In effect, we're locked out."

"Oh," said Max. "I guessed something pretty dire had occurred. What happens, now?"

"Metaphorically speaking, we may have to shoulder our pencils and squared paper and trudge glumly out of Eden," said Bill.

"Do you mean we have to abandon Tunny?" said a very concerned Max.

"Not necessarily. I hope not. All along, I've been convinced there must be a way of successfully attacking a single message."

"What happens now then?" repeated Max anxiously.

"Well, John Tiltman wants us all to put our thinking caps on to see what new approaches we can come up with. In the meantime, Ralph will get out the last of September's messages. This gives me the opportunity to pursue a few ideas I've had for a while now. What about you, Mr Newman? There may be less to do in Ralph's team now."

"I think I'll go and see Gerry," said Max who obviously had something weighing on his mind. He knocked on Gerry Morgan's door.

"Max. You've heard the latest?" said Gerry.

"Yes," said Max. "This setback is serious, I understand. It has prompted me to raise something with you, something that has been on my mind. You see, Gerry, I've been wondering if I'm in the right place, if I made the right choice coming here. Don't get me wrong, the work is interesting and I can see how important it is for the war effort, more than I could have possibly supposed when I agreed to join you. But I can't say I feel I'm contributing much. Perhaps, there is too much linguistic bias in the work. I'm sorry to throw this at you when there is plainly a major crisis on. It's nothing to do with the people who have been extremely welcoming but maybe we both need to consider how I can best be employed."

Gerry Morgan was not altogether surprised at this from Max Newman. Ralph Tester had hinted to Gerry that Max appeared a little ill at ease, remarking that such a senior figure cannot hide his disquiet for long.

"Actually, I think," said Gerry, "this latest development is the answer. I'm going to need you back here to work with me on this situation. I believe we need to seek a way forward that is more mathematical than linguistic. In fact, it may be the solution is purely mathematical. I wrote a paper on letter subtractor machines in which I promulgated a number of mathematical solutions, albeit based on a much simpler rotor enciphering machine than Tunny. I'll give you a copy to read." He paused to gauge Max's reaction before continuing.

"Ralph's section will continue with September's messages and will monitor messages coming through in the new manner. If we still get identifiable depths then hopefully, with Alan Turing's method, we can get the wheel patterns for that month but we will only have the wheel settings for those messages in depth. We will have no way of finding the wheel settings for any other messages which means we cannot decipher them. So, we're asking everyone in my section to address themselves exclusively to this setback. That's what the Research Section was set up to do. And, as I say, I believe we are looking at mathematics to help find a solution. That is why I'd like you alongside. A fresh pair of eyes, and all that."

Max was not entirely convinced but was encouraged enough by Gerry's words to stay his hand.

"Let me have a look at that paper of yours, Gerry. Oh, and by the way, Alan's US visa has come through and he'll leave for Washington in a couple of days."

Bill was back in his element. Now that he was relieved of supporting the Testery and that Alan Turing had departed, he could re-join his personal battle with Tunny. He took to walking round the Park grounds, hands behind his back, his mind concentrated on the latest Tunny problem, finding the usual hut chatter and noise disturbing. The weather was typically October, dull and at times, the early morning fog lingered. He enjoyed the walks to and from Mrs Batchelor's house to the Park, feeling the damp fresh air on his face and savouring the autumn with its changing colours and the cherry red hips and haws in the hedgerows.

When he was just thinking, he found the quiet of the grounds more conducive to clarity of thought. Max Newman, noticing Bill's disappearances, asked one of the others if Bill was all right. The answer was a shrug of the shoulders and the comment that it was typical Bill.

With all the impediments the Germans had put in their way since he had originally discovered the construction of the Tunny machine, Bill began to think that rather than looking for a way around this latest setback, maybe it would be more productive to go back to the basic encipherment equation. Their knowledge of the process had grown considerably and although the Germans had made various security enhancements the equation was the same; the chi wheels and the stuttered psi wheels each added a layer of encoding to the plain text to produce the ciphertext. He could look again at each of these elements, possibly picking up on a feature Alan Turing had used in his wheel breaking method.

Bill had noticed that Alan Turing added the first letter of a key stream of letters to the second letter, then the second letter to the third letter, the third letter to the fourth and so on to produce a new stream of letters, a known mathematical technique of identifying and measuring changes called delta-ing. Bill was intrigued that Turing's new delta-ed stream revealed information otherwise hidden in the undelta-ed stream and he reasoned that such a technique may be usefully exploited when applied to individual impulses of the basic encipherment equation. He decided to undertake some analysis and went to see Ralph Tester to obtain some material.

"I gather you are still getting a few depths," Bill started. "Do you have an October message I could use for some analysis, please? A successfully decoded one and preferably fairly long."

"We are still getting a few depths. It's really quite surprising considering. You would think, Bill, that with all the new security, they would make sure depths were eliminated.

It was pretty obvious that messages on the same link with the same 'Q number' would be in depth and so it has turned out. But that only allows us to attack a fraction of what we were decoding these past few months." He leaned over and picked up a folder. "Here, take this recent message from the Berlin/Salonika link. It's 3,200 characters. Is that good enough for you?" Bill took the papers. Curious at the request, Ralph added, "What are you looking at, Bill?"

"Oh, just an idea," replied Bill with his customary vagueness.

Bill took the message papers back to the Research Section room and set himself up in a corner where he could work on his own, where he could develop his ideas in relative isolation. The others recognised the signs and left him to his own devises.

He decided to write out a delta version of the encipherment equation for the first impulse. It was particularly tedious as he had to work out the delta for each character pair for each element of the equation. A dot followed by a dot was a dot and a cross followed by a cross was also a dot. But a dot followed by a cross or a cross followed by a dot was a cross. It was very time consuming but he had to start somewhere. He studied the result. The numbers of dots and crosses were almost exactly equal and since nothing else struck him, he decided to leave matters there for the day. The next day was his Saturday off and he had invited Cedric over for the weekend. But when he got back to Mrs Batchelor's, there was a letter from Cedric saying regretfully work and a touch of flu meant he would have to put off the visit.

Cedric not coming gave Bill the opportunity to resume his analysis. He became so engrossed that he spent long hours on both Saturday and Sunday working. From time to time, the recognition that he was hungry sent him to the cafeteria which now catered for the daily three shift system operated by many huts. For what they were, the subsidised meals and snacks were fine, although the quality was of little importance to Bill. He ate on his own, his mind still ticking over.

After further study of the delta version of the first impulse, he decided there were no firm conclusions to be drawn other than the delta stream was random. What next? Maybe, he reasoned, the corresponding equation for the second impulse might reveal something if set alongside the first impulse since the psi wheels all moved in step when they did move. It meant another long drawn out passage of writing out the streams of dots and crosses, another long period of total concentration to ensure no mistakes. One bonus was that the others drifted off after lunchtime on Saturday and he had the place to himself. Gerry Morgan had jokingly admonished him for coming in on his day off and said he should not work too long but added, again jokingly, that Bill would probably ignore him. Bill did, not in any way deliberately, simply because he became so preoccupied.

On Monday morning, Bill found a circular on his table headed 'Bletchley Park Home Guard', on which was a handwritten note from Gerry Morgan to the effect that everyone as appropriate should make sure they attend the enrolment evening. His heart sank. Civilian men were required to enrol; only senior staff members were exempt. Having thought he had avoided any sort of military service, he was now faced with having to put on a uniform, learn to fire a rifle and patrol the country lanes in the dead of night. One sentence in the circular cemented his alarm at the prospect. It stated that those enrolling would be subject to military law.

He had heard jaundiced stories of the Home Guard from his brother, how amateur the platoons were and how they were ill-equipped. Bill thought it was a volunteer force but the circular made it plain that enrolment was a requirement. He considered asking Gerry if he could be excused but decided to do nothing for the moment. At lunchtime, he met Jack Good and mentioned it to him. Jack too had misgivings but said he would reluctantly attend, pressured because his boss, Alan Turing, had already joined up before leaving for Washington. Bill felt he had little choice but to tag along.

In the afternoon, Gerry called a meeting of everyone to see what ideas people had on the Tunny problem. It was clear none of the others had made any sort of progress. Bill gave very little away and Gerry did not press him knowing Bill would only speak out when he had something fairly solid. Max said he would be better working with someone and Gerry agreed the two of them should work together. James Wyllie also said he was rather out of his depth on his own and would be more use helping someone else. Gerry, noting Bill was working long hours, offered him James to which Bill agreed. The meeting ended rather downbeat.

With James's help, Bill finished the delta-ing of the second impulse. He was not expecting it to produce any fresh conclusions on its own and began analysing it alongside the first impulse. The two psi streams appeared much alike which Bill had expected. He knew that when the psi wheels did not move on one step because of the stuttering effect, the next symbol would be the same as the previous symbol, and whether dot or cross, the delta would be dot. This, he analysed, was about 40 per cent of the time. But, he wondered, for the other 60 per cent of the time when the psi wheels moved on one step would there be a random 50 per cent of dots in the delta-ed form? He asked James to add the two psi streams together, to produce a delta-ed stream and to count the proportion of dots. All this took time even though James worked at a pace which Bill acknowledged he could not match. Meanwhile, Bill considered his next steps.

"68.7 per cent," James finally announced with a flourish.

"Ah," said Bill. "I was expecting about 70 per cent. That vindicates that my next piece of analysis is worth attempting. I know it is onerous, James, but this next step will be critical."

"Oh no, not more delta-ing!" bemoaned James.

"This is the plaintext, the language bit," said Bill encouragingly. "We need to carry out delta-ing on the addition of the first and second impulses of the plaintext this time but on say four messages to get a good average. Ask Ralph if we can have three more recently decoded messages and we'll take two each. The longer the messages, the better for our averages."

"Ah, well this is more up my street," said James. "What are we looking for this time?"

"I want to see what the proportion of dots is in the one plus two impulses of the delta plaintext. If you remember the equation is: the ciphertext is equal to the contributions of the plaintext plus the chi wheel plus the psi wheel. We've just discovered that the contribution of the psi wheel is 70 per cent dot in the delta-ed one plus two impulses. That is well outside the randomness of 50 per cent you might expect the Germans were aiming for. Maybe they didn't think of looking at the delta of two impulses added together. If the plaintext delta is over 50 per cent dot then we may simplify the equation by a method of linear algebra and solve it statistically."

"You've lost me," said James. "I'll just stick to words and letters."

The two worked meticulously on the plaintext streams of their four messages. Bill stayed on late having told Mrs Batchelor he would eat at the Park. He was anxious to get this next piece of analysis finished.

"59.2 per cent," said James on completing his first message.

"That's interesting," said Bill. "Good. It's more than I expected."

Later, Bill produced 60.8 per cent for his first message which again was an encouraging result.

"62.1 per cent for my second message," said James. "What now? Do you want me to finish your second message?"

"Er, no," said Bill. "Can you analyse why these rates are well above the random 50 per cent, much higher than I thought might be the case."

Bill finished his second message and the average of all four came out at 61.1 per cent. "This is looking good!" he said somewhat surprised yet delighted. "What have you got, James?"

"Well, there appear to be two influences. Well, one influence really but two aspects. The main influence is the high proportion of double characters in the plain text. This is partly due to long drawn out punctuation marks such as +++MAA8889, which is: move to figure shift pressed three times, full stop, two dashes, move to letter shift pressed three times and a space. That produces a string of nine consecutive dots in the delta of your 'one plus two'. This type of operator repetition appears to be a regular feature. Also, influential but maybe to a lesser extent is the language of the German military which has many repeated letters like the 'M' in 'commander' and the relative high frequency of bigrams such as 'EI', all producing dots."

"I think we are getting somewhere," said Bill.

"It's the first Home Guard evening tonight, isn't it?" said James who was exempt from the Home Guard due to his being in the military already. He knew Bill was in dread of the whole idea. "I hope they don't march you into a wall," he said mischievously. "Not like I did once on the parade ground with one of my platoons!"

Bill, not wishing to be reminded, refused to react to the taunt.

The Home Guard enrolment evening was somewhat chaotic. He and Jack had to join a queue as the process to sign on everyone who turned up took longer than expected. Bill soon became impatient, hating wasting time. There was a lot of noise; names being called out, banter and general hubbub. In all, it was not a good start. Eventually, everyone was marshalled into rough ranks for an address by the Officer Commanding, Major Lucas. Bill and Jack stood well to the back, Bill looking for an early means of exit.

"Gentlemen," the Major began. "We have a splendid turnout. Thank you for your patience but more importantly, thank you for your enthusiasm for what is an important role in the defence of our country. As many of you will know, the Home Guard was formed in 1940 to act as a secondary defence force in case of invasion by the forces of Germany and their allies, to try to slow down the advance of the enemy, even by a few hours in order to give our regular troops time to regroup. Whilst we are training and honing our skills, we have another important role. Home Guard units across the nation are the eyes and ears of our towns, villages and countryside on the look-out for anything unusual, for spies and parachutists or clandestine fifth columnists.

"I have a training programme which will bring us into line with other local units so we can support them together with other local civil defence units. What can you expect?

"Well, initially, we have a varied programme of drill, weapons training, unarmed combat, observation and reconnaissance duties. Later, we will move on to defensive positions.

"As you may know, weapons and uniforms are in short supply. I hope to have some Short Magazine Lee-Enfield rifles shortly and with the co-operation of the authorities here, I hope to establish a rifle range. Uniforms will be provided in due course; in the meantime, for all Home Guard duties, you should wear the armbands already handed out.

"Now, I know it will be difficult for some of you to attend regularly due to changing shift patterns but otherwise, attendance is a requirement to ensure everyone receives the necessary training for this vital role and so that we can act as a cohesive unit.

"Gentlemen, that is all for this evening. Again, thank you for your keenness to join the many thousands of men right across the country who dedicate their spare time to the Home Guard and in the security of the realm. We will muster the same time next week. You may dismiss."

"What have we let ourselves into?" said a concerned Jack rhetorically on the way out. Bill said nothing, his mind in a whirl. So far, he felt he had grown into this place and had become comfortable knowing he was contributing along with his peers. And now this!

Before Bill could move to the final stage of his analysis, Gerry called another progress meeting. Gerry and Max were still investigating a possible angle which they articulated at length. Bill found he understood little of it and had little confidence in that little. He himself was still non-committal on his own idea. No one else had any firm news. Unusually, at the end, Gerry allowed some discussion to develop about the state of the war in view of the news from North Africa that the Eighth Army had commenced a major battle against Rommel's forces. Gerry had a copy of The Times and read out one section of the report that stated 24 Axis supply ships had been sunk or damaged by our submarines in the Mediterranean during October. He caught Bill's eye as if to say the breaking of the Italian Hagelin codes was still working well. The meeting broke up with people in a slightly better frame of mind on the news.

In a rather hoarse voice, Bill addressed James. "Let's get back to it. What I need next is to prove my calculations by a practical example."

"Are you all right?" asked James. "You've been coughing a lot today and you seem a bit shaky."

"Just a bit of a cold I expect," croaked Bill, although he knew that was playing down how unwell he really felt. "This is what we need to do," he said wanting to press on regardless. "We should take a deciphered message and add the first and second impulses of the ciphertext and produce the delta, and do likewise for the chi contribution. We then need to make a comparison of the dot counts. I anticipate the ciphertext will agree with the chi contribution in about 55 per cent."

"Where does that come from?" James wanted to know.

"The probability of the psi contribution we calculated to be about 70 per cent dot and we estimated the probability of the plaintext being dot at about 60 per cent. Combining these two probabilities gives a mathematical probability of about 55 per cent dot agreement between the ciphertext and the chi." Bill paused, trying to stifle a fit of coughing and failing.

"Why don't you get yourself off to your bed, Bill? You're doing yourself no good here. If it were me, my wife would have had me tucked up in bed with a hot toddy long before."

"We need to check my calculations," Bill repeated.

"I tell you what," said James, "you set me up with the test and I can then progress it while you get yourself off."

Bill found his relationship with James quite odd. James was clearly playing second fiddle to Bill simply because of Bill's knowledge of Tunny and of mathematics meaning James's skills were not always the pre-eminent requirement. Yet, James was about 10 years older than Bill, an Army Captain, married with several small children and an established lexicographer of some repute. In that respect Bill felt quite junior. It was this latter aspect that swayed Bill to take James's advice.

He felt a little better in the morning, struggled through most of the day before being despatched early again by James. Progress on the test had been made but there was no conclusion yet and a frustrated Bill trudged homewards in the damp gloom. The next day followed the same pattern except that an assessment of the test so far on less than 1,750 letters was showing encouraging results. Bill went home early again as his flu caught up with him in the afternoon.

Friday saw improving results for 2,250 and 2,750 letters. But this did nothing for Bill's health and James persuaded him to take the whole weekend off which he spent reading and writing some letters. He pressed on during Monday and Tuesday.

By the end of Wednesday, the result of the 3,200-letter message was clearly above random at 54.7 per cent. Bill discussed with James the two conclusions he could draw. Over a message of that length, the small margin above random, whilst only 4.7 per cent was, in Bill's eyes, easily large enough to be statistically significant. The results at counts of letters lower than 1,750 were less conclusive.

"My method works," he said with evident satisfaction. "But it needs messages of at least 2,000 letters, probably more, to produce valid results."

"That's remarkable," said James impressed that Bill's prediction should be so close. "But how do you know a different setting won't produce a similar result?"

"I've been thinking about that over the weekend," said Bill.

"You can't leave it alone, can you, Bill! Go on."

"I estimate the correct setting will give statistically the highest result because other settings will have different chi elements and these elements will bias the count towards the random 50 per cent. Here, I've written down the equations that support that view. We will need to run some test examples. Impulses one and two have a combined periodicity of 1,271; that is before the combined pattern of the two wheels begins to repeat itself. The combined periodicity is the periodicity of impulse one, the wheel of 41, multiplied by the periodicity of impulse two, the wheel of 31."

"What! We haven't got to go through 1,271 sets of deltas to prove your theory, have we?" said James horrified at the scale of the task.

"No, no, only a few samples based on the 3,200 message. And I have some ideas on how to simplify that process; one idea being a rectangle of sides 31 and 41 tabulating diagonally the addition of the two delta-ed ciphertext streams."

"What are you going to do now, then?" asked James.

"I think I'm sufficiently satisfied of my hypothesis to take it to Gerry," said Bill. "Are you coming with me?"

"Actually Bill, I don't think I can add anything. In any case, I want to take an early lunchtime to work out train times to Scotland with the station ticket office. I shall be writing to my wife this evening about going up to see her. You go and see Gerry."

Bill, feeling marginally better, prepared himself. He collected together various papers in support of his pitch. He steeled himself; whatever the circumstances, he was loath to make any sort of presentation.

He put his head round the open door to Gerry Morgan's office. Max was there talking animatedly about something. Gerry saw Bill and waved him in and indicated he take a seat. Bill listened for a few minutes as the two of them enthusiastically told him about the state of their own investigations which appeared still to be about the complex idea they talked of earlier. Eventually, Bill butted in.

"Now, my method is much simpler," he blurted out brashly.

Both Gerry and Max were somewhat startled by the uncharacteristic manner of Bill's interruption and at the boldness of his statement.

"You have a scheme?" Gerry queried, quickly regaining his composure.

"Yes," said Bill rather regretting his nervous and presumptive opening remark.

"Well, you had better tell us about it," Gerry ordered.

"My hypothesis is that given a sufficiently long string of message letters, if you lay all 1,271 pattern combinations of the delta of the first and second chi impulses combined against the same delta of the two ciphertext streams, the highest dot count should statistically reveal the start points of the two chi wheels."

The words 'delta' and 'statistically' immediately caught Max's attention.

"Tell us more," he urged.

"From the beginning," added Gerry wanting to slow Bill down a bit and get behind the proposition which, knowing Bill as he did, he expected to be highly probable if not more so.

Bill expounded his hypothesis and showed them his sample findings. It did not take Max and Gerry long to grasp the significance of Bill's theory. Inevitably, they had some questions.

"Why the first two impulses?" Gerry asked.

"There are 22 million combinations of starting positions for all five chi wheels," Bill stated. "For the first two, it's 1,271. Also, the expected proportion of dots is slightly greater than in the case say for impulses four and five combined."

Question followed question. Bill was able to satisfy his two mathematician inquisitors to the point where the only question left was what to do next.

"I think," said Bill, "we need to set up some further tests which set out to affirm my hypothesis both positively and negatively. As I said in answer to one of your questions, I have not yet attempted to prove my calculation that an incorrect setting produces a result biased towards random. I am satisfied that the correct setting produces a statistically significant result around 55 per cent. We need to prove that all other results cluster around 50 per cent."

Gerry started to row back from his initial enthusiasm when he realised the sheer volume of calculations required to pursue this line of attack.

"We need to think about how we could do this," said Gerry. "It's not just the comparison of the 1,271-wheel pattern combinations, it's also producing the delta streams of added impulses."

"You have seen the result that James and I worked through," said Bill. "It took the two of us perhaps six days, not full time though as I was struggling with a cold. Because the chi wheel patterns are set for a month, once that delta-ed stream is mapped out it doesn't have to be done again until the next month," he argued. "Next, I want to run a few negative samples, that is with combinations known to be incorrect and so should result in near random scores."

"Maybe I could help with that," offered Max, thinking this was more in his line.

"Can we look at this more tomorrow," said Gerry looking at his watch. "I have to leave now for another meeting. Let's pick up again the same time tomorrow."

Bill's hacking cough returned later that afternoon and James sent him home early yet again. Bill still felt grim in the morning but was determined not to miss the meeting. The only solution he had to the volume problem was more manpower, perhaps requesting two from the team to help him and James undertake one positive and a couple of negative tests at least.

"Right, let's resume," said Gerry. "I've been thinking this is a most important breakthrough. More important than anything else we have going, including our idea, don't you think Max?"

"Agreed," said Max.

"This is what I suggest. Rather than spend time on some known incorrect runs, why don't we take a recent message that Ralph hasn't touched, one not in depth, and tackle that with Bill's hypothesis, all 1,271 chi wheel combinations. I think we need to do this before we can consider the way forward."

"I could agree to that," said Bill, happy to endorse Gerry's brute force approach.

"It will be tedious and we'll have to see if we can streamline the process. As it happens, I was in a meeting with Freddie Freeborn later on yesterday. He runs the Hollerith Section, if you didn't know, which records data on punched cards. I mentioned this volume problem to him and he suggested using stencils. That sounds like something we could pursue. Can I leave it to you two to see what you can come up with in the next few days? You can hold on to James; also Max can join you. I'll get one of the others to help you too. Keep me in touch though, please.

"Oh, and by the way," he concluded, "I've mentioned this to John Tiltman and he's behind us on this."

Bill tagged along with Jack to the next Home Guard evening which turned into an embarrassing disaster for both of them. Trying to hide at the back during the first drill practice in the hall, both he and Jack were conspicuous by their ineptitude even compared to the other novices. Jack just lacked coordination and Bill struggled to concentrate, his mind on the next stage of his hypothesis. Their clumsiness did not go unnoticed. Next, outside came a hand grenade throwing demonstration and practice. Jack whispered to Bill confessing he had not been at all sporty at school and had never thrown or bowled a cricket ball. It showed when it came to his turn. He stood sideways as shown, pulled the pin on the dummy grenade, leant back and threw. But the grenade only went a few yards and he fell awkwardly instead of throwing himself flat on the ground as instructed to avoid the blast. Bill was no better. He pulled the pin but in doing so, dropped the grenade. Everyone jokingly pretended to take cover. In his embarrassment, Bill picked up the grenade, threw it underarm and forgot to flatten himself on the ground. All of which brought even more laughter than Jack's pathetic effort.

Back inside the hall, there followed a short but alarming Military Training film demonstrating unarmed combat with one exercise showing an unarmed British soldier tackling a German sentry and placing him in a Japanese strangle hold.

"The idea of me doing that," Jack whispered, "is about as remote as me swimming the Atlantic; and I can't swim!"

As they left the hall, a dejected Jack said, "This is not for us, Bill. There are plenty of them. Surely, they can manage without us. Maybe I'll have a word with Major Lucas; for us both, if you like. What do you think?"

An equally dejected Bill readily agreed.

In the morning, Bill struggled on. James's polite enquiries about the previous evening's events were impolitely ignored.

Ralph Tester provided an October message of 4,000 letters of ciphertext that was not in depth and therefore had not been subject to any decoding attempt. Over the next few days, they developed the idea of representing the first two impulses of the ciphertext stream added and delta-ed on a paper tape stencil using a perforator linked to a keyboard, holes indicating dots and blanks indicating crosses. They then devised a set of paper tape stencils representing all the 1,271 possible pattern settings of the first two chi wheels in the one plus two delta format from the known October patterns. Each of the chi stencils then had to be laid over the ciphertext stencil and the common dots counted. It was a long and monotonous process for which a careful log had to be kept. While the others pressed on with the process, Bill nervously took counts every 500 letters.

His first concern was that the results of this first of 1,271 runs would be well outside his expected range of five or six points either side of the random 50 per cent. As, one by one, each of the eight 500-letter counts came in close to random, he began to feel reassured. The final result for the whole of the 4,000-letter message of was a satisfactory 49.2 per cent dot.

The group reviewed the outcome, pleased that the result was within the forecast range. Since it was the initial test run of very many, they agreed there were no other conclusions to be drawn.

"Only 1,270 more runs to go," quipped James to groans from the others.

What did exercise their minds was the effort required to produce this one result and what could be done to hasten the process. It was decided to double up on the stencils so that two pairs of settings could be carried out at the same time. Over the next few days, Bill monitored the results closely, his confidence growing as result after result came in close to random.

At his digs, Mrs Batchelor continued to be concerned at Bill's health which had improved but he was left with a nasty persistent cough. When he was first poorly, she had moved into mothering mode making some special hearty meals and doing what she could to make him comfortable.

"You really should take time off to get properly better," she said repeatedly. But Bill still went in saying it was vital.

"If you don't get yourself better, it will only come back worse. Take my word for it," she warned knowingly.

Bill, however, persisted in going in because this period of testing his theory was just too important yet he could not explain any of this to Mrs Batchelor. Concentrating during the day, he largely forgot about his condition but inevitably, it worsened in the evenings which did not go unnoticed by the knowing Mrs Batchelor. Gradually, he did improve but could not shift it altogether.

He did, however, take the whole weekend off and stayed indoors in the warm, wrote some letters and intended to study some equations Cedric had included in his last letter. But he found his mind returning to the problem of a faster process for the 1,271 chi wheel setting combinations. Having a number of completed tests, one obvious course he considered was to run the tests on less than the 4,000 letters of ciphertext, maybe 2,600 which would allow for two runs of the 1,271 combinations. He would need to review his intermediate counts to see if their results were sufficiently consistent to make such a reduction valid for test purposes. He began to look at Cedric's equations but feeling totally drained, he lay down on his bed and slept for hours.

At Tuesday evening's meal, Mrs Batchelor asked if he wanted to listen to a speech Mr Churchill was giving on the wireless later. He said he would and came down to the sitting room in time for the beginning of the broadcast. They listened to his every word. As Mr Churchill spoke, Bill could envisage that small, bent, pale figure who gave that address outside Hut 6, and again marvelled at his oratory, this time speaking at the Mansion House following the rout, as Mr Churchill called it, of Rommel's army in North Africa.

"We have victory, a remarkable and definite victory. A bright gleam has caught the helmets of our soldiers, and warmed and cheered all our hearts," said Mr Churchill to warm applause.

"The Germans have received back again that measure of fire and steel which they have so often meted out to others."

He went on to caution, "Now, this is not the end. It is not even the beginning of the end. But it is, perhaps, the end of the beginning."

They both agreed it was a most uplifting speech.

"The best bit of news we have had in years," sighed Mrs Batchelor contentedly. "But it's late and I must to my bed."

The following morning, Bill bumped into Michael Crum and wanted to know how he had got on.

"I've been working on this depth of 40. Can you believe it, 40 messages sent without changing machine setting! Don't their operators know what they are doing? It's a bit difficult without some obvious cribs but I'm getting there. The next stage is to get some key stream. By the way, the traffic has ceased. Just before our victory in the Battle of El Alamein. Funny that?"

All week, the production of results from Bill's analysis of a lesser number of examined ciphertext letters continued. The approach appeared valid but when a result was not consistent, the remaining letters were examined. No one count stood out. They all knew that the one they were looking for could be the next one or the very last one. Bill reported to Gerry.

"The results we have so far support my theory. The more test runs we complete the wider the range of results but so far nothing is statistically outstanding. We are getting quicker at it though," Bill said hoping to allay Gerry's possible concerns at the length of time it was taking. "We have nearly halved the number of letters in each test but sometimes when a result is not consistent, we complete the whole 4,000 letters. Then the final result regularises. This tells us that there may be passages in the plaintext which give inconsistent results."

"Press on," said Gerry. "Let me know when you have something interesting." He was reluctant to commit more bodies to the effort at this stage, but was prepared to do so should an outstanding result come through.

There were some false starts which got the team excited but to their disappointment, in the end the counts fell in line with a random score. But then on test run number 853, the count stayed high through the 1,000 letter mark, then through the 1,500 letter mark, even improved through the 2,000 mark. The excitement mounted.

"This looks like it!" said James. He could hardly contain his delight, the antithesis of Bill whose expression was almost unchanged.

"We'll need to work through the whole 4,000 letters," stated Bill calmly.

The others in the room, hearing the growing excitement came over to see what was going on. Run number 853 was progressed steadily in an increasingly excitable mood.

The final count came in at 55.2 per cent dot, well above the next largest score. They all sat back contemplating this moment which, for most of them, was quite momentous after all their efforts. The whole room was abuzz as the final score was announced. Even Bill allowed himself a faint grin. But he had already reminded himself that there were still a further 400 or so test runs to go, any of which could throw his theory into doubt. He and Max went to see Gerry.

"What's with all that noise going on?" Gerry demanded good-humouredly. "Some good news, I hope."

It was Max who spoke. Gradually as he had become familiar with the process and possibly because Bill was under par, he had taken more of a lead role in the group. Bill was content to let this happen as it gave him more room to think beyond the current stage which, if completed satisfactorily, would give them two wheels only out of the twelve. The next phase would be to find the other three chi wheel starting positions.

Gerry was plainly delighted with progress and encouraged them to grind on to the end. He suggested then they all get together with John Tiltman to review their findings.

Bill felt wretched towards the end of the afternoon, not having contributed a great deal since the meeting. Seeing Bill worsen, James again told him to pack it in for the day. The atmosphere was noticeably more smoky than usual that afternoon. Because there was always someone smoking a cigarette or puffing on their pipe, the hut had a permanent whiff of tobacco smoke about it but that afternoon, it seemed to be worse. Some said it was caused by emissions from the coke stove due to the wind direction but it all made for an unpleasantly stuffy room which did Bill no good.

In the morning, Bill looked ghastly and this time, James wheeled him round to the newly opened sick bay. Mrs Meade, the medical officer, diagnosed a bad bout of flu and ordered him to bed in one of the single-bed rooms. Bill weakly protested but the look on Mrs Meade's face told him there was to be no argument. She wanted to keep an eye on Bill because there had been a number of cases recently of pneumonia and of tuberculosis among the Bletchley Park staff brought on, she was convinced, by the stress of the work and the close working conditions. She did not think Bill was that seriously ill but wanted to be certain.

Bill was shivery, aching and coughing and in no shape to protest further. Soon, he was tucked up in a bed with a hot water bottle and Mrs Meade's remedy, a honey and hot water drink.

"I usually put lemon juice in with the honey," she said, "but you can't get lemons no more."

He woke up several hours later and became agitated. Hearing him awake, Mrs Meade came in.

"I can't stay here," he fretted. "Mrs Batchelor will worry if I don't go back this evening. I haven't got anything. I should get back to work."

"We'll take care of everything," said Mrs Meade soothingly. "You just lie still. Your colleague James came round. He has gone to see Mrs Batchelor and will tell her and get a few things so you can stay here. Here is the best place for you. So, don't worry."

After several days in the sick bay, Mrs Meade felt Bill was well enough to travel home to Cheveley on the strict instructions that he took a complete week's rest and recuperation.

At Cheveley, Bill's mother made a fuss of him. She was quite in her element as she had two invalids to look after since Bill's father had been unwell again and he too was at home. The fire was well banked up with coal and she baked and cooked and fussed from morning till night.

There was the inevitable inquisition. His father gently quizzed him hoping, but not necessarily expecting, to learn something of what Bill was doing for the war effort. By now, though, Bill was quite practiced at batting away that line of questioning and his father soon gave up. The state of the war was what his father talked about mostly after that. His mother was more interested in his health and welfare. What was his digs like? Did Mrs Batchelor look after him properly? Was he eating properly? Did they make him work long hours? She was glad there was a cafeteria where he could eat. The subscription for the cafeteria was £1. 2s. 6d a month he told her and the food was quite good, although not as good as Mrs Batchelor's cooking. Sometimes, he did work long hours, he said, but he could get out and go for walks in the grounds. Despite this information, she was unconvinced and adamant his illness was proof he was run down.

"Will you be home for Christmas?" she wanted to know when the time came for him to return to Bletchley.

"I'll try but can't be certain. We have a lot on at the moment. Maybe I can get away for a couple of days. I'll let you know. Look after Dad. Here, take this," he said handing her five of the new war-time pink and blue one pound notes. "I don't spend much."

His mother gave him a disapproving look yet, with just a touch of mock hesitation, accepted them.

When Bill arrived back at the Research Section, Gerry welcomed his return saying he hoped he was fully recovered.

"By the way," he added, "I've had a message from Major Lucas to say you have been excused from Home Guard attendance for the time being and placed on a reserve list. It seems he was oversubscribed. Good to know people are so keen!"

For once, Bill's face gave a trace of emotion, a flicker of blessed relief at his reprieve. The look on Gerry's face told Bill he knew exactly how Bill felt about the Home Guard.

Gerry convened the meeting with John Tiltman a couple of days after Bill returned when the final test runs were complete. Again, Max Newman took the lead role in explaining the set of results. Run 853 remained the stand-out score, the remainder were within a two point range either side of random. Gerry turned to Bill wanting him to set out the ensuing steps to find the other chi settings and how he saw the route to finally decoding the message.

"The next stage is to run similar tests on impulses four and five which have periods of 26 and 23. The number of tests is, therefore, much less, 598, but I anticipate the correct settings could be statistically slightly less prominent because there are probably fewer duplicates to delta. We shall see. That leaves impulse three to complete the chis. I think we may approach that by combining it with the strongest of the other results."

"What then?" inquired Colonel Tiltman.

"The chi settings will then be known and the stream can be added to the ciphertext to leave us with a combination of plaintext and psi from which we need to separate out a length of psi."

"Rather like reading a depth?" put Colonel Tiltman seeking confirmation of his understanding.

"Comparable, yes," said Bill. "Obviously, the psi stream is not plaintext but it has its own peculiarities. The stuttering effect will produce many double letters and we should be able to exploit this non-random feature to set the remaining wheels."

"It all appears promising," said Gerry. "Still some way to go but I think we should pursue this at least to see what the ciphertext and the chi combined look like." He glanced over at Colonel Tiltman for support.

"I agree," said the Colonel. "The sheer volume of calculations is a concern, though. Hopefully, this next stage will be less time consuming."

Bill and his group pressed on. Wheels four and five were eventually set but an acceptably significant score was only achieved when the comparison was made with the entire 4,000 letters of ciphertext. Wheel three proved easy when combined with the known setting for wheel one. They had acceptable scores for all five chi wheels.

"A tremendous achievement," announced Max acknowledging the work of the others.

"I'm glad Bill knew what he was doing otherwise we'd never have got this far," said James. Bill, as usual, showed no outward sign of triumph.

"The scores have a high probability of being correct," said Bill, "but they are not certain. The proof is if we can decode the message on these settings. The next step is to combine the chi stream with the ciphertext stream. If we can separate out a stretch of that result, we should be able to set the psi and motor wheels. I need to think about how we might do that."

The next update meeting with Gerry did not go well. Bill presented two options for setting the psi and motor wheels; a statistical method and a more traditional depth-reading type technique. When it came to deciding which approach to adopt, there was a lively, even heated, argument.

Ralph Tester had joined them and he was strongly in favour of the traditional way which he said his team were well versed in and would produce more certain results. Max Newman favoured the more mathematical, statistical approach arguing that Bill's statistical attack had borne fruit, proof that this was the way to go. Although Max had only very recently joined them, his air of sagacity and intellectual insight carried much weight in Gerry Morgan's mind. Gerry knew he would have to decide one way or the other; he did not have the resources to manage both. He kept looking at Bill but to Gerry's annoyance, Bill gave nothing away. In the end, Gerry directly asked Bill which route he recommended.

"I've no strong feelings either way," said Bill, to Gerry's further irritation.

Bill did not want to take sides. He had a foot in both camps.

"At this stage," Bill added in his typically understated manner, "I suppose we should experiment with both."

"You are right, Bill, we should, but at the moment, we don't have the resources so first I think we should opt for the traditional route. Can you give us support please, Ralph, if we need it?"

Afterwards, Gerry took Max on one side, concerned that Max should think he had gone back on his earlier word.

"I actually think we should develop the mathematical approach, Max, but for now, we have to take the faster, more certain route. We can bring in statistical analysis when we know the whole process works. I also think you will learn a great deal from the traditional method. We are on the cusp of something extraordinary here and I firmly believe mathematics will deliver the way forward. Stick with it for now and at the same time, think ahead how we can address the volume problem should Bill's procedures prove to be the significant breakthrough we think it is. Our role in the Research Section is to bring developments to a routine. How do we get Bill's procedures with its attendant high volumes to a timely routine? That is the question."

Max acquiesced and accepted the challenge.

Back in the main room, Bill set out the stall for this next phase.

"To separate this stream made up of the plaintext and the psi contribution, we need some cribs," he explained. "The Testery people are much better than I am at this and we may need to call on their help. But let's try ourselves to start with.

"We have here the patterns of the psi wheels for this month that the Testery broke earlier from a depth. The task is to find for each psi wheel where in its pattern it was positioned at the beginning of the message. Remember the psi wheels have a length of 43 characters on psi one, 47 for psi two, 51, 53 and 59 for psi five, also that they all either move on one step or stay still depending on the motor wheels. When they stay still, they contribute the same letter to the key as the previous time. In other words, there are very many duplicated letters in the psi stream. This is what we have to exploit. By placing a good crib under the stream we generated earlier, we may find useful bits of psi characterised by many duplicated letters. If we can join up some of these bits with clever guesses, we may be able to get a long enough string of the psi stream. Take out the duplicates caused by the motor wheels and we have some 'pure' psi for which we can match up the individual wheel patterns against the known patterns the Testery found earlier. Bearing in mind the lengths of the wheels, we can extend this 'pure' psi backwards to the beginning of the message and we have our settings."

"What about the motor wheels," asked Max. "Don't we need these to set up the Tunny machine?"

"Alongside the psi setting, we can analyse the distribution of duplicated letters and build up probable patterns of both motor wheels," said Bill.

"You've lost me again," grumbled James. "I think I'll understand it better as we go along."

"It is somewhat artistic," said Bill. "Jerry Roberts in the Testery is a master at it. He can instantly spot a possible position for a crib by adding in his head letters that will produce a string of duplicates in the psi. Let's start and see where we get."

Without help from the Testery, they managed to set the psi and motor wheels and took all the results to Ralph.

"How confident are you, Bill, that you have the correct settings?" Ralph tested.

"I would be surprised if we were wrong," said Bill. "If we are, it's back to the drawing board."

Ralph's team set up the Tunny machine with Bill's settings and the operator began typing in the ciphertext. Gerry Morgan had come in to witness the final piece of the process. Everyone held their breath. Gradually, word by word, recognisable German plaintext appeared. Applause rang out. Broad smiles were everywhere. It began to sink in to everyone this was a crucial moment. Having been locked out of single messages, they were back in business.

Gerry, Bill, Max and Ralph went to see Colonel Tiltman. Everyone was in high spirits. Ralph suggested Jerry Roberts should tackle a second message with Bill's help. It was agreed that solving the volume problem was now the priority and Colonel Tiltman tasked Max to look into this.

"You're an odd cove, Bill," Jerry said later when the two were working on the second message. "You did all that tremendous work to get out that first ciphertext yet you didn't ask what the message was about!"

Bill thought for a moment.

"I guess, I do get a bit involved in the technical side of things," he said obliquely.

"A bit!" exclaimed Jerry. "You can say that again. Anyway, it was a very interesting message with some extremely high grade intelligence. Of course, the military boys only asked for more. They always do. I said we're working on it."

A Young Bill with His Parents

Bill at Trinity College, Cambridge

Cedric Smith at Trinity College, Cambridge

The Mansion, Bletchley Park

The Lorenz cipher machine

A Bletchley Park Tunny Machine

A Bletchley Park Robinson Machine

A Colossus at Bletchley Park

Gerry Morgan, Head of the Research Section, Bletchley Park

Alan Turing, senior Bletchley Park codebreaker

Tommy Flowers, who designed and built Colossus for Bletchley Park

Ralph Tester, founder and Head of the Testery, Bletchley Park

Captain Jerry Roberts leading codebreaker & founder member of the Testery, Bletchley Park

Memorial to Bill Tutte, Newmarket, Suffolk –unveiled 2014

Chapter 8
Depth of One

With the experience Bill and James had gained on the first message and with the skilful Jerry Roberts, they made good progress on the second message. Bill introduced one improvement to reduce the workload. He had analysed the results of the first message and reckoned 2,000 letters should be sufficient in most cases which proved to be the case.

One afternoon, Max Newman asked Bill to spare him a little time to go over some ideas he had on the volume problem.

"I've been speaking to a few people about how we get over the sheer volume of calculations in your theory. Taking the construct of one delta as one calculation, in order to run the 1,271 combinations of the patterns of just the first two chi wheels, the number of calculations runs into many millions. So, a solution to be practicable must be capable of that order of volume. The answer has to be a machine, a very high-speed machine, an electro-mechanical machine. And that is setting the chi wheels only. Talking to Ralph, the steps in the process after chi setting require 'artistry', as he puts it, and does not lend itself to a machine. But that is not where the volume lies. So, I've based my thinking on a machine, or a connected set of machines, that sets the chis only. Do you agree?"

"Yes," said Bill, "although at this very early stage, any machine should be capable of much adaption as our experience grows."

"Indeed," said Max. "Freddie Freeborn likes the idea of using punched teleprinter tape, like using a stencil. Another idea I'm looking at is sliding photographic plates over each other. However, what I'd like you to do for me, Bill, is to cast your eye over this functional specification I've drawn up to make sure I have it correct. You have a greatest understanding of everyone, I am told." He paused on his way out.

"By the way, I expect you have met Alan Turing. He was a student of mine, you know. I helped him publish his paper, *On Computable Numbers*. If you haven't read it, you should."

On the way back, Bill took the opportunity to see how Michael Crum was getting on.

"So far, Bill, this is what I have," said Michael. "The machine is not a Tunny machine but is a teleprinter type that the Germans refer to as a T52. It has ten wheels with periods ranging from 47 to 73. While the patterns of the wheels have remained unchanged, they can be set to different start positions so the key is constantly changing. Five wheels can be selected to provide a key added modulo 2 to the plain text. The five impulses produced are then transposed by a key provided by the other five wheels to produce the ciphertext. It seems to be used principally by the Luftwaffe. The powers that be here have called it Sturgeon."

At the beginning, Bill rather saw himself in the role of mentor to apprentice Michael but with this piece of reverse engineering similar to his own, the roles were much more equal.

"What now, Michael?" said Bill.

"The ten wheels are combined in groups of four in a complicated relationship and I'm looking for a simple way to describe it."

"Let me see," said Bill.

He considered for a few minutes the relationships Michael had discovered.

"This is a job for a graph theorist," he declared mimicking Jim Wyllie. "How about a regular pentagon, like this? The five vertices each have four connections, or relationships, two sides and two diagonals."

"That's it, Bill! Excellent," said Michael. "I need to write this up and conduct some statistical analyses to make reading messages quicker. I reckon it could be possible to get a break from depths of just four or five. This machine may well reappear on another link soon and let's hope they don't tighten up their security as they should. Thanks for your help, Bill."

Bill found this T52 interesting and still felt a little put out that it had been given to Michael. There were, undoubtedly, some statistical improvements that could be made in attacking it. Maybe he would get an opportunity to be involved should it come up on a new link.

The Christmas rota came round. Bill and Daphne were to hold the fort. Bill did not mind that much. He had last Christmas off and he knew others had young families to go to. Christmas Day itself was quiet but the cafeteria ladies, somehow, managed to put on a traditional lunch which was thoroughly enjoyed by all. Daphne asked Bill to join her and her husband so he was not on his own. He had sent a card to his parents saying he hoped to be home the second weekend in January and would ask Cedric over. By return, he received a card signed by all the family saying he would be missed which he put up in his room, the only item of festive decoration. He did miss being with his family at Christmas, especially the children.

The year ended misty and cold with rain turning to sleet but at least working by the stove, he was warm and he could get on in relative peace and quiet. The fumes from the stove still irritated his throat but thankfully, the habitual pipe and cigarette smokers were absent.

Everyone returned in the New Year and the rhythm of the place resumed. The second message that he, James and Jerry had been working on was successfully completed, the content of which was even more important than the first, Jerry assured him.

Bill made his promised post-Christmas visit to his family despite the poor weather.

"Come on in, come in," urged his mother when he finally arrived home. "This awful fog looks set to linger all day. Put your coat up and come by the fire."

"How are you, Dad?" asked Bill.

"This weather doesn't do me any good," bemoaned his father. "I'm not doing too much at the moment."

"Stay in the warm, then. Oh, I have something for you. A late Christmas present. Here."

Bill produced a quarter bottle of Scotch whiskey from his coat pocket. "A colleague of mine was home in Scotland over Christmas and he brought me this back. I won't drink it but a wee dram will do you good, as my colleague would say. A hot toddy to go to bed with."

His father's eyes lit up as he took the bottle, looked at the label and gave it an approving pat.

"Be sure to thank him from me, son. That's a grand present."

"I have something for you, Mum," Bill called out. His mother wiped her hands on her pinafore and came over, rather coyly as she was unused to presents.

"It's a cake," said Bill handing over a round parcel. "Not any cake. It's Mrs Batchelor's special recipe fruit cake! She baked an extra one for you. She felt sorry for you because I was not home for Christmas."

"Oh, look at that wonderful cake. I must write and thank her."

Lola and the children came over in the afternoon. Brother Joe was on shift. The children were wildly excited when Bill produced a bag of sweets each.

"Look what I've got, Mum!" shrieked young Joey. "Pear drops, lemon sherbets, jelly babies!"

"I've got liquorice, Fry's chocolate creams and barley twists," shouted Jeanne.

"Don't eat them all at once," warned Bill. "I had to save up a lot of coupons for those."

Cedric arrived in time for Sunday lunch. Bill's parents always welcomed Cedric whose company they thoroughly enjoyed though underneath they were disapproving of his stance on National Service but out of respect for their son's best friend left that unsaid. They asked him about his work at the hospital.

"The other day," he said, "I had a visitor from the University who came to the hospital and asked for Dr Smith. Only to be told they had no doctor of that name there. As it happened, I appeared and the visitor said, 'There he is!' Of course, the hospital did not know I had been awarded my PhD!"

"You're making that up. You're teasing us," said Bill's mother.

"No, no it's true, really. And once when I decided to take the bus to the hospital rather than go on my bike, the bus was very crowded and a refugee and his wife got on. She could get a seat downstairs but her husband had to go upstairs. When the conductor came round saying, 'Fares please' she replied, 'The Lord above will pay!'"

This must be another tall story, Bill's mother thought; Cedric is such a raconteur. But he assured her it did really happen.

After a very amiable lunch, Bill and Cedric wrapped up and went for a long walk, during which the topic of conversation was mostly mathematics. Cedric even admitted to working on some theorems over Christmas. He did ask after the other Trinity people at Bletchley Park. Bill related how he and Jack Good had briefly experienced the Home Guard at which Cedric expressed his approval at their swift retirement from military service. But Bill did not have much news of the others. Sometimes, he met them briefly in the cafeteria but otherwise, their paths did not cross.

On his return to Bletchley Bill was summoned to a big meeting with Commander Travis, the new head of Bletchley Park. Colonel Tiltman, Gerry, Ralph and Max were to present a case for an experimental machine to tackle the chi setting issue and Gerry wanted Bill along. Bill had seen a copy of the briefing paper sent to Commander Travis and was surprised to be invited to such a high-powered meeting. Gerry said Max would make the presentation much to Bill's relief. They all trooped into the Commander's spacious office.

"Ah, Mr Tutte. We meet again!" said the Commander to everyone else's surprise. "I keep hearing about your exploits on Tunny."

After shaking hands all round, he settled his large frame into his chair. "Gentlemen, let's get down to business."

Colonel Tiltman opened by emphasising the importance of the Tunny work and the need to have a means of attacking single messages now the Germans had improved their security.

Max then gave an outline of Bill's method and the proof that it worked. In his precise and measured manner, he briefly covered a number of options considered to bring the theory into the realms of practical use.

"My recommendation as per the briefing paper is this: in order to achieve the very high volumes of calculations and counts, we read photo-electrically two punched tapes, the message tape and the wheel tape and combine the signals before counting. Readily available teleprinter paper tape will run mechanically past the readers on a tape rack and the signals from the readers sent to a combining unit designed by Dollis Hill using existing telephone know-how and hardware. This combining unit can be variously wired via a plug-board to select the desired run. A valve and relay counter capable of reading 2,000 characters per second designed by Dr Charles Wynn Williams of the Telecommunications Research Establishment will make the counts which will show on a display panel."

"This Wynn Williams," said the Commander, "did some work last year on Mr Turing's high-speed bombes which I seem to remember did not proceed. Whilst this proposal sounds very different, is Mr Wynn Williams's high-speed counter technically proven? I've heard these valves are not that reliable," he inquired.

"I knew of Charles's work at Cambridge before the war," said Max in his authoritative manner. "The science is not new. Charles published his paper on it in 1932. If handled properly, these valves are reliable."

"What sort of time are we looking at to set one pair of chi wheels?" the Commander wanted to know, peering over his dark rimmed glasses.

"Half an hour is the estimation I've been given for a 2,000 letter message," Max replied, a statistic which seemed to impress the Commander who then addressed his questions to the others.

"Ralph, how do you see this fitting in with your Section?"

"We just need the chi settings," said Ralph. "I'm not sure machines can help with the work my people do so I think it's right to concentrate efforts on the chis."

"Gerry?"

"We have not come up with anything else that can attack a single message. Bill's breakthrough is shown to work. I think we have to do this. Tunny is too important."

"Bill, are you happy that this proposal is viable from a theoretical point of view? Will it do what your scheme requires?" questioned the Commander.

"I am content with the functional specification, so yes, I believe so," Bill answered cautiously.

"Gentlemen," Commander Travis summed up, "you know well enough how scarce materials are. We have difficult decisions to make with many projects competing for resources. Without doubt, if the intelligence Tunny can provide was not so very important, your request would have been in the waste paper basket long ago. As it is with Mr Turing's bombes and your Tunny decoders, we have come to rely more and more on such machines. I will approve your prototype on the basis proposed. I trust your assurances on performance will be met. I must be informed at the earliest opportunity if this appears not to be the case. Keep me informed, please."

"Bill," said Gerry on the way back, obviously puzzled by something. "What did Commander Travis mean when he said to you, 'We meet again'?"

"Oh, we shared a car once, on the way in from Adstock. His chauffeur didn't turn up one day. He lives out there," said Bill as a matter of fact. "Didn't I tell you?"

"You drove in with the head of Bletchley Park and you didn't tell anyone! You're a dark horse at times, Bill. You really are," said Gerry with a mild shake of his head.

Later that day, Gerry came across Bill standing by the window, hands behind his back, gazing into the distance.

"What now?" said Gerry feigning exasperation.

Bill turned, not picking up on the irony in Gerry's voice, and for once, his usually impassive expression gave a hint of concern.

"What if the Germans really tighten up their procedures? Since October, they have been changing the psi wheel patterns monthly instead of every three months. What if they change all the wheel patterns even more often than that? Operator laziness means we are still getting some depths but what if they tighten controls and we don't get any? None at all. All our efforts will have been in vain because we are still totally reliant on depths. All that potentially vital intelligence beyond reach."

"What are you getting at, Bill?"

"I'm convinced there is a way of totally breaking a single message."

"You have an idea?"

"Embryonic."

With Bill's record, Gerry was only too willing for him to explore his embryonic idea.

"Do you want to pursue it?" he asked. "I'm sure they can manage in the Testery without you now as long as you are on standby."

"I don't expect it will be quick, if it works at all. I think it will need a long message too."

"I'd be really upset if it was quick," stated Gerry flatly. "That would mean we have missed a simple trick. I'll square it with Ralph."

The next day, Bill found a note for him on the table attached to a rather long ciphertext. The note was from Jerry Roberts; it simply wished Bill good luck. Bill examined the cipher. It was dated yesterday and was 15,000 letters long, possibly two messages merged into one long one, a feature that was becoming more common.

One day while Bill was working on his hypothesis, Jim Wylie came over and said he had been asked to help the Testery with a problem. Apparently, a mysterious change in the encryption of some messages on the Rome/Tunis link had locked them out. Attempts to break two messages apparently in depth all failed.

"I think Ralph asked for your help but Gerry didn't want to disturb you so he suggested I should go instead," said Jim.

"What is it?" asked Bill.

"I don't know yet but everyone seems a bit worried about it."

Bill was a bit put out that he had been bypassed on a Tunny problem but did not show it.

"Let me know what's going on, please," he asked in a tone that was more a polite command.

"Of course," replied Jim, understanding Bill's concern.

But Jim's updates over the next few weeks were of growing anxiety in the Testery that the problem was sticking. In contrast, Bill was making steady progress working alone at his table. Gerry Morgan made several tentative enquires on progress but Bill gave little away.

After three weeks of intensive effort, Bill felt he was ready for the ultimate test of his theory. He gathered up a set of papers and made his way over to Ralph Tester.

"Bill, what can I do for you," said Ralph in his amiable way.

Uncharacteristically, Bill made a startling statement.

"This is the first message to be broken on a depth of one!"

Ralph stood up.

"You haven't done it?" he said incredulously.

"Can we run these patterns and settings through your Tunny decoder? That's the only way I can know if my hypothesis is reliable. I believe it is but of course, I could be wrong. It relies on the weight of evidence so even if the theory is sound it's possible I may have interpreted the evidence incorrectly or maybe I have simply made a mistake along the way. The next stage is to run a test on my findings. If you have an available slot on one of your machines, can we set up a test run, please?"

Bill watched as one of Ralph's ATS young ladies set up a Tunny decoder according to his findings, firstly with the patterns by means of U-shaped pins and then the settings using uniselector switches. Then she started typing in the 15,000 letter ciphertext. Bill was very impressed with the way she touch-typed the string of letters which, by their nature, appeared total gibberish. They all waited. Gradually, the teleprinter attachment started to clack as it printed the decoded letters.

"Here we go. This is it," said Ralph building the suspense.

First, a recognisable preamble address and serial number began to appear. Then the message itself began printing out in military German with much punctuation.

"You've done it!" declared Ralph before many letters had been printed. They all knew that if Bill's findings were incorrect, the machine would have spilled out nonsense.

"It is just staggering what you have done. Had it not been you, Bill, I would have thought this a set-up. Have you told Gerry?"

"I wanted to run a test first," said Bill. "I suppose he should be told now."

Seeing the German plaintext print out, Bill felt a surge of satisfaction far greater than he had felt before, although his countenance gave away little evidence of his delight. All along, he had been convinced a single Tunny message could be broken. And now, he had achieved it without a depth, only by prising open a weakness in the German's seemingly impregnable system. Of course, much had happened since he was given the Hellschreiber file and all the experience gained in the meantime was undoubtedly crucial in reaching this point as was the help he received from his colleagues. Primarily, his delight was because his hypothesis had been proven. But there was a secondary satisfaction; there had been a multitude of opportunities for making mistakes, yet quite obviously, he had made none.

Initially, Gerry was displeased with Bill that he had not been informed of this news before Ralph but supressed his annoyance in the light of its notable significance. He had called Colonel Tiltman who was on his way over and had asked Max to join them. When the group was assembled, Bill was asked to run through his method. Normally, he would be reluctant to make such a presentation especially without preparation but he was unusually flush with success.

"I had a 15,000 letter message," he began. "First I organised it into groups of 20 to make sure I didn't lose myself in the delta-ing. I delta-ed the first impulse plus the second impulse of the ciphertext as in the chi setting process. My theory was that such treatment of the ciphertext impulses produced a badly damaged version of the similarly treated chi wheel impulses. I hoped that it would be at least 55 per cent correct and therefore analysis of a sufficiently long message may lead to a good estimation of the first two chi wheel patterns. I used a rectangle."

Gerry, Max, Ralph and John Tiltman remained silent, absorbing Bill's reasoning.

"I populated a rectangle of 41 rows, representing the first chi wheel periodicity and 31 columns, representing the second chi wheel periodicity, a total of 1,271 cells. In the cell corresponding to its position in the delta-ed cipher stream, I placed a dot or a cross as appropriate. After 1,271 positions, the period repeated itself and in this way, each cell was populated with 11 or 12 dots or crosses. I examined each cell and took the majority, dot or cross. If, for instance, a cell had nine dots and three crosses, I would score that cell 'plus six'. If another cell had five dots and seven crosses, I would give it a score of 'minus two'. I called these the weight of evidence."

"The longer the message," said Gerry, "the greater the weight of evidence."

"In principle," said Bill. "But some cells were found to have equal numbers of dots and crosses and no initial decision could be made on those."

"But," said Max, "those that did have a good majority score were still the addition of two unknown elements. How did you break that down?"

"I was reminded of a simple mathematical puzzle," said Bill, "involving an addition table for pairs of unknown positive whole numbers. If say, for example in the cell where a column and a row intersect there is the number eight. That might mean the number five contributes to all the cells in that column and the number three to all the cells in that row, or some other combination adding up to eight. Given that all the cells of a table are populated according to that rule, then if just one contributory number is known then all the remaining unknown contributory numbers can be deduced. Such a table is analogous to my rectangle."

"Go on," said Gerry intrigued.

"Look at this version of my rectangle. I examined the rows and chose one that appeared to have the highest aggregate score ignoring negative signs. Of the scores in that row, I chose the highest eight or nine and set them, dot or cross according to their positive or negative weightings, in a new row at the bottom of the grid in their respective columns. That gave me a tentative fragment of chi pattern for the second impulse. Taking the first character of this fragment, say a dot, I could then work out a tentative contribution of the first chi impulse for each cell in that column. If a cell had a positive score, I assigned it dot, negative a cross. If the chi two contribution common to all cells of that column was dot, where the addition for a particular cell was assigned a dot then the chi one contribution was dot. If a cell in that column was assigned a cross then the chi one contribution was cross, and so on. That gave me eight or nine columns of tentative chi one patterns. I took the majority of these eight or nine scores to give me a weighted chi one pattern."

"These are all still in delta format at this stage, are they not?" said Gerry seeking confirmation of his understanding.

"Oh yes," answered Bill. "With that tentative chi one pattern, I could rework each cell in each row, all 1,271. I could now take the majority of each column to give me a tentative chi two pattern. Some of my original choices for the initial fragment may have changed. Therefore, I needed to rework the chi one pattern. Again, some changes may have occurred and so I would need to rework the chi two pattern again; and so on until they converged and no further changes occurred when the process was repeated. I now had two estimated patterns for delta chi one and delta chi two impulses."

"So, you repeated the whole process for chi three and chi four impulses?" probed Max.

"Yes," said Bill. "That rectangle is, of course, 26 by 29, 754 cells so from the 15,000 letter ciphertext there would be 19 scores in each cell. So, I had patterns for delta chi three and delta chi four impulses. For estimating chi five, I delta-ed chi four and chi five impulses and used the chi four pattern already obtained. As a check, I did likewise with chi one and chi four using the chi one pattern already obtained to check the chi four agreed with my earlier estimation from the three/four analysis. It agreed."

"But you still have the delta format?" said Gerry.

"Undelta-ing chi streams is relatively easy as analysis has shown the Germans constructed their patterns according to the rule that the number of crosses in each chi and delta chi pattern should be as nearly as possible half the length of the wheel. With all five chi patterns, the message could then be decoded using existing methods."

Bill paused and looked around the others. Their reactions were muted as though they could not quite believe what they had just witnessed, never expecting to see the day when a single Tunny message encoded by this fiendish machine could be totally broken by hand. Amazement turned to more practical matters. Colonel Tiltman was the first to respond.

"How robust do you think your method is?" he queried.

"This method is weaker than my 'one plus two' method since I have used no statistical theory, unless you count taking those majority verdicts as statistics. The longer the message, the better the weight of evidence of course, but also the content of the message may need to be favourable like this message which had an inordinate amount of punctuation. No doubt though, my method can be improved upon. If the early estimations could be verified statistically that would be a worthwhile progress check. Perhaps a machine like the one Max is developing could be adapted to carry out this rectangle set of procedures."

"We are in the same realms as your 'one plus two' method so far as practicality is concerned," said Gerry. "There are far too many calculations to introduce this now as a routine. It looks like another machine job. But meanwhile, it could be a vital back-up should no depths appear. See what refinements you can make, Bill."

"It's too late to make changes to the chi setting machine now being built," stated Max emphatically. "The latest is we should have a prototype for testing in late April or early May. If we mess about with the specification now, we will put the project back months."

"I agree," said the Colonel. He paused a moment. "Bill. We've been somewhat stunned by your discovery and have been talking around the consequences. But before we go any further, I have to say this is a red-letter day for the Research Section; possibly we will see no greater piece of codebreaking than the series of breakthroughs you have made over the last 15 months. We have been catching up with you ever since with machinery to turn your discoveries into practical routine and we have more to do it would seem. I'm hearing from the service chiefs the intelligence value from Tunny decrypts is of the highest order and is likely to be of increasing value now that the Americans are becoming more involved in the European theatre. The significance of your work cannot be underestimated. So, a big 'thank you' is in order."

"Hear, hear," echoed the others tapping the table in concurrence.

Bill felt very uncomfortable at this unexpected and overt praise from his superiors and sought to deflect it.

"The whole team was involved, really," he said rather tamely.

"In the short term, Bill, I suggest you refine your rectangling method as Gerry has suggested. Max, please keep in close touch with this in the light of your new machine.

"Gentlemen," said the Colonel in conclusion, "I might add here an emphasis, an emphasis that you should pass on to all of your teams. Whilst it's understandable people might be tempted to talk of success, there is an imperative for absolute secrecy about our progress on Tunny. It does no harm to remind everyone from time to time of their obligations. This is an apposite moment to do so."

Bill went to see Jim Wylie ostensibly to tell him about his rectangling method but his ulterior reason was to find out what the problem was that Jim and his Testery colleagues had been working on.

At last, Jim said he had some news and gave him a debriefing on the problem and on the solution that had only just been developed after three weeks of anxious investigation. It transpired that another line of dots and crosses had been added to the motor key stream. This addition was based on the pin position, in or out, of the second chi wheel one position back.

"I worked with Donald Michie," said Jim. "He's new to the Testery. He's been on the cryptanalysis course you went on. He's very young but exceptionally bright; quite measured though. Anyway, when we had finally bottomed it out, Ralph wanted to catch up on recent messages and a group of us offered to go flat out round the clock. I've only just recovered. They have called this new security modification the 'chi-two limitation' but it's not so much of a problem once the pattern of the second chi wheel is known. In effect, it varies the number of times the psi wheels stand still. Next thing is that I have to write it up. We'll have to stop there, I've got to go and see Ralph now."

Bill thanked him. He was still somewhat piqued that he had not been asked to look at the problem and made a mental note to study Jim's text. He wanted to make sure he was fully aware of every Tunny development.

Gerry looked out of his room and saw Bill finishing his discussion with Jim.

"Bill," he called from the doorway. "Can you pop in?"

Bill followed Gerry in, wondering what he wanted.

"Michael was just about to give me an update on Sturgeon. I thought you would like to hear it."

"As you know," said Michael, "traffic from North Africa stopped after El Alamein, except for an odd single message sent soon afterwards from the Caucasus which we successfully attacked because it was made up of several passages in depth, the content of which was information on the Russian front. For a number of weeks recently, however, a new link we've called 'Salmon' has appeared between German headquarters and Mariupol in eastern Ukraine. Messages on this link proved much more difficult to break. The reason we discovered was the Pentagon combining feature was absent, five wheels provided a letter of key and the other five provided the permutation key. Message content was nothing more than operator chat though. Then," he paused for emphasis, "from decodes, we learned the Germans realised the T52 was very badly compromised. They issued rather alarming instructions that all top-secret messages were to be encoded on Enigma before being transmitted on the T52 save when no other means was available. Among other instructions, one required the removal of the device which allowed the operator to set all the wheels back to their original positions. Presumably, they have been horrified at the volume of depths being sent. Incidentally, decodes have mentioned two types of T52, a/b and c. It would appear that recent transmissions have been on the T52c as they are talking about an adaption to that model. What that adaption will be, we don't know but for wheel setting without depths, we are probably faced with looking at much larger numbers of characters than Mr Newman's tape machines are intended."

"Thanks, Michael. We'll just have to monitor the situation to see what we are up against."

Michael got up to leave and Bill followed suit. But Gerry said, "Hold on a second, Bill, I have something for you. Two things in fact."

Bill hoped Gerry wanted him to be involved in Sturgeon but Gerry pulled over a file.

"Commander Denniston has sent this up from London asking if we can have a look at it. He says it is five-figure traffic between the French Military Mission in Washington and Gustave, Algiers. Gustave, he says is the signal code for General Giraud, the C-in-C of the French armies in North Africa."

Bill looked puzzled.

"I thought the French in North Africa were on our side now," he said. "Why are we spying on our allies?"

"I can't say for certain," said Gerry, "but I think there are still surreptitious plots and manoeuvres going on between the Allies, De Gaulle and Giraud. Anyway, the French Mission in Washington is there to negotiate supplies for the rearmament of their forces in North Africa and that's fraught with complications and shipping shortages. Problems all round! So, I guess Commander Denniston has been asked to keep an eye on what the French Mission is telling Giraud and vice versa. Have a look and see what you can make of it. At least it will be a change from Tunny for you."

"You said there were two things," said Bill.

"Oh yes," said Gerry picking up a memorandum. "This is a copy of a note from Max to Commander Travis. Have a read of it."

Bill read the memorandum at his usual steady pace. The first line was interesting. Max was indicating his machine could be used to set not just Tunny but Sturgeon as well. This was the first he had heard of Sturgeon being linked with the machine and he hoped it would give Sturgeon greater prominence. Testing of the machine was going well, wrote Max. Then there was mention of a chap at Dollis Hill called Flowers who knew of the work on the chi-setting machine and who had suggested an entirely different machine. This Mr Flowers reckoned the data on the tapes could be stored and processed electronically within the machine. Mechanical movement would thereby be avoided altogether and speeds up to 10,000 letters a second could be possible. It would need a very large number of valves, 5,000 or so, and 2,500 relays but this Mr Flowers reckoned it could be done. Citing some justifications, Max was recommending this line be followed up at once alongside the current work.

"What do you think?" said Gerry.

"I like the idea of Sturgeon being set on the machine," said Bill.

"I think," said Gerry, "that is just an idea at this stage rather than a specific plan. What I really want to get are your thoughts on this suggestion of Mr Flowers. I can just about get my head around the currently proposed machine, although the science of the counting and combining units is beyond me. But how can you store the dots and crosses of a tape stream in an electrical machine that then does all the high-speed stepping and counting? We thought the supposed capability of 2,000 characters a second of the present design was almost unbelievable. This is five times faster! And all done by valves and relays without anything moving? Max seems convinced it should be pursued, and it would be without question a major step if it could be done. And that must be a big if. Max calls it a much more ambitious scheme but I just can't see it as possible; to me it seems, well, science fiction. We really can't afford the time and resources on something that fanciful. We don't even know if this first machine will work yet. You took the Sciences, Bill. What do you think?"

"I was a research student in Chemistry," said Bill. "I know a little about electrical networks but I've not heard of storing and manipulating data electronically within a machine. Valves are usually used as amplifiers but I believe they can be used as very high-energy electrical switches yet how you would use them for this purpose, I don't know. And how you would configure such a vast number of valves I can't imagine. One thing I would say is that I was impressed with Frank Morrell when I dealt with him, so I imagine any suggestion coming out of Dollis Hill must have some merit."

"Mmm," mused Gerry. "I gather this chap, Tommy Flowers, has done work for Alan Turing and Alan speaks highly of him. We'll have to wait and see if this goes anywhere."

A few days later, Bill received a surprise message, coincidentally asking him to meet a Mr Flowers in the Main Building. Curious, Bill went along.

"I'm Tommy Flowers," said the tall, sandy-haired man in a dark suit. He had a high forehead, heavy round glasses and eyes that spoke intelligence. Despite an engaging smile, he appeared somewhat reserved.

"You must be Bill Tutte. Thank you for coming along. Max Newman and Frank Morrell said I should speak with you about my proposal for a machine to replace the

Tunny setting machine currently being built. I gather the current machine follows your logical sequence of steps or rules and that you helped Frank at the initial stages. Let me explain. In my opinion, the current machine has some inherent weaknesses, not in its ability to process your set of rules but in the practical running of two tapes. My idea is to do away with the running tapes and replicate the data on them using valves, possibly 5,000 would be needed. Speeds of 5,000 to 10,000 per second would be possible"

"I have seen a report by Max outlining your idea," said Bill.

"Oh, good," said Tommy Flowers. "Before putting forward a formal proposal, I just wanted your opinion. Frank said you had a good understanding of the current design. Can you see any reason my idea will not work?"

"I am not familiar with valves so I can't really say," Bill answered cautiously.

Tommy Flowers gave a brief review of the technical set up he envisaged. From his limited knowledge, Bill could not see any fault with it and said so.

"Will it run your sequences, do you think?"

Bill quite took to Mr Flowers. They were both of similar dispositions and Mr Flowers spoke in terms that Bill could follow.

"It sounds extremely ambitious," said Bill. "I've not heard of storing and manipulating data electronically within a machine. Has anything like it been built before?"

"No," responded Tommy Flowers categorically, "and I would know. Without being big-headed, I don't think there is anyone, anywhere who has the practical experience of valves that I have. I am convinced this will work."

"I don't have your technical knowledge of valves but if a large bank of valves can be set up to replicate the operations of the current machine then I see no reason for it not to work. Having said that though, it is a conceptual leap in the dark and I have to wish you luck in trying to convince the powers that be to give you a green light."

Tommy Flowers stood up.

"Thank you, Bill. I rather suspected you would not be one to put the dampers on my idea. It will work. All I need to do is convince the sceptics. I'm sure we'll meet again."

On the way back, Bill thought Mr Flowers very impressive and very likeable. As to his unprecedented idea, it will be interesting to see if it ever flies.

"What progress on Gustave?" asked Gerry the following week as he passed Bill's table.

"It's taken me back to my course days," said Bill. "But I've identified a few depths and whilst transmission is in five figures, I am working on the theory that it is a four-figure code from a code book reciphered with an additive key which I'm stripping out. At the moment, I have yet to reveal the whole reciphering process though. That will take a bit longer."

"Let me know when you have something more," said Gerry as he moved on.

The work on Gustave took another week before Bill felt he had taken it far enough. He knocked on Gerry's open door to get his attention.

"Do you have a moment? I've come to a point on Gustave when we can perhaps send him back," said Bill.

"What have you got?"

"I have solved it in principle. With the reciphering stripped out, we have a diagonal and columnar transposition of a four-figure book. I haven't identified which book but no doubt, the Diplomatic Section will be able to from their library. I have solved one day only as I imagine this will be enough for Commander Denniston's team to take it from here. I've written it up."

"Thanks, Bill. Let me have the report and I'll send it on. But there is something you need to know. There's another urgent Tunny problem come up in the last few days on the Herring link," he said, sounding unusually downbeat. "I find it curious the Germans seem quite restless with machines that have been running for some time. This problem though looks rather serious and could be more serious than the one Jim and Donald Michie have just solved. Before you start anything else, I want you to look at it. You've seen their 'chi-two' solution, I take it?"

"I'm aware of their solution but I haven't read the write-up yet," said Bill.

"You need to read that first. It may be useful," he instructed. "Come and see me tomorrow and we'll discuss what to do. Before you do that, there is some news on Max's machines. The machine to run two tapes should be ready in two months which is good news for once. Messrs Flowers and Morrell, though, have put forward an amended proposal for the more ambitious machine by which the message is still run on tape and the valves used only for the wheel patterns. This new proposal was put to the powers that be here and was received with considerable scepticism, I gather; the main concerns being the generally held view that valves were unreliable and that the machine would take so long to develop that the war would be over before it could be built. Success, it was thought, could not be guaranteed for a machine for which there was no precedent. It was left to Dollis Hill to develop it on their own if they wanted to. In the end, I think common sense has prevailed."

"So," said Bill to himself, "Tommy didn't get his green light. A case of the exigencies of war stifling innovation."

Chapter 9
Robinson

"A word," said Gerry.

Bill sat down slowly, apprehensive at Gerry's sombre tone.

"I really thought we'd got on top of Tunny, what with the latest hurdle overcome and the tests on Max's machines going well. Yet for some reason, the Germans seem uncertain of themselves. Whether they have concerns about aspects of Tunny's security, I don't know but they keep tinkering with it. This time, I really am concerned. There was mention on the Rome/Tunis link, Herring, towards the end of last month that an 'attachment 42.42' would be brought into use. The following day, an apparent depth was not readable. Attempts to read several other depths have similarly failed even taking into account the chi-two limitation. It would appear that whatever new attachment they have introduced, it has locked us out yet again."

Gerry looked grim. Bill was aware he had other problems on his plate, especially Japanese military and diplomatic traffic, and sensed this latest setback with Tunny had got to him particularly with the advent of Max's new machine and the responsibility for success that brought.

"I want you to get onto this quickly, Bill. Jim can help you. Fortunately, this change happened after we had broken some March messages so you can expect these unread depths to have the same wheels patterns. One of these unbreakable depths was 6,000 letters long which may prove susceptible to your 1+2 chi setting method. That may be a place to start."

Gerry looked directly at Bill.

"There's a lot riding on this, Bill; more than usual. It's not just the intelligence but Max's new machines are due on stream soon. Keep me closely in touch, please."

Bill nodded his understanding of the task and the gravity Gerry attached to it. Could this possibly put Max's machines in jeopardy? But he was far less anxious about the situation than Gerry; rather the opposite. He was relieved to be back on home ground, resuming his contest with Tunny. Bill recognised the urgency, yet Gerry, knowing he worked at his own moderate pace, had handed him the task, a demonstration of Gerry's trust in him.

Bill took the file of papers.

"I'll see what I can do with it," was all he said.

"Oh no!" exclaimed Jim when Bill explained what was needed. "Not more days and weeks of delta-ing."

"Until Max gets his machine, I'm afraid so," said Bill. "Last time, we were out to prove something. This time, we don't know quite what we're looking for so as well as being 100 per cent accurate, we need to be alert to anything unusual. At least the 6,000 letters of the first depth should give us plenty to work with. We'd better get started."

A week later, Bill gave Gerry a brief but encouraging progress report.

"The work is going satisfactorily. Four of the chi wheels have been set so far, Gerry. But it is too early yet to say what the new attachment does."

Once all the chi wheels had been set, Jim applied the usual Testery methods to produce a new stream. Oddly, this new stream contained a passage of very many repeated letters. Bill studied this unusual result and came up with a hypothesis that the underlying clear language might contain a long sequence of z's followed by a long sequence of 9's which proved to be correct. That allowed them to set the psi wheels and decode the message. Unfortunately, the translated message was unimportant and of no help to them in understanding why the depths were unreadable.

"What now?" asked Jim.

"The motor key next," said Bill.

He was already thinking beyond the motor key when Gerry asked how they were getting on.

"We'll have the motor key by tomorrow," Bill told Gerry, "but that alone may not give us any answers. We shall have to decode the second 6,000-letter depth. That should be straightforward on the assumption it was enciphered with the same initial settings. We'll have to see what that gives us."

"Slow progress," bemoaned Gerry somewhat frustrated. "If only we had Max's machines…let me know as soon as you have something."

Decoding the second message in itself gave no clues but soon after Jim began working out the motor key of the second message, he stopped and his heart began to beat faster. He went back to the beginning and checked his workings.

"Bill," he called. "Bill, look at this! The motor keys are different. They should be the same surely."

Bill looked over his shoulder and smiled. Whatever was causing this, it was the reason the depths could not be read.

"You're on to it," said Bill with a sense of excited anticipation. "Finish the stream first then we'll have a look."

He went to see Gerry and explained their findings that the two motor keys differed.

"The difference can only be explained," said Bill, "on the assumption that the motor key is a function of the clear language, or of the cipher, as well as the initial state of the machine."

"Ah," said Gerry, pleased at last and relieved that it would appear the problem would not be terminal. "In the language of cryptography, this is called an autoclave where some element of the plaintext is incorporated into the machine's key. If this is to become a regular feature though, we have real problems; depth reading will be impossible and the decoding process more difficult. But let's find out exactly what is going on. More to do yet, I'm afraid, Bill."

Considerable analysis of the two motor keys and the two plaintexts led Bill and Jim to discover that the fifth impulse of the plain language two places back came into play. Not only that but that impulse had been added to the chi-two limitation Jim and Donald had recently discovered. The stream of the resulting sum had been added to the motor key stream generated as usual by the two motor wheels. Fragments of the motor key without the limitations could be identified and from those fragments the settings of the motor wheels could be worked out and so the whole machine was broken.

"I see now why the depths were unreadable," Jim said. "What a dastardly, cunning attachment!"

Gerry called a meeting to discuss the situation. Ralph Tester and Donald Michie from the Testery came along. Bill outlined their findings.

Gerry was still downbeat. The chi-two limitation was internal to the machine, he explained, and was, therefore, predictable once the second chi wheel pattern was known. This autoclave was external to the machine and variable. It posed a much more difficult problem if used routinely.

"You know, chaps," said Ralph, ever the motivator, "what's been achieved here is a triumph of the hand methods of statistical analysis. This is the first time a Tunny machine has been totally revealed on an unknown motor key, so well done. Mind you, those long repeats of z's and 9's appear to have made it exceptionally easy! On a more serious note though, I imagine these attachments can be switched on and off. We have to hope that we still get some traffic without these limitations, enough to get the month's wheel patterns and enough to keep the show on the road. We'll just have to work a bit harder, that's all."

As the meeting broke up, Ralph Tester turned to Bill.

"Jerry Roberts has something for you, Bill. Pop in and see him."

"Ah, Bill," said Jerry. "If you have a few minutes, I have something to show you that might interest you," he said mysteriously. From his expression, Bill sensed this was unlikely to be frivolous and followed Jerry across to the other side of the Testery room.

"Take a look at this," said Jerry pushing a handwritten script in front of Bill. It was lengthy and had lots of scribbles and crossings out leaving Bill a little confused as to what it was. He looked up at Jerry quizzically.

"This is my original translation of a Tunny message. I've just finished checking a typescript which has been sent over to Intelligence. I don't usually do translations. Once I've made a break-in, I move on to the next message, just pass on my break-in to the wheel setters. But this one looked interesting. You've seen many Tunny decrypts but possibly, I suspect, none as important as this one. I know you've not been overly interested in the content of messages but this one is rather different."

"Why is that?" asked Bill.

"It's from General Field Marshal von Weichs, Commander-in-Chief of Army Group South to the German High Command, and see, it's headed 'Comprehensive appreciation of the enemy for 'Zitadelle'. Citadel, we've learned, is the code name for a planned major German offensive against the Russian front at Kursk. Not only does it set out the German view of Russian defences in the area but it also indicates their plan of attack, a pincer movement against the salient. See how detailed it is. Look here at the list of various Russian units, their location and anticipated movements. And look here, he says, 'According to information from a sure source'—code for spies possibly—'the existence of the following groups of strategic reserves can be presumed', and he goes on to list them in detail. You can see he anticipates stubborn resistance to their attack by 90 enemy formations and talks of dug-in tanks."

"When is this attack going to be launched?" asked Bill.

"No date is given. Maybe the Germans are still bringing their forces to the area to await Hitler's order. At the end here, he summarises the situation giving his opinion that the Russians are setting up defensive positions rather than forming up for an attack. I like this bit. Von Weichs says even if they bring up reserves, they won't be able to forestall his attack. Usual cocky Germans! You can see just how significant a message it is."

"What happens to it now?"

"My guess is Churchill will have read it before he goes to bed tonight. I wouldn't be surprised if the contents weren't pretty quickly conveyed in a note to Stalin; without the source being revealed of course."

"Don't we trust the Russians with our sources? They're our allies."

"Not that far," said Jerry pointedly. "Not like we trust the Americans. But you can see, Bill, just how much strategic information and detail can be in a single Tunny message, unlike Enigma messages which are seldom more than a couple of hundred letters long."

"I see what you mean," said Bill getting up. "Looks as though something big is brewing."

"Exciting stuff," said Jerry. "Tunny is really very important, Bill. And it's all thanks to you. Even the Russians may be thanking you!"

"I'm not sure about that, Jerry. I can't understand Russian anyway!"

It was a busy time in the Research Section. A Portuguese link using the Hagelin machine was being attacked and continuing progress on Japanese naval codes was being made. Max Newman was heavily engaged in setting up a new section to handle the new machines, the first of which to arrive were special Tunny machines. At the same time, a group of Wrens arrived and initially, began training on the special Tunny machines, creating to very exacting standards the tapes for the new chi setting machine when it arrived. Alan Turing, back from Washington, was interested in these machine developments and had several meetings with Max and even went over to Dollis Hill.

In mid-May, Gerry called a Tunny review meeting. Bill reported he had been writing up the limitation results and looking at possible methods to improve existing Tunny processes. Max reported progress in setting up his section. The latest delivery date for his chi setting machine was the middle of next month. He reported that sufficient versatility had been incorporated into the design that it may be possible to set the other wheels too as had been suggested. Max mentioned again that he thought it would be possible to set Sturgeon messages on his machine, not just Tunny messages.

"Ah, now," said Gerry picking up a typed sheet of paper. "Some news on Sturgeon has just come in. A capture no less, in Tunisia! The technical report has just arrived and it is definitely a Sturgeon. But from the description, it is not the type we have seen as the wheels do not combine. It is labelled T52b. We're not aware of any traffic sent on that model. The danger is, of course, that should the capture become known by the Germans, they may well abandon Sturgeon altogether, unless, that is, they feel the adaptions they have made make them feel secure. When we'll get to see the actual machine, I don't know. How would I feel if it had been a Tunny machine that had been captured? Strange to say but I think at this stage, I'd rather a Tunny wasn't captured."

Bill did not say anything but the developments renewed his interest in becoming involved with Sturgeon if possible.

"Bill," Max started, "are you a theoretical statistician? I'm looking for one on my team."

"No," Bill replied. "I know some statistics but probably not to the level you want. But I know someone who would fit the bill. Jack Good, he's with Alan Turing."

"Ah, yes; his name has already come up as a suitable candidate," said Max.

With that, the meeting broke up but Bill held back.

"What is it, Bill?" asked Gerry.

"Can I change my holiday dates in August, please?" said Bill sheepishly.

"What, again!" exclaimed Gerry clearly irritated.

"My friend, Cedric, can't now get the dates we arranged, I'm sorry."

"Leave me a note and I'll get back to you tomorrow," said Gerry, an unusually sharp tone in his voice.

Bill quickly scribbled the dates on a scrap of paper and scuttled out of the room.

The following evening, he wrote to Cedric stating the week commencing Sunday, 29th August was now fixed and immovable.

At the next Chess Club, Bill went over to Jack Good to tell him his name was in the frame for joining Max Newman.

"It's all arranged, Bill. I'm moving over shortly. Max wants me to look at ways of improving machine processes using pure statistics. It will be interesting to find out what you've been up to! Donald Michie is also moving over from the Testery. It all sounds jolly interesting. We should be seeing a lot more of one another."

At the end of the first week in June, Bill was introduced to a visitor by Gerry Morgan.

"Bill, this is William Friedman, Chief Cryptanalyst of the US War Department in Washington. He's over here having a look around."

For a moment, Bill was dumbstruck. Was this really the world-renowned cryptanalyst mentioned on his course? He certainly fitted the bill, a tall, distinguished-looking man with a high forehead, piercing eyes, a small moustache and dickie bow tie.

"Good to meet you, Bill. John Tiltman has told me a great deal about you and from what I understand of your efforts on Tunny, you must be a very bright young man indeed. I hear you have a machine arriving any time now that can process your Tunny solutions. Shame I won't be around to see it as I have to return to the States before it is due to arrive. It sounds a very interesting development."

"Mr Friedman," Gerry said, "has dropped by to find out a bit more on Sturgeon following the recent capture. As Michael Crum is not around, perhaps you could brief Mr Friedman on what we know."

"I'll try," stuttered Bill, still somewhat overawed at finding himself in the presence of such an eminent personage.

Bill rattled off a résumé of Michael's findings which Mr Friedman followed intently.

"Interesting," he reflected, "the introduction of these T52 machines by our German friends seems to have been uncharacteristically problematic, if not chaotic. This may be a symptom of their cryptographic architecture, or lack of it. I get a strong sense each of their service arms commission and develop their own bespoke cipher systems. They don't appear to have a central overarching control and pool of expertise. Typical of German armed forces to act in isolated towers when mutual cooperation could save them a lot of trouble."

The phone rang.

"Your colleagues are here," announced Gerry.

"Oh, they've arrived at last. Thank you, Gerry. Well, it's been nice to meet you, Bill. Keep up the good work. Thank you again, Gerry, for showing me your Research Section. Very impressive. You know, we visitors from the States are absolutely amazed by what you have here at Bletchley, beyond all our imaginings. Forgive me now but I must go."

He stood up, shook hands and strode off.

Bill and Gerry exchanged a look of amazement.

"Yes, the William Friedman," said Gerry slowly with the emphasis on the word 'the'. "I was told he could see whatever he wanted when I was asked a week or so ago to give him a briefing on what our Section does. It's all evidence, I guess, of the increasing intelligence cooperation with our American allies. I'm glad you could meet him."

It was a week or so later that Gerry Morgan came out of his room and rapped on the nearest table to catch everyone's attention.

"For those who are interested, there is a test about to begin in Hut 11 of Max Newman's new chi setting machine."

There was an immediate scraping of chair legs on the floor as people quickly stopped what they were doing and got up to make their way to see this keenly anticipated machine. From the usual quiet, intense atmosphere, an excited chatter filled the room as everyone headed for the door. No one was going to miss this, least of all Bill.

But as they entered Hut 11, the chatter abruptly stopped. Everyone gazed in awe at this machine that virtually filled half the room from floor to ceiling. It was enormous, nothing like anyone had ever seen before. At one side was a tall stack of assorted electrical components with wires, plug boards, switches, valves, rows of small lamps and a display unit. At right angles to this bank of electronics was a structure of angle iron rather like industrial racking only without the shelves. Within this structure was a curious array of wheels and pulleys with teleprinter tape threaded this way and that. Without knowing its purpose, no one could possibly guess what it did or what it was for.

Bill looked around. All the Testery people were there. John Tiltman was already talking to Max Newman. To one side stood Jack Good and Donald Michie looking anxious. There was a pair of senior looking people in earnest conversation who Bill thought might be Mr Freeborn and Mr Heil, the Senior General Post Office representative. There were two men checking over the machine and a young lady in uniform standing by with a clipboard. Max Newman, rather nervously, addressed the group now squeezed into the other half of the room.

"We have here the prototype counting and stepping machine specially designed to discover Tunny chi wheel settings. Let me introduce Harry Fensom from Dollis Hill and Alan Bruce from TRE who have helped design and build it. Without going into too much detail, I'll explain what we hope will happen. You can see these two teleprinter tapes. This one is a specially prepared loop of the message ciphertext we are testing. The other tape loop represents the known chi wheel patterns. The two tapes are run against each other with photo-electric cells reading the holes in the tapes, sending electrical impulses to this combining unit here which mimics Bill Tutte's '1+2 Break-In' processes. The signals from the combining unit are transmitted to TRE's high speed counter up there. This display unit here gives us the counts, but we only want counts of significance and we can tell the machine to display only counts over a certain parameter by using these switches here. We're going to run a test on two wheels of the Tunny machine, the chi one wheel which has 41 positions and the chi two wheel which has 31 positions, stepping through all 1,271 combinations against our message ciphertext tape of 4,000 characters. The machine can run at 2,000 characters per second and the whole run should take approximately one hour."

Max looked across at the two engineers. "Is that about right?"

They both nodded.

"I should add that the message is one we broke by hand earlier so we know what results the machine should produce. You may wish to come back in about an hour's time when we should have all our results. All right, Harry, start her up."

Harry Fensom disappeared round the back of the machine and threw a switch. The pulley system started to whirr. But just moments later, smoke appeared to be coming from one of the electrical units. Harry rushed round the back again. The assembled audience did not know whether to dash for the exit or laugh.

"It's all right," said Harry reappearing somewhat red-faced, "it's just a resistor overheating. I've fixed it."

The machine built up to running speed and an array of panel lights began to wink in a seemingly haphazard fashion. No one left. Everyone was simply entranced by this contraption which seemed to be thinking. After a short while, Alan Bruce called out pointing to the display.

"First count showing!"

The young lady in uniform leant forward and wrote down the display on her pad.

"What have we got?" asked Alan raising his voice above the noise of the machine.

"The count is 2,077 for chi one at position one and chi two at position three."

Max addressed the audience. "We set our parameter for this test at 2,070. This count is only just above so I don't expect it will turn out to be the setting we are looking for. A purely random count would be close to 2,000."

The whole group was transfixed, waiting for the next count to be called out by the young lady in uniform.

"2,127 for chi one at position seven and chi two at position 20," came the next call. Further counts came at intervals.

"2,088 for chi one at position 33 and chi two at position 15."

"2,239 for chi one at position 29 and chi two at position 12."

"Now that one, 2,239, is significant!" Max emphasised.

Several other counts above the parameter were displayed before the run came to a halt but none was closer to 2,239 than 2,127. Harry and Alan had beaming faces. Max, looking equally pleased, turned to the expectant gathering.

"It works! It works! The correct setting for that message was, indeed, chi one at position 29 and chi two at position 12. Congratulations, Harry and Alan, and also to your teams. One hour for what would have taken days by hand. Gentlemen and lady, I believe we have entered a new age in cryptanalysis."

Spontaneous applause broke out. Those around Bill turned and shook his hand. He had every confidence that his theory was sound but nevertheless, seeing it verified by such an amazing machine was very satisfying. He was, though, typically rather less satisfied with the vigorous handshakes.

Most of the gathering stayed on for a while chatting excitedly, asking questions and peering closely at this weird contraption. Bill, on the other hand, sidled off as soon as he could.

The atmosphere in the canteen was positively animated following the news of the Sicily landings. Bill could overhear those on the next table commenting enthusiastically about the first major assault by the Allies on the soft underbelly of Europe, how it was a first step on a steep road to Berlin; even, that it augured well for success with similar operations across the much narrower waters of the English Channel. Those in the military discussed the huge logistics of the air and sea attack and warned of the difficulties faced by any invasion force. It was only 24 hours into the assault, cautioned one voice, and success was not yet secured. Nevertheless, the news had lifted spirits. For once, Bill dared to think of the end of this war and of returning to Cambridge. But the thought was only fleeting.

"Seen the papers today, Bill?" asked Jerry a few days later as he caught up with Bill as they both headed for the canteen.

"About Sicily? What's the latest?" said Bill.

"No, no, not Sicily. More good news. They're saying the German enterprise at Kursk has failed, the first of any summer German offensive anywhere in Europe to fail. I wonder how the Russians were able to hold off the German attack, Bill. Perhaps a little bird told them lots about German intentions? A little British bird, perhaps. Maybe they had time to reinforce their defences? Without doubt, it's a significant setback for Germany, particularly after their defeat at Stalingrad. Mr Von Weichs is not so cocky now!"

"I wonder who could have told them," Bill said and smiled, joining in Jerry's banter for once.

Chapter 10
The Rounders Young Lady

The holiday with Cedric did not quite work out; not that Bill was surprised as it seemed doomed from the start. Cedric kept changing the dates until Bill told him the end of August could not be altered; in truth, he was afraid to approach Gerry Morgan for yet another alteration. More than that though, none of Cedric's proposals for the holiday came to fruition.

His first idea was to explore the River Thames around Eton and Windsor and he had asked Bill's mother to see if her relations in Burnham, where Bill's family originated from, could get any rooms. When that did not come off, he wrote to a number of guest houses but felt their charge of three pounds ten shillings a week or more too much. He asked his father and a friend to make enquiries for rooms in London but nothing came from that. Two weeks before the holiday was due to start, Cedric wrote suggesting cycling west of London staying at Youth Hostels.

But Bill knew the whole idea was fated when he read the next part of Cedric's letter. He wrote that his cycle was giving an awful lot of trouble nowadays—both pedals had fallen off, the bell didn't work and there was a spoke missing from the back wheel. That was not all. He went on to complain that he had two inner tubes for the front wheel, one of which goes down for no discoverable reason at all, while the other goes down because it has a hole in the metal part of the valve. Further, he wrote the pump makes no impression on the tyre—in short, the bike wasn't dependable and he wouldn't go on tour with it. Not to be discouraged though, he cheerily suggested it might be all right for something like short trips out of London, where a failure wouldn't be a disaster.

Oh, dear, thought Bill, *Cedric and bicycles just do not get along.* In the end, the holiday was a day with Cedric in Cambridge, a day trip by train to London and the rest of the week at home.

Afterwards, he felt the holiday turned out surprisingly well, mainly because the days he spent at home had somewhat assuaged his guilt at not going home more frequently. His mother wrote regularly. Often, she would ask when he could next get home; and often her letters revealed her concern for his father's health, recently mentioning he had reduced his hours with Mr Taylor.

Whilst his father tried to make light of his ailments, it was clear to Bill he was not able to work the long hours he used to do at this time of the year, when habitually after supper, he would tend his garden and vegetable patch till dusk. Now his father appeared reconciled to spending the evenings just pottering around or sitting outside, glad, for once, to have someone's ear other than his wife's. In the daytime, Bill took Joey and Jeanne for long walks, much to the grateful thanks of their mother, Lola, for getting them out from under her feet during the school holidays. The ambient mood of those hours sitting with his father in the warm evening air, in the tranquillity of the garden, engendered a shift in the balance of their relationship and in a way, forged a greater closeness that had not been there before. Normally, Bill lacked perception of such things but the change was sufficient even for him to sense it. Neither had it gone unnoticed by his mother who busied herself contentedly darning socks or patching clothes leaving her menfolk to talk about what menfolk talked about.

Bill was always conscious that he was, by far, the youngest in the family. He once worked out from a grant application form his father had filled in that his father was 43 when he was born. And no one explained how it came about that his only sibling, Brother Joe, was 16 years older than him. By nature, his father was quiet, undemonstrative, and the difference in their ages coupled with the academic world Bill inhabited, of which his father comprehended little, meant they were never that close. Paternal support was always steadfast nevertheless; there was no tension. In turn, Bill was always respectful but a divergence between them had grown, particularly over the years since he went to Trinity College. This short break, however, favourably reversed the dial, which perhaps had already begun to happen once Bill was no longer a student but held a salaried position with the Foreign Office. But for the first time, Bill realised his father was getting on in years; no longer the stout and hardy figure he had always known. He now seemed vulnerable with his white hair and moustache and eyes that had lost their keenness. This vulnerability appeared to put them on a more even footing. Also, since Bill could not discuss what he was doing, the academic gulf between them lessened in significance. As a consequence, in those few days, the dial turned appreciably. They were more at ease with each other.

For that reason alone, Bill felt the holiday worthwhile.

Not long after returning from leave, Bill was strolling by the Main Building with Rolf Noskwith. They had lunched together for a rare catch-up. The day was warm and balmy and it had brought out the rounders brigade who were engaged in a fierce battle on the front lawn.

"Good hit!" rang out and the small, hard, leather-cased ball landed near Bill who managed to stop it with his foot. A young lady who was sitting with a lively group on the grass nearby had tried to catch it, missed and came over to retrieve it. She smiled as he handed it to her. Slightly embarrassed, Bill could not help but smile back.

"Thank you," she said politely with a cheeky little smile, turned and threw the ball underhand to the nearest player, quickly re-joining her friends who were caught up in the high spirits of the match.

Rolf was interested in the latest mathematical banter between Bill and Cedric and they sat awhile on a bench chewing over Cedric's latest proposition. They were about to return to their work when the group of young ladies who had been sitting on the lawn came by, no doubt also returning to their Huts. Bill happened to look up just as the young lady with the rounders ball passed. It was one of those moments when it was impossible not to acknowledge each other.

"Hello again," she said somewhat self-consciously but without stopping.

Bill was flustered. "Hello," he mumbled but she was almost out of earshot by the time the word came out.

"You know her?" asked Rolf.

"Oh no," said Bill. "No."

"She is around I think, a room in Hut 6, on Enigma," said Rolf. "A quieter one," he said without further explanation. "Quite keen on you, Bill, my eyes tell me," he added teasingly.

"Huh!" was Bill's response. But the encounter did leave him feeling a little disconcerted. He hoped it did not show.

As he walked back after Rolf had left, he was reminded of the girl at Churchill's speech. He still had a clear picture of her face. Today's young lady was definitely not the same young lady as the disappearing Churchill young lady, though by comparison, he mused, today's young lady was perhaps even prettier.

But by the time he sat down at his table and resumed his analysis, the switch in his mind had been thrown and he was completely immersed in his work.

At the Chess Club, Bill managed a few words with Jack Good. He was interested to know how he was getting on with Max Newman and his new machine.

"Progress is slow," said Jack. "There have been quite a few teething problems as you might expect but some successes too. The girls call the machine, 'Heath Robinson', after the cartoonist with his wonderful contraptions. Max is a bit frustrated because he is anxious to show results. Donald and I keep suggesting some experiments but he says we must concentrate on getting messages out." Jack looked around to see if anyone could overhear them.

"Don't let on," he continued in a lowered voice, "but Donald and I come back in the evenings when Max has left and conduct some experiments. The machine is actually very flexible and we can set up test runs which give us some valuable statistical data. There is a lot we could do but we have to tread carefully. Max is good though. He does occasionally allow us some experimental runs but by then we are pretty certain the results will be positive and lead to improvements in our routines."

Earlier in the evening, Bill had been matched with Leslie Yoxall. He had seen Leslie around but they had not really spoken since they first met. They chatted generally without, as usual, asking what work each other was engaged in. In the match, Bill was white, opened with his Evans Gambit and won. He went home quietly pleased.

"How are you getting on with the latest Halibut and Conger traffic?" asked Bill as he passed the table where Michael Crum had sheaves of paper spread out.

"I have to admit, I'm a bit stuck," said Michael. "Maybe you could cast an eye. I have been racking my brains why my method is not working."

"An adaption was expected, wasn't it? Have you found out what has changed?"

"I am coming to the conclusion that the wheel patterns have been changed but I have not proved it yet."

"What are you looking at?" asked Bill.

"I have been working on a July depth of five. There is a depth of four in August but I haven't tried that."

"Maybe trying that and comparing results may give a clue," suggested Bill. Seeing an opportunity to learn more about Sturgeon, he continued, "I'll give you a hand if you like. I could do with a bit of a break from what I'm doing."

They worked on the August depth. Michael began by outlining his method of attack. At one point, Bill stopped him and pointed to a formula Michael had written down, $Z = \pi(P+ \Sigma)$. Michael explained the formula represented the machine's basic operation, where Z and P represented the cipher text and plain text streams, respectively and the Greek letters pi and sigma represented the key streams of the permutation and the addition effects, respectively. The five impulses of the plaintext letter, P, were added to impulses from five selected wheels, each wheel set to a start point of its fixed pattern, giving the first part of the key. The impulses of that first part of the key, P plus sigma, were then subjected to a variable permutation, pi, created from the other five wheels, again from set start points of their fixed patterns. Bill admired the formula's simplicity. Michael went on to explain further that his attack relied on a probable crib and a feature he had developed to exploit the permutation element of the key. Because, Michael pointed out, the permutation element simply reordered the five resulting impulses of the first key, P plus sigma, the number of dots and crosses in the resulting ciphertext, Z, must be equal to those in the first key.

The method was long and tedious. For each letter of the second message opposite a crib letter of the first message, a group of up to ten possible letters was produced. With a string of five or six groups of letters, it was possible to tease out a German word, or part word, so long as the crib was good and in the right place.

After much work over a couple of days, to their surprise, they managed to decipher a short passage from each message which Michael recognised as operator chat. He then showed Bill how he worked out the wheel order and wheel settings all of which confirmed the wheel patterns were unchanged. But the exercise also confirmed this August message was enciphered on the same non-Pentagon version encountered earlier in the year on the Salmon link. That left the possibility the July depth was enciphered on a new version of the T52 machine.

Always polite, Michael thanked Bill for his help but said he would tackle some of the Conger messages next which, if enciphered on the non-Pentagon machine, should not be difficult in view of the profusion of depths available. He would leave the recalcitrant July message for the time being.

Bill found Sturgeon very interesting. As he returned to his own work, his mind was turning on the possibilities of a statistical approach particularly to the permutation element which he felt had scope for a deeper mathematical approach. One thing appeared certain though, that Max's machine would be required to handle the very large number of permutations and comparisons. But that would not stop him musing on the logical sequences needed.

"Ah, Gerry, have you a moment?" It was John Tiltman, newly promoted to Brigadier, who had poked his head round the door.

"My congratulations, John, on your promotion."

"It is congratulations all round. I hear your promotion to Major has come through too. Thoroughly deserved, I might add. Before I ask a favour, Gerry, what's the latest here?"

"Well, on Sturgeon, as you know, we managed to get out in part that August Halibut depth of four after much effort. In the end, it turned out to be encoded on a non-Pentagon machine. Bill Tutte helped Michael with that. The similar September and November Conger traffic between Athens and Berlin was extraordinary with hundreds of messages sent in depth and accordingly read. The traffic stopped at the end of November. The depth of four was only operator chat as has been all the Conger traffic and of no intelligence value. You may be aware Bill is keen to take over the work on the Sturgeon machine. He's said a few times that he thinks he can get a working hypothesis for breaking it for Max to take on to his Robinson. The July Halibut depth of five, we could not shift much to Bill's consternation. He asked me to let him have a go at it but I told him to leave it for the time being. Bill grumbles at the missed opportunity but really I think he fancies the logical, cryptanalytical challenge.

"Anyway, he has been helping on the Portuguese Hagelin stuff from Berkley Street. The changed London to Lisbon military attaché codes took longer than we thought but was broken using statistical methods and they have been sent back to Berkley Street for decoding. Actually, we discovered the Portuguese are pretty hopeless with their cipher security. I don't think they understand what they should be doing. You'll remember the Italians eventually introduced a book system for their indicators leaving sufficient gaps in the 101 million or so combinations to ensure no overlaps. Well, the Portuguese are regularly overlapping messages, seemingly ignorant of the implications. Bill has undertaken a brief investigation into the parity properties of these overlapping keys with some interesting results. We know, for instance, changing one letter on one wheel leaves approximately half the key stream unchanged. The other half is changed by plus or minus the kick on that wheel. I'll let you have his report."

"All good stuff keeping Berkley Street quiet!" said the Brigadier. "You're quite right, by the way, to lever Bill away from Sturgeon. Michael is quite capable and we can't afford two people on it." He paused. "The actual reason I came to see you is to seek your support. We're having a country dance evening next week to cheer everyone up before Christmas. I know it's not your scene, but it would be good if you could encourage your people to come along and put in an appearance yourself."

"All right," said Gerry with fake weariness, "I'll show up. But just for a couple of drinks, mind; I'm not into this charging around the floor you do!"

"Good man, Gerry. See you there."

With that, the Brigadier departed with a broad grin on his face.

The canteen was full and abuzz with noisy conversation as usual. A group of young ladies from Hut 6 were still talking animatedly as they got up from the table to return to their duties. One of them, Grace, held back her friend, Connie, pulled her close and spoke into her ear.

"Connie, over there, the one sitting on his own, that's the chap I told you about; the one at the rounders game, remember? I saw him again the other day when I was waiting in the queue for transport. He's quite good looking, don't you think?"

"Grace! You're always chasing dreams. Why don't you go over and say hello? Ask him to walk you out."

"You know I couldn't do that! Besides, I don't know anything about him. I wonder who he is though."

She gave Bill a last glance as they left.

That night, Grace recorded in her diary the sighting of the good looking young man, careful as always in what she wrote not to disclose any official secrets. She noted her impressions: quite handsome looking and tallish but not lanky tall. She speculated on his character: thoughtful perhaps, quiet, gentle, intelligent with a faraway look in his eyes. But what was he really like, she wrote? What was his name? What did he do? He obviously knew Mr Noskwith, one of the senior people at work. Was he clever too like Mr Noskwith? Questions, questions but no answers. Connie was right, she wrote—I am a dreamer.

Just as Bill was leaving for the evening, Jim Wyllie came up to him looking quite pleased with himself.

"I have a bit of news, Bill. I've been given a new task; part-time for now. Apparently, one function of the Research Section when it was set up was to standardise, as far as possible, the nomenclature of systems and methods of solution. A glossary of terms with definitions was supposed to have been prepared but nothing has been done until now. Do you know Professor Vincent? He is a rather distinguished Cambridge Professor of Italian and he works for Colonel, sorry Brigadier, Tiltman. Well, he has asked me, knowing I am a lexicographer, to start this cryptographic dictionary. It is a jolly good idea, don't you think, so I said I would be happy to take it on. Be like the old job. But I will need lots of help. So, you may find me asking for a definition of something, or ask you to review some definitions."

"I'd be happy to, Jim. Quite a task, that. I wish you luck."

"Now then, Bill, about the dance," said Jim changing the subject, "are you coming along on Saturday night? It should be good."

"It's not for me," said Bill. "I don't know any country dances, least of all any Scottish kind. I'm no good at dancing anyway."

"No matter," pressed Jim. "You don't need to know any of the dances. There's a caller and nobody minds if you get it wrong. It's fun. Join the Christmas spirit."

"Really…" Bill began but Jim played his trump card.

"John Tiltman has organised it. So, you could just come to support him, couldn't you? You don't have to join in any of the dances if you don't want to. Come on."

"Oh. If you insist," groaned Bill.

"Good man!"

Saturday evening came and it took all of Bill's courage to enter the Recreation Club. He had been boxed into agreeing to come not only by Jim Wyllie, but Gerry Morgan had also said he hoped to see him there. He deliberately arrived late, just in order to show his face, not intending to stay. He hung around at the back near the doors for a short while and actually, he thought, *This is not so bad after all.* The music was foot-tappingly tuneful, if loud, and everyone was enjoying themselves enormously, especially the dancers who rhythmically wove in and out in fantastic patterns. John Tiltman was in the thick of it, sporting tartan trousers. Even those not dancing were whooping and clapping in time to the music.

Then he noticed her, the rounders young lady. She too was in the thick of it, grinning broadly, swaying this way and that with great gusto. She seemed to know all the moves, swinging her partners wildly round and round before moving onto the next. He marvelled at her confidence and enthusiasm and strangely for him, he rather envied her being able to enjoy herself with such abandon. The dance came to an end and everyone clapped in breathless delight. There was an interlude and he watched her as she made her way to a table on the other side of the room where she slumped on a chair in mock exhaustion. The table was all-female, her friends from Hut 6, Bill imagined; she seemed to know them all very well. Bill kept in the shadows. Oddly, he was pleased she was there but had no intention of doing anything about it.

Later, Jim Wyllie spotted him and literally dragged him onto the floor to make up numbers for a set and before Bill knew it, he was being spun and dragged in all directions as the music played a Scottish reel. Suddenly, he was in the arms of the rounders young lady. She smiled in recognition and promptly took his hand above his head and vigorously spun him round and round before weaving on to the next man in line. Bill had no time to gather his thoughts. In and out, round and round went the dancers in a swirl of colour and music. And when, finally, the music stopped, he was opposite the young lady again. She clapped with exuberance. His clapping was hesitant and tepid. She grabbed his arm and steered him to a vacant table.

"I'm Grace by the way. We met at that rounders match, if you remember."

"I know. Hello. I'm Bill," he stuttered.

"You're not into country dancing, are you? Not everyone is. But its great fun, isn't it? We did a lot of country dancing at school and university, festivals and that sort of thing. I even danced before the King on Empire Day at Lochinch Castle."

Bill did not know what to say to that. He thought he should be polite and asked, "Would you like a drink?" Going to the bar would give him a moment's escape.

"A lemonade shandy, please. I'm quite thirsty after all that."

Bill got two small shandies from the bar. There was a brief embarrassing silence.

"You know Mr Noskwith?" she asked attempting to open up a conversation. "He's one of our senior people. I don't know him as such but I see him from time to time."

"I don't know him well," said Bill. "We were at the same university."

"Someone said he was at the same university as Mr Turing. Do you know him too?"

"He interviewed me originally. I've had a few meetings with him since, but I can't say I know him."

"Finish your drink," she prompted looking over at the band. "The next dance is about to start."

With that she took his hand and dragged him onto the floor. The music started again and this time, there were arches to duck under and he had to grab the waist of the girl in front while someone grabbed his waist from behind. There were more twirls and weaving and Bill was almost out of breath by the time the dance ended. Grace came over to him.

"Phew! That was great, wasn't it? You did very well. But I have to go now. My bus is going in a minute. You can walk me to the bus if you like. Hold on while I get my coat."

Bill was not sure what to do. Her request took him totally by surprise, such that he froze to the spot. He could see her hastily talking to her friends and then she disappeared to get her coat. Moments later, she reappeared and they walked briskly the short distance from the Club building to the waiting area for the busses.

"I've had a lovely time. And I enjoyed our brief chat," said Grace. "Thank you for seeing me to the bus."

A voice called out. "If you want this bus, love, you'd better hurry!"

"I must go. Good night, Bill."

He offered a stilted, "Good night." It was all he could say. He could not even manage her name.

Grace skipped the few steps to the bus and hopped on as it began to move off. Moments later, the bus was gone and there was silence.

Bill stood in the cold night air, bewildered, perplexed and flustered. He was brought out of his daze by voices as more people spilled out from the dance. During the walk back to Mrs Batchelor's house and in his room, his emotions were running wild. Nothing quite like the last hour or so had happened to him before. He had been taken right out of his normally controlled world into a whirlwind of music, dance and a young lady called Grace. He supposed he was flattered by her attention. But then he realised she must have thought him hopeless. She was a wonderfully vivacious, confident dancer; he regretted his social ignorance and ineptitude. He vowed never to go to such an occasion again; not to make such a fool of himself ever again. Unhappy, he pulled the bed covers over his head. But his heart was still thumping and his mind still turning.

Bill would, as best he could, steer a course to avoid situations he found difficult. People like his older brother said he was missing out but he did not see it like that. He was content to make his way in his own narrow tunnel, sheltered from life's intrusions and brickbats. Yet here was someone, Grace, whom he hardly knew and who had tempted him out of his safe harbour like a mythical Siren. How come she could have that effect on him? Who was she that he succumbed before he even realised? And yet…she could see how gauche he was, yet she did not reject him as others might have done. She drew him into conversation, propelled him on another whirlwind around the dance floor and even asked him to see her to her bus home. What did she see in him?

It then occurred to him the evening had ended abruptly, in a blank. Was he supposed to say something, to ask her to walk out? What was he supposed to do? He had no idea; the situation was alien to him. Did he want to see her again? He couldn't say. Normally, he would aim to forestall any such potential encounter so perhaps it was best that nothing had been said, best it was left there. Anyway, it was all too difficult, too fraught with complicated feelings to fathom. He wanted it all to go away, to be rid of all this emotional upset but it was hours before he eventually slipped into a fitful sleep.

He was not due to go in to the Park the following morning, being a Sunday, but he felt doing so might provide the distraction he needed after last night, erasing the evening's events from his memory, allowing a return to normality. He would do some work then go back for Mrs Batchelor's Sunday roast, spending the afternoon writing some letters and reading—normality blessedly resumed.

Christmas was a dull affair. Bill had written to his mother several weeks beforehand to say he would not be home, explaining he had no leave left and adding he would even have to work on Christmas Day which fell on a Saturday. He had bought a Christmas card and sent it with some postal orders and some ration coupons hoping his mother could buy a little something for everyone. A card from the family duly arrived for him that even little Joey had signed which he opened on Christmas morning and put up in his room, a small token of the spirit of Christmas. Included with the card was a letter from his mother. His father was not too good, she wrote: the cold weather did not suit him. To illustrate how cold it had been, she quoted the local newspaper proudly recording nearby Santon Downham the coldest place in England at only 17 °F the other week.

The ladies in the canteen had made a big effort to lay on something of a traditional meal and had put up some paperchains around the walls. Mrs Batchelor too cooked a splendid roast chicken dinner on Boxing Day with one of her special recipe cakes for later, the ingredients courtesy of a food parcel from a relative of hers in Canada. Bill told her how much he appreciated her cooking which, he said, truthfully reminded him of his mother's home cooking, commenting further his mother was a cook and housekeeper by profession. This pleased Mrs Bachelor no end as she prided herself in her cooking.

For Grace, the Christmas period was equally dull being away from home and on an evening shift, but she and her colleagues in the Hut had made the best of it as the workload was lighter than usual. It was just after one o'clock in the morning of New Year's Day when she got back to her room in her digs. Often, she found it difficult to wind down after a late shift; tonight she was even more awake than usual. There were no New Year celebrations as such but the shift had ended on a high note with heartfelt Happy New Year wishes all round. In reflective mood, she sat at the small table in her sparsely furnished room and opened her diary. She picked up her fountain pen, unscrewed the top and paused to gather her thoughts. Eventually, she started to write:

'There is very little to balance this New Year's Day of 1944. Despite the war and its universal sorrows, for me personally, the account is in credit. The last few months have been happy ones for me, mainly because I have a well-paid job amongst pleasant people which means that the little trivialities of life don't bother me so much as they used to do. And I don't have to bother whether it is a question of spending or not spending, working or not working.

'I think I'm learning to appreciate my friends, old and new, much more than I did but even so, I know the best thing in life hasn't reached me yet. I know it is something for which I can do little in the way of searching for, at least not just at the moment. Perhaps when I find it, it will turn out to be something rather different from what I now hope. I have not yet reached the stage of desiring much more than an earthly communion. I see one possible source from which to receive it but I am not one of those who can easily seize fate by both hands and twist it into something desired. And I've yet to find that all comes to he who sits and waits. I wish I were more audacious and could grasp the biggest things in life but where vision is lacking there the will fails. Reason is not one of my strong parts and my suburban upbringing prevents the magnificent embracing of wild if grandiloquent dreams. So, of me—perchance this New Year will unleash a courageous, more intrepid me. That should be my resolution.

'So, bless them all and me. Bless also the coming new year.'

With nothing more to say, she screwed the top back on her pen, closed the diary and felt ready for bed.

By then, Bill had been asleep for a couple of hours, no New Year's resolutions having been considered let alone written down.

"I have just come back from a Section heads meeting," announced Major Morgan having called everyone to gather round, "and I want to briefly tell you some of what was discussed. You will all be aware of the pressures we have seen in recent months and those pressures will continue, if not increase, in the first months of this year. Resources everywhere are stretched, particularly in the Testery where their decoding of Tunny has almost trebled in the second half of last year with the introduction of the Robinson machines, and recruitment and training has struggled to keep pace. Their workload is only likely to increase further when more efficient Robinsons arrive soon. Some of the work we are doing now may, therefore, have less priority, but for now, we will continue with the Croatian Quisling transposition traffic and other Balkan traffic until Colonel Jacob's unit is fully staffed. We'll continue with the Portuguese Azores traffic and with the study of one of the Italian Navy cryptographic systems sent to us following the Italian armistice. The Japanese diplomatic code book work will hopefully be passed to Berkley Street shortly. Now, I know all the talk recently is about when the Allied invasion of mainland Europe will be launched, especially after the early progress against Kesselring's forces in Italy. But as we know that progress has stalled due to bad weather and will be hard going. My message is that we'll continue as we are for now but leave will be restricted and we may well have to move to full six day working soon. Also, be prepared for our priorities to shift very rapidly as the war situation changes when some of us may need to be deployed to help out operational units."

A voice from the back raised a concern. "When do you think we will have to move to six day weeks and will we have to go on shifts if we move to other units?"

"Not for now," said Gerry. "But should we be deployed to help operational units then obviously we will have to fit in with their work patterns. Any other questions?"

"What does 'leave will be restricted' mean?" It was the same voice.

"On a case by case basis and only when workloads allow," answered Gerry firmly. "Any more questions? No. Right then thank you for now and let's return to our work."

There were some murmurings as people digested Gerry's announcement but they were brief and the usual muted atmosphere soon returned. Bill heard a few grumblings about possible shift work, but he was not averse to the idea of working at night. He had done a little in the early days when he had quite liked the hushed surroundings and lack of interruptions.

The Brigadier breezed by saying, "Bill, this should interest you."

Bill followed him into Gerry Morgan's room.

"Dollis Hill are installing a new machine in Block F for Max. It's not another Robinson, the latest of those is running very well; Dollis Hill have made some very useful improvements to the original. No, this is the machine Dollis Hill have developed on their own. The one that has only the message tape running and the wheel patterns stored using lots of valves and relays somehow. It's beyond my understanding. However, it has been tested at Dollis Hill, been dismantled and brought over here. They are putting it back together now. So, stand by for a trial run shortly. Should be interesting, especially in comparison to the Robinsons."

"Mr Flowers has built it already?" said Bill. "I thought it would take years."

"Apparently, they have been working on it day and night for ten months, knowing they didn't have years. Anyway, I thought both of you would like to come along when they switch it on. I'll let you know.

"Now to why I really came. Sturgeon appears to be on the go again," said the Brigadier. "Harold Kenworthy's people have been picking up teleprinter traffic between

Königsberg and Munich, probably 'Halibut', and between Athens and Berlin probably 'Conger'. They can't be sure it is a version of the T52 but they think it may well be. Is Michael Crum still on sick leave?"

Gerry nodded. "Still not sure when he'll be back."

"Perhaps Bill ought to have a look at this Sturgeon traffic then, Gerry, at least till Michael is back."

Bill's eyes lit up.

"One aspect to look at," said the Brigadier looking across to Bill as if giving him direct instructions, "is a test to apply to the ciphertext to indicate positively when traffic encountered is Sturgeon. Too often, we're not sure if it is Tunny or Sturgeon. Now, I'll let you have a copy of a brief report that has only just found its way to me on two machines captured in Naples which appear to be Sturgeon type machines. It may be helpful. I have asked for the machines to be sent here. Harold is sending the ciphertexts over to you now. Let me know as soon as you have anything useful."

With that the Brigadier turned and made for the door. Gerry raised his eyebrows at Bill as if to concede Bill had got his way on Sturgeon after all.

Suddenly, the Brigadier stopped, turned slightly and said over his shoulder, "By the way, the machine is called Colossus." He then raised his hand in a half wave and was gone.

"Well, you had better pass on that Portuguese stuff and pick up Sturgeon again," said Gerry. "Colossus, eh! Be interesting to see if it lives up to its name and reputation."

Bill thought Mr Flowers must be a genius to have built his machine in such a short time. He could hardly wait to see it. Meanwhile, back to Sturgeon. Since the Germans had tightened Sturgeon security, this version, if it was a new version, might be a harder nut to crack. And devising a test to differentiate between the two cipher systems should prove an interesting exercise.

He read the Naples report and was disappointed to find it was written by a British signals officer who quite clearly did not know what he had in front of him. There were, however, a couple of interesting nuggets of information. The officer noted the label on one machine had been altered from T52b to T52d. The other machine had a label T52c but it appeared some of the mechanism had been removed before capture. There was a physical description of the machines in which the officer noted that both of them had ten discs, each of which had many electrical contacts embedded in the circumference with no two discs having the same number of contacts. The number of contacts ranged from 47 to 73. The report ended with the officer simply recording the date and place of capture and commenting that he had not seen anything like the machines before and could not say what their function was. The report had a number of handwritten annotations on it indicating it had been passed around a number of military intelligence departments for some time before someone recognised its significance and sent it to Brigadier Tiltman.

The ciphertexts arrived later that day but before looking at these, Bill needed to bring himself up to date. It was clear from all the work done so far and from the captures that the basic machine remained the same.

From the file, he could see that Michael had recently been working on a general tool for reading depths, painstakingly developing a catalogue of 512 squares mapping all the possible alphabets resulting from any assumption of a plain/cipher pair of the 32 teleprinter characters. The squares prompted him to consider the relationship between the four elements of the formula Michael had devised. He felt the relationships could be represented by a cube of 32 cells by 32 cells by 32 cells where one of P, Z or sigma can be placed in a cell within the cube and the three elements become the coordinates of that cell. He assessed pi could not be placed in the cube as in most cases it was not uniquely determined by the other three. He decided to return later to this cube idea to see how, or if, it could be usefully employed. Still in the file was the untouched depth of five from July last year.

Next, he took an initial look at the new ciphertexts from Knockholt. Surprisingly, all the Halibut messages were very short, the opposite of the August batches, and the Conger messages often long. Did that have a meaning, he wondered. He would look at the indicators after the lunch break. He wrapped his coat round him on the way to the canteen to ward off the February chill. The heavy clouds warned of rain or sleet.

"We meet again."

Bill turned recognising the voice. It was Grace.

"May I join you?"

"Yes, of course," he said but there was a hesitancy in his voice.

"You can usually be sure of seeing someone you know in the canteen. It's where everybody meets; that is when they're not on unsocial shifts. I'm back on normal shift at the moment thank goodness. Late shifts play havoc with my sleep. Do you work shifts?"

"Fortunately, no," said Bill panicking and already looking for an escape.

"I'm sorry about rushing off like that after the dance. I didn't mean to but the last bus was about to leave. Can you forgive me? I was hoping we could meet up so I could explain. It must have seemed very rude of me. I didn't know how to get in touch with you. I nearly asked Mr Noskwith if he would give you a message but I didn't dare. I'm glad I saw you today."

"You don't need to apologise," mumbled Bill nervously. He looked at his watch, an old strapless wristwatch he kept in his jacket pocket. He found checking the time a useful ploy when escape was needed. "I should be getting back."

Since the dance, Grace had dreamed of walking out one day with Bill, just being together, talking and getting to know each other. If she was not quick, the chance may be gone. With her heart racing, she plucked up courage.

"I'm going over to Bedford on Saturday to do some shopping. Would you like to meet me afterwards? I don't suppose you want to follow me around the shops but we could walk along the Embankment by the river. It's lovely along there. It helps me forget this war. Say yes!"

Faced with such a decision, Bill would default to a 'No, thank you'. But the look on her face beguiled him again and he found himself saying, "Yes." Then he immediately regretted it. But it was too late as Grace immediately pressed home her advantage.

"We could meet by the Swan Hotel by the main bridge. It's only a few minutes from the station. Everyone knows it, just ask. Can you make two o'clock? No, say half past one; it still gets dark early. It will be lovely."

"The Swan Hotel, on Saturday, at half past one," said Bill quickly seeing the opportunity to end the encounter. "I really must go now."

"Saturday, then," said Grace smiling broadly. "Goodbye, Bill."

"Goodbye," he said, sliding away as swiftly as politeness allowed.

Outside, he stopped. He was cross with himself. He had vowed not to get involved. So why had he? He couldn't say; he'd been silly. He resolved not to go. He should go back inside straight away and tell her. But he stalled; he could not face it. He would just not turn up, or cancel it somehow. Maybe he could ask Rolf to give her a message. Why did he let this happen? He set off back, troubled that the matter was unresolved.

The afternoon seemed to drag. Unusually, his concentration was superficial; the lunchtime encounter with Grace still niggled. He made progress nevertheless. All the indicators were of the special radio Q-code number type, QEP now instead of QSN as earlier, pointing to those messages with the same QEP number being in depth. Bill carefully organised the messages into same number sets. Many sets had only two or three messages which were too few to be of interest but there were a few sets of four messages. Michael maintained that four messages in depth were the absolute minimum for breaking, ideally many more. Fortunately, two sets were of the longer Conger kind, the obvious place to start.

Later in his room after supper, the whole lunchtime affair came back to haunt him. Yet somehow, now, he felt less angry with himself. There was just something about her, that against all his instincts, he had found himself saying 'yes' to her rather than 'no'. Perhaps, he mused, she was more the Goddess Peitho than a Siren. The Goddess Peitho, he remembered reading, was the Greek Goddess of Persuasion, to whom, by her honeyed enchantments, nothing was denied. Recalling the dance evening before Christmas, he might also ascribe to Grace the Goddess Terpsichore, the Goddess of dance. Maybe she was some of all three.

He started telling himself that maybe she wanted to be just friends, platonic friends. It did not occur to him that she might see a relationship beyond that. Neither did the possibility of something beyond that occur to him. When his university friend, Arthur, got married a year or so ago, the notion that one day he might marry did, very fleetingly, cross his mind but that notion had long since been forgotten. Other than close work colleagues, he didn't have any friends at the Park, apart from perhaps Jack Good and Rolf Noskwith; not that that ever bothered him. The end of this war was nowhere in sight so maybe another colleague/friend who understood the work and the conditions there could help pass more pleasantly some of the little spare time he had. She went to a university, she said, so at least they had that in common.

Maybe he could get away early enough on Saturday to go over to Bedford, a place familiar to him, just to see what transpired, his change of heart persuaded by Peitho's winning charms.

"Bill!" he heard and turned to see Grace hurrying across the Swan Hotel forecourt towards him.

"Bill, you found it. I'm so pleased." Breathlessly, she added, "You haven't missed anything; I didn't spend too much in the end. Just some new shoes. Look. Nothing special, I'm afraid."

She was radiant, her cheeks red from the cold. It was a crystal-clear afternoon, cold but dry.

"This way," she steered him. "It's lovely along the Embankment. I had digs here for a short time. It's much nicer than Newport Pagnell, much nicer. There's the boathouse," she said pointing across the river. "It's exciting to see them in their long, sleek rowing boats."

They walked by the river under the bare trees, swans gliding over to them in the hope of titbits. Mothers, often in twos, pushed their prams with their little ones copiously wrapped against the weather. Out of earshot, a mother pointed Bill out to her friend wondering why he was not in uniform.

Grace talked about herself and her upbringing in Scotland and in the north of England. Bill said little. He found her easy to listen to, catching a hint of Scottish lilt in her voice and finding her phraseology attractive. He could identify with her very modest background about which she was quite open. She did not appear to be seeking sympathy or indeed any response. Bill was glad her questions to him were few and far between. His answers gave little away but she did not press him. She walked close to him. There were occasional brief silences during which she glimpsed his abstracted gaze, but there was no awkwardness. At one point, she considered approvingly his quiet, thoughtful demeanour, comparing him to the raucous, overbearing types she had suffered at a recent evening out in Wolverton. She knew which she preferred. The quiet moments did not bother her.

They walked as far as the arched ornamental foot bridge and turned back. Grace remarked more than once how much she liked this part of Bedford especially in the summer with everyone out enjoying themselves. This made Bill feel a little ill at ease because he had not said he knew the Embankment well from his spell in the town at the end of his course, thinking he should avoid mentioning the Bletchley Park courses which were still continuing. He had heard the courses conducted there now taught Japanese, at least sufficient Japanese to aid codebreaking.

As they neared the Swan Hotel at the end of the Embankment, Grace was slightly peeved that Bill had not broached what was to happen next. In the end, she again took the initiative.

"I can catch the train back to Bletchley with you and then take the Park bus back home. I think there will be time for a cup of tea at the station café. We could warm up there."

Bill agreed without expression. They headed for the station.

Grace deliberately sat opposite Bill at the café table. She ordered a pot of tea and two toasted tea cakes. Bill fidgeted. Grace grew a little uncomfortable at the interval before the tea arrived.

"Thank you for coming," she said to break the pause. "I hope I haven't bored you. By the way, just back there," she said pointing to the way they had come, "is a statue of John Bunyan, the famous literary son of Bedford. I vowed to read his *Pilgrim's Progress* but shamefully, I never did. I read a lot and I like to write, poetry sometimes. I suppose English was my best subject at university. I just write for myself now. I find it relaxing. Have you heard of John Bunyan?"

"Oh yes," said Bill, knowing no one could have lived in Bedford and not been told of John Bunyan. "He was a preacher too, I believe. But I've not read anything of his."

Grace had harboured a curiosity she could contain no longer.

"Where did you go to university?" she asked as casually as she could manage.

"Cambridge," said Bill. "I shall go back hopefully when all this is over."

"Oh," said Grace. "What to do?" she added, fishing for more information.

"I'd just started my doctorate when I was asked to do some war work," he replied, again offering little more.

"They'll have you back, will they?" she said, still fishing.

"I have a Fellowship, so yes."

"A Fellowship!" she exclaimed. "You're far too young, surely. I was taught mainly by graduate students your age at my university. I don't suppose any of them were Fellows. They just stood up and read the lecturers' notes. Most of the lecturers had been called up. What are you doing for your doctorate?"

"Something on graph theory, I hope," he said. Then seeing her incomprehension, he explained, "A branch of mathematics."

"Oh, I see now. I might have guessed. Mr Turing and Mr Noskwith are mathematicians too, I think."

She looked at the café clock.

"We'd better go; our train is due."

They walked out on to the platform.

"Just look at that gorgeous sunset," she remarked wistfully as their train arrived. They sat next to the window looking out onto another platform where a stationary engine had smoke drifting from its stack that caught the pinks and reds of the sunset.

"That sunset is the sort of thing that inspires me to write," she said pensively. "But from here, even with imagination that smoke turns it to an autumn brown at best. I guess it's very difficult to wax lyrically about a railway cloud."

Bill was quite surprised at this melancholy, seeing a different, sensitive side to her. He wondered what her poetry might be like; free verse perhaps. Whatever her style, to him, it was an appealing quality especially when added to her looks. Bill rarely took critical notice of people's physical features but in odd moments that afternoon, he had observed her closely. He thought her enchanting with a Mona Lisa-like smile, an inner beauty. Her face was longish with a more pointed rather than rounded chin; cheek bones high-ish; forehead high-ish; eyes bright and sparkling. Her hair was long, full and down past her shoulders, dark brown and lustrous. She was undoubtedly prettier than her friends. There was a flaw, however, a slight gap between her front teeth. Bill was pleased she had a flaw; perfection should be reserved for mathematics.

Despite all this, his mind was muddled. He could not unscramble his emotions or determine his feelings towards her. Yet, the idea of Grace as a friend was agreeable; but he had no notion of how to cultivate that idea. He was still confused about what he should do next other than to escape somehow. Again, Grace made the running.

"Here," she said as the train drew into Bletchley Station. "I've written my address on this piece of paper. It's difficult to keep in touch with changing shifts and so on. Maybe we could do something like this again. Write to me if you like."

He took the piece of paper as the train juddered to a halt.

Bill was relieved to see her bus was waiting. Even so, there was a slightly awkward goodbye, due in part to her hope he would offer his address in return. In his anxiety, though, all Bill wanted was to exit and lacking in experience of such a situation, did not recognise her expectation. Later when his head was a little clearer, he realised that perhaps out of politeness, if nothing else, he should have proffered his address. The afternoon itself was pleasant enough, the walk by the river particularly so, and Grace's fondness for writing appealed to him. Just a friendship with Grace could be fine but the fact that she was a young lady seemed to complicate matters in such a way that he did not know how to play his part. That tended to throw him. He hated complications or matters left pending. Grace, in spite of everything in her favour, posed a complication. What to do?

When Grace arrived back at Newport Pagnell she went straight to her room, threw down her shopping and slumped onto her bed. Why, why had she been so forward? Against her nature, she had steeled herself and manoeuvred the rendezvous, hoping he would then meet her at least half way. She had tried so hard all afternoon. But he didn't seem to grasp how hard she was trying. She hadn't minded that he said little and she was pleased to have found something of his background, especially the bit about being a Fellow at Cambridge University. But he could have given a bit more. What hurt the most was that he did not even offer to write down his address. Did he not want to meet her again? It seemed like a rejection. Why did she leave herself so open? She had such expectations of the day and it had all gone so well until the end. At least she had not shown him her disappointment. But she could contain her emotions no longer. She curled up on her bed and sobbed.

Chapter 11
Colossus

On Monday, Bill began his examination of the two sets of four Conger ciphertexts, each set with QEP indicators in common. With such long messages, he expected to find many repeats if they were truly in depth or near depth as had been found in the August depth that had been successfully broken. Over the next days, he looked for repeats but there were none. He analysed the shorter Halibut sets of four and the outcome was the same; no repeats. Was this latest traffic subject to a new security feature added to the August machines or did the Germans have a new version altogether? There had been references in Enigma and Tunny decryptions to T52c, T52ca and T52d, and there was that T52d reference in the Naples report. Michael was pretty sure that the T52c version, the Pentagon machine, had been the version the Germans suspected of being very insecure. Bill reckoned the T52ca was probably an adapted version of the T52c to improve its security and the T52d a new version with further security features. What was he faced with?

Messages with the same QEP indicator number but no repeats pointed to the use of an autoclave type function whereby a letter of plaintext was influencing an element of the key. That hypothesis was supported by the occurrence in the clear text message preambles of such phrases as 'Mit KTF' and 'Ohne KTF' which Bill knew meant with or without clear text function. The German's use of an autoclave meant no depths, and depths had been the only means so far of breaking Sturgeon traffic. He had been right to think these latest Sturgeon links would be hard nuts to crack yet he was still confident that a way could be found albeit requiring a considerable number of calculations, maybe many more than Tunny required. But those onerous calculations could probably now be done on Max's new machines. All that was needed were the right step by step sequences.

During the week, when not deep in thought on Sturgeon, the problem of Grace rose to the fore. Bill sought out Rolf and confided in him about his dilemma. Immediately, Rolf said in his faltering English that Bill should write to her.

"Tell her you had big impression and forgot to give her your address. Say you had a beautiful time and would like meet again. Offer to take her to Cambridge. Show interest in her. Say you'd like to read her poetry. She favours literature so tell her the sort of books you like; if you read that is. You could tell where home is and what family you have. Girls like that stuff I'm told. Sometimes, they're a bit mystery to me but they are sensitive creatures and want attention, I believe. She looks lovely girl and hope still is keen but you will lose her if you do not act quick. You have to, how you say, pull out all stops on this, Bill but think she is worth it."

He took Rolf's counsel and that evening, penned Grace a letter. Not knowing really how to go about it, he settled for writing almost word for word Rolf's advice. At the letter box the next day, his hand hesitated but he let the letter drop.

With that off his mind, he returned to the issue of Sturgeon. He remembered seeing one set of Conger messages with the same QEP number, all prefixed 'Ohne KTF' probably meaning the autoclave was absent and therefore were almost certainly in depth. It was one last hope. When he found the set, he sighed in disappointment. There were only two messages in the set, insufficient for an attack.

He went to see Gerry with his initial findings on Sturgeon only to get a response from him that was altogether negative. Gerry pointed out that only one pair of messages, long ago, had produced any intelligence at all. All other broken messages had been operator chat. Only depths of four or more could be successfully attacked and he suspected those from last August and September were most probably test messages as nearly all of them had been on a single QEP number. And now with the suspected introduction of an autoclave function, depths were no longer available. Gerry was concerned it was getting more difficult to justify the effort against Sturgeon unless a way forward could be found soon. Despite Gerry's downbeat note, Bill was undeterred, still engaged in the quest for a solution based on mathematical hypotheses. He returned to the quest but knowing time for answers was running out.

On Saturday morning, excitement ran high as the group from the Research Section made its way over to the recently completed Block F, a drab, functional-looking, single story building of concrete and brick. They had been told the Colossus machine was about to run its first test, a machine that supposedly would surpass even the amazing Robinson machines in speed, accuracy and flexibility. Anticipation of its arrival had been keen, expectations of its capability undoubtedly exaggerated. They all trooped into a room totally dominated by a very large, very complicated looking machine with racks of electronic components reaching to the ceiling; a bewitching array of relays, switches, plug cords and displays. To the right, protruding about six feet into the room was the same type of framework as the Robinson machine, like a bedstead on its side, decked with pulleys around which ran a single tape.

The visitors' eyes widened at the sight of such overwhelming complexity.

All the senior people from Bletchley Park were there, including those who had been sceptical that such a machine could be built before the war ended, let alone work. Max Newman, Jack Good, Donald Michie and others from the Newmanry were gathered at one end of the room together with the Testery people, including Ralph Tester and Jerry Roberts. Tommy Flowers was there with Harry Fensom whom Bill remembered from the Robinson demonstration. Tommy Flowers noticed Bill and gave a brief, nervous smile in recognition. Max stepped forward.

"Well, gentlemen. Remarkably, we are here to see the first test run of the Flowers Machine we now call Colossus. It is no exaggeration to say Mr Flowers and his team have worked night and day for many months to design, build and test this extraordinary machine just installed here in our new Block F. The aim of the machine is to speed up the initial processing to break Tunny messages, a need that has gained great urgency in recent months. I'll let Mr Flowers introduce his machine."

Tommy Flowers moved to the front. He was nervous, more from having to address the assembled gathering than for his machine's performance. His audience stood in awed silence, the anticipation palpable.

"We have tried," said Tommy, "to improve on the Robinson, which works but has had some design and reliability issues. My machine, as you can see, has only one looped tape on the pulleys on which the message is recorded. Everything else, including the double delta calculations, is done internally. The output scores, the chi wheel settings, will appear here on this display panel and will be printed on this electric typewriter. The machine is designed to run many times faster than the Robinson. You will see the tape running at about 40 miles an hour. Back at Dollis Hill, we ran it up to 60 miles an hour when it flew into pieces like confetti which obeyed Newton's laws of travel, getting everywhere! So, although the machine could read up to 10,000 characters per second, we have limited it to 5,000 characters a second."

His face was deadpan as he delivered this last sentence but his audience looked on incomprehensively, unable to conceive such a fantastic speed.

"We tell the machine what to do with these switches and plug boards." He looked over to Max Newman. "Shall we run it?" Max nodded. "Of course, we already know the answer we are looking for on this run. Right, Harry. Off you go."

In moments, the machine came into action with the gleaming pulley wheels whirring faster and faster, the tape building up to a frenetic, whooshing speed. On various panels lights winked in apparent randomness. There was a hypnotic *tick, tick, tick.* Each tick, Harry explained over the general hum, was the tape completing a circuit, completing a single statistical attack on the message. All of a sudden, the typewriter clacked into action as if by magic, then stopped, then the carriage violently leapt back to its rest ready to type the next score; all this without any human intervention. The audience watched in total fascination.

The typewriter burst into action a dozen times in the next ten minutes, and then the whole machine sighed to a halt.

"What should we have?" Tommy asked Max.

"We're looking for significance at chi one, position 20 and chi two at position 11."

Tommy tore a strip of paper off the typewriter, looked at it and passed it to his nearest visitor, pointing to the highest score which was read out.

"The highest score is for wheel one at position 20 and wheel two at position 11."

It had taken ten minutes. There was silence. For a moment, everyone in the audience was dumbfounded. They could hardly believe what they had just witnessed. Excited chatter then broke out. Jerry Roberts caught Bill's eye. He was beaming from ear to ear.

"That seemed to work," Tommy Flowers declared flatly. "Let's try again to see if we get the same answer."

Harry Fensom reset the machine and started it again. Once more, the audience was mesmerised, watching one part of the machine and then another, trying to anticipate when the typewriter would spring into action. After ten minutes, the machine stopped. This time, Tommy handed the torn-off page to Ralph Tester on the other side of him.

"Exactly the same, wheel one at position 20 and wheel two at position 11," said Ralph. Tommy passed him the first sheet. "And the two highest scores are exactly the same," he added, his voice like an amazed member of an audience on stage at a magic show.

Bill looked across at Commander Travis. He wore an expression of disbelief, all his early scepticism dispelled in two short tests.

"One more?" called out Max playing to the gallery. There were nods all round.

The third test gave the exact same output as the previous two, something unheard of with the Robinsons which rarely counted exactly the same scores on repeated runs. The machine had behaved brilliantly.

Tommy Flowers cast an eye round the room at the stunned reaction. He shook his head. "They just didn't believe it!" he said to himself. "They didn't understand what I was proposing. I don't think even Max really understood what I was telling him. Maybe they will believe me now, now they have seen it with their own eyes."

Commander Travis moved forward and the hubbub subsided.

"Mr Flowers, you and your team are to be congratulated on a splendid achievement. Your machine is truly remarkable. I sincerely hope your valves prove as reliable as you predict. If so, your machine will be an invaluable addition to our capabilities at a time of greatly increased necessity. Well done indeed. I look forward to regular reports on its use."

With that he and the other senior people departed leaving the Newmanry, the Testery and the Research Section people to mingle around chatting excitedly, electrified by what they had just seen.

Jack Good came over to Bill.

"What do you think of that?" asked Jack, more animated than usual.

Bill had taken little notice of the appearance of the machine. His mind was turning over the possible use of such a machine beyond setting the chi wheels.

"It is certainly an amazing machine. I hope you know how to drive it, Jack. With all those plugs and sockets, you might expect it can be made to do more than its present role."

"I think we are both thinking along the same lines. We'll see what we're allowed to do with it. Exciting though, don't you think!"

"Indeed," said Bill with his habitual brevity.

On the way back, Bill overheard Gerry Morgan remark to one of the group that Mr Flowers was undoubtedly a genius. Bill, who had never doubted Tommy Flowers, was, nevertheless, silently in complete agreement.

Over the next couple of weeks, Bill addressed his mind to the Sturgeon problem. Was there a weakness to exploit? The original glaring weakness was a button that allowed the operator to reset all the wheels to their message setting, the reason so many depths had been seen. That particular weakness had been eliminated by changes the Germans had made. A second weakness, the Pentagon arrangement, had also been identified by the Germans and jettisoned. The workload of the machine was phenomenal, the number of combinations of wheel order alone was over three and a half million. With each wheel having starting points ranging between 47 and 73, even with Colossus, a workload attack looked questionable. Perhaps some sort of approach based on knowledge gained through Tunny was needed.

All the evidence pointed to the wheel patterns being fixed, unlike the Tunny machine where the patterns were regularly changed. But Bill noticed all the wheel patterns started with a dot, followed by a cross and all the patterns had an almost even distribution of cross and dot. These characteristics, he decided, may well not be significant otherwise the German cryptographers would not have allowed them. They may be of help when all the start points of the wheels, the settings, are known and wheel order is sought, but on their own were probably not of value. Michael had told Bill that it was more than likely a centrally issued key book held by both ends of the link set down for a particular key period which five of the ten wheels were to be used for modulo 2 addition and in what order. The almost even distribution of crosses and dots meant this first part of the enciphering process was nearly random. The remaining five wheels produced a key for the permutation process. The setting for each of the ten wheels was selected by the sender from a table held by both sender and recipient and communicated to the recipient at the beginning of each message by means of the QEP number. Michael had explained that so far as the permutation effect was concerned, the choice of five wheels and a multitude of settings sounded complicated but the result was simply to reorder the dots and crosses produced by the first part of the process,

Bill decided the permuting possibilities of the machine appeared to present a possible point of attack and set about studying the permutation process.

In coming to this decision, he reasoned that that part of the process offered far fewer possible combinations than was at first apparent. With five teleprinter impulses from the first part of the process, the half-encipherment he called it, there were not 120 possible combinations as would be the case for five different impulses but a maximum of 32 because the five impulses were made up of only two different impulses, dot and cross. Did the actual permutation routine offer further help? That was the question.

When he arrived back at his digs, there was a letter on the hall table where Mrs Batchelor usually left his correspondence, a letter addressed to him but in unfamiliar handwriting. Curious, he picked it up and took it up to his room. It was from Grace. She wrote that she was very glad to get his letter and was especially pleased to read about his family and Cheveley. Did he go home often, she asked? At the end, she said she was on late shift for the next two weeks. After that she had arranged to go home to see her family in Crosby near Liverpool as she had some leave due that she had been told to take now otherwise it would soon be very difficult to grant. She would write when she got back. Surprisingly, there was a post script. She had enclosed a poem as he had requested. It was about her childhood, written for a first-year assignment at university. He unfolded the separate sheet of paper and read:

Where shore meets ocean and ocean meets shore,
Loch Ryan sits looking towards the west, watching ferries come and go across the Celtic Sea.
There, I have wandered in all weathers from early Spring to late Autumn,
Feeling the westerly winds and tarrying to watch the setting sun.
I have marvelled at the return of shy primroses year after year,
Their delicate pale cream flowers withstanding the late winter gales.
I have rejoiced at the re-emergence of those bright harbingers of Spring,
The golden daffodils, trumpeting the triumph of hope over winter's despair.
I have trod gently through glades of bluebells, their subtle shades lit by dappled sun,
Making me half believe a world of little people throve beneath my human feet.

Where shore meets ocean and ocean meets shore,
The River Mersey flows out into that self-same Celtic Sea.
On Crosby Sands, I've watched the boats sail out carrying their passengers to Dublin;
Remembering walking as a child down the banks of the Liffey towards the strand, to look back towards my far homeland.
I have walked the shore there in a city both familiar and strange,
Where faith has made odd heroes of ordinary men.

Where shore meets ocean and ocean meets shore,
I have walked all day from Blundellsands to Hightown and back to Blundellsands,
Talking of religion and why men die in defence of their beliefs,
Talking of Crusaders and the world of medieval knights,
Wondering whether one day I might be called to sacrifice myself like they.
I have walked all day from Blundellsands to Hightown and back to Blundellsands,
Past dunes covered in tough marram grass and sheltering delicate bee orchids,
Wandering and wondering what life might hold in store,
Whether I shall be blessed by a miracle of great beauty or meet troubles lapping at my feet,
Where shore meets ocean and ocean meets shore.

He sat back. His first thought was that the poem was rather moving, impressed at how accomplished she must be to write so eloquently. There were a number of place names he had not heard of before and he would have to look them up. He read the poem again as there was much in it to absorb. Her emphasis on the wide outdoors and the wonders of nature had a special attraction for him, as did her uncertainties about the future which mirrored his own anxieties of what lay outside his confined and ordered compass. He could relate to it and relate it to her, what he knew of her. Was he reading too much into her words? Maybe, but a third reading left him enchanted. She had beguiled him yet again.

A couple of evenings later, he wrote to thank her, expressing his admiration for her eloquence. He bemoaned his own lack of linguistic skill which he doubted would ever improve as he was burdened with the impossible task of mastering mathematics. He hoped she would enjoy her no doubt well deserved leave.

The Sturgeon machine's permutation routine was, to Bill's mind, unnecessarily complicated. Michael had written down his understanding which Bill studied. He read that, although the five permutation wheels produced a set of five impulses that could be interpreted as a teleprinter letter, the machine did not use it as a letter but as a series of dots and crosses. The permutation consisted of a series of interchanges between adjacent impulses in the half-encipherment letter, so reordering them. The interchanges took place in a fixed order, one and five, then five and four, four and three, three and two and finally two and one. Whether or not an interchange took place depended on the dots and crosses in the series generated by the permutation wheels, a dot being operative and a cross being inoperative.

Michael had written an example with ●xxx● the five permutation impulses. He had numbered the impulses of the half-encipherment letter one, two, three, four and five. Because the first permutation impulse was a dot, that triggered the interchange of one and five of the half-encipherment impulses, now reordered into five, two, three, four and one. Since the next three permutation impulses were crosses, the second, third and fourth possible interchanges were inoperative. But the fifth interchange was operative because the fifth permutation impulse was a dot and so two and one changed places. The original order of one to five was finally reordered into two, five, three, four and one. Michael completed his example with the plaintext letter B added modulo 2 to the letter F, the product of the first five key wheels, giving the half-encipherment letter 'H'. 'H' permuted by ●xxx● produced the cipher letter 'I'.

Bill considered the process for a while working logically through each element and its consequences. Then at one point, his heart began to race as it occurred to him the second impulse of the half-encipherment letter could only end up in positions one, two or three of the ciphertext letter. The machine's routine meant it could never end up in positions four or five. Another logical consequence was impulse three could never end up in ciphertext position five. Had he found a chink in Sturgeon's armament? With enthusiasm, he set about proving his hypothesis and in doing so finding the distribution of the five impulses of the half-encipherment letter under the 32 possible combinations. He began laying out his findings in tabular form and realised the columns could be assumed to represent true inverse probabilities, a statistical concept he had come across but with which he was not that familiar. He would have to consult Jack Good, the master statistician, to understand it better.

At that point, Michael Crum returned from sick leave. He had told Bill some time ago he was prone to bouts of ill health and that he had even been tutored at home because of it.

"I'm feeling stronger now, thank you," he answered to Bill's enquiry. "But I have been thinking about my failure to make progress on the July depth and I think I may have a hypothesis. The idea came to me that maybe the Germans had built in a motor mechanism that stuttered some of the wheels like Tunny. What do you think, Bill?"

"That is a distinct possibility and worth pursuing," said Bill.

"You can imagine it's been so frustrating at home not being able to discuss the idea with anyone let alone write anything down. Of course, Ma and Pa have no idea what I do here."

"When you have settled in, I'll show you some statistical progress I have made. It is at a very early stage but I think has possibilities."

A little later, Michael came back from seeing Gerry Morgan who had told him he could pursue his hypothesis for the July depth. Bill showed Michael his permutation attack and described how it should be possible with his discovery to set the second wheel with the aid of a reasonably long crib, say 40 letters. Once that was set, it should be easier, he explained, to set wheel three even though there was less statistical data for that wheel, and so on.

"Next," said Bill, "I want to link this with characteristics of the plain language by mapping pairs of half-enciphered letters, which incorporate non-random plaintext, against pairs of ciphertext rather like I did with Tunny."

Michael ginned; tangible progress at long last.

Bill felt comfortable working alongside Michael whose first-class intellect had been ably demonstrated by his earlier Sturgeon discoveries. Bill knew he was in good company as he had learnt Michael had a first-class honours degree in mathematics from New College, Oxford before becoming a Harmsworth Senior Scholar at Merton College. He also took to Michael's very gentle character. The son of a clergyman, his maxim before he said anything was, 'Is it true, is it kind, is it wise?'

The two of them set upon their hypotheses with calm enthusiasm.

At his digs, there was a postcard on the hall table and a letter obviously from Cedric. The picture postcard was an old photograph of a large, austere-looking building and along the bottom was the legend, 'Merchant Taylors' School for Girls, Great Crosby, Liverpool'. It would be from Grace. He immediately turned it over. She had written briefly that she was having a restful time with her family, reading and going for walks. Then she wrote that the picture was of her old school, adding that she had hated it there. She stressed the last words by underlining them but did not explain why. The postcard confirmed at least what he had thought earlier that she had not rejected him.

Cedric's letter was unusually uninteresting. He wrote that the hospital was very busy and short-staffed. He was working long hours saying his shift ended at six o'clock that evening and he was on duty again tomorrow at half past one in the afternoon until half past twelve the following afternoon with few breaks. But he could not complain as everyone had to work long hours.

As he put Grace's postcard with her letter and poem, he was reminded of his own unhappy days at his school in Cambridge. He hoped she had not been picked on remorselessly as he had been. He might ask her what lay behind her comment, to show interest as Rolf had said, but could that open himself to questions of his own school experiences? It might it be better to say nothing, he decided. He found he was actually looking forward to a letter from her when she was back.

A letter from her eventually arrived and beguiled him yet again, tempting him with a countryside walk with the Bletchley Park Club's hiking group. After the long winter, the idea of a spring-time Sunday walk among the trees with their fresh green leaves in the morning sunlight had great appeal, the group side of it less so but he agreed.

The hiking trip lived up to Bill's expectations, enjoying in his own quiet way both the scenery and Grace's company. Afterwards on her way back to Newport Pagnell, Grace felt pleased how it all went; pleased her slowly, slowly strategy appeared to be paying off. That evening, she wrote in her diary:

'A lovely day with Bill in Ashridge Forest in the Chilterns. Connie, Mary and Marjorie persuaded me to join the Hiking Club on a day out with the promise of bluebells. Wanted me to bring Bill—curious to meet him no doubt. Bus dropped us at a pretty village Aldbury, has a village green with a ducking pond and stocks. Walk was steep at first but easy after that. Bill was very quiet—the girls were unfair asking lots of questions. They got fed up with the little he did give. We dropped back behind the group. Bluebells were exquisite. Nature lifts the soul so, especially in torrid times. Bill very knowledgeable on countryside. The beech trees, he said, would be spectacular in autumn (Note to arrange another trip then). Hedgerows full of pretty little birds I'd not seen before—yellowhammers according to Bill. Refreshments back in Albury at The Valiant Trooper ancient alehouse said to be from the 1750s.

'Wish Bill would give more—the girls said they could not understand what I saw in him, unkindly why I waste time on him. He is better with just me but could give me more too. He is not cold but neither is he warm—although in possession of a dry wit. Is there a brilliant mind behind that distant exterior? Yet for all his faults, I do believe, with gentle, patient, guiding hands he could be *la réponse à mes prières*.'

Both Michael and Bill were making progress when later, Gerry Morgan called them in. His face was uncharacteristically serious. He was aware his usual soft-touch style of management was not appropriate for what he was about to impart, a very unpalatable directive from on high.

"First," he said, "more good news on Colossus. Twelve have been ordered, sanctioned by the War Cabinet no less. If you haven't seen the Colossus Michael, I suggest you go along to the Newmanry and watch it in operation. It's fascinating. But I have to tell you that following your progress report for me last week, Michael, the news on Sturgeon is not so good. Instructions have been issued to cease monitoring Sturgeon traffic altogether."

He paused to see their reaction. There was a dismayed silence.

He continued, "Your report, Michael, went to the top here and there was a discussion about the need to husband resources and for good intelligence on the German Army. Also discussed were the cryptanalytical difficulties faced in attacking Sturgeon machines as outlined in your report. Consideration was also given to the small number of exploitable Luftwaffe links and the limited intelligence that could be derived from them. In consequence, the decision is to concentrate on Tunny traffic."

Silence persisted. The news was a hammer blow to Michael after many, many months of work with some notable successes. Bill could not believe what he was hearing, just as he was prising open a statistical breach, something he was convinced could, given time, be made routine.

Gerry rightly expected Michael to be bitterly disappointed. He did, however, have one morsel of comfort for him.

"I managed to get John Tiltman's agreement for Michael to spend a few more weeks on the July message so at least we can understand the German's latest changes to the T52 in case of later need, and also to see if a routine can be devised to differentiate at an early stage between Sturgeon and Tunny traffic."

He had no such comfort for Bill.

"Your statistical work, Bill, will have to be suspended. Over the next few days, can you write up your hypothesis and the point you have reached so that's all in the file."

Bill leant forward as if to say something but Gerry held up his hand to stop him.

"I realise this decision is a big disappointment to you, gentlemen, but I have to remind you, we are at war and whilst we may not always agree with our superiors, we must carry out their instructions. This is an instruction," he added for emphasis. "On this occasion, I happen to agree with them for reasons you will see later."

That last sentence took any wind left in Bill's sails, for without Gerry's support, any protest was likely to fall on deaf ears.

"What happens to us then?" asked Michael rather forlornly.

"I will be making an announcement in the next couple of days," was all Gerry would offer. "I know this is a big disappointment for you both, but there we are. There is other more important work to be done."

Back at their table, Michael, despite being thoroughly demoralised, could see how disconcerted Bill was at this turn of events. He was the first to speak.

"I did not see that coming," he said with a pained expression. "I seem to have a brief reprieve but I don't see the sense in you not being allowed to develop your hypothesis. I don't know what to say, Bill. I know how confident you are on this statistical work. I suppose we will just have to wait and see what happens."

"Logically," said Bill asserting his contention, "if you are allowed to continue with the July message to understand the latest changes then I should be allowed to develop a statistical routine. I was going to say that to Gerry but he was in no mood to listen. Why didn't he tell us what we would be doing next? I don't like all this not knowing. I thought Gerry was more trusting. Maybe I should go and see him tomorrow."

Michael had not seen Bill quite so expressive before, showing such a measure of frustration.

"Don't be too hard on him, Bill," said the equable, more forgiving Michael. "He may be under orders not to say just now. I don't see him changing his mind, Bill, even if you went to see him. And I don't see how he could say what he has in mind for you until the announcement; it wouldn't be fair to the others. I think some of us in the Research Section have been rather lucky not to have been too subject to orders, more having a bit of a free rein to see where our investigations take us. Perhaps that is coming to an end as the Allied invasion of Europe nears."

Bill calmed down a little. Perhaps the wise Michael was correct. Perhaps, Gerry was constrained.

Reluctantly, he admitted, "You are probably right." But his acquiescence belied his anxiety about not knowing his immediate future.

All evening, he was unsettled, resentful. It irritated him being told to stop what he was doing and having to wait to be told what to do next like a disciplined schoolboy. He wondered whether he could make a case to Gerry Morgan that he should be allowed to continue with Sturgeon. It was only a matter of time before he would have a suitable routine that could plug into Max's new machine. Surely, it was worth the time and effort? With Michael's help, it would be even quicker. He rehearsed a sales pitch in his head. But on his way in the following morning, reality set in and he half abandoned his idea, giving up altogether after a further brief discussion with Michael. His state of mind though did not improve much.

The next day, Bill was met by Michael as he arrived.

"Gerry has called the Section together at half past nine. Sounds like some big announcement. Is it the invasion, do you think?"

The atmosphere as they all gathered in Gerry' room was charged with nervous anticipation. Gerry arrived and took the front.

"Thank you for joining me," he began. He stood erect, looked around to engage his audience, some papers in his hand but he did not refer to them. "We are entering a critical point of the war. You will all be aware from press speculation that the Allied invasion of the near continent is expected any day now. No, I don't have information on the date; we will hear the same as everyone else. When it is launched, though, it will be a most difficult and dangerous time. As part of the preparations, there are severe restrictions on movement around large areas of our southern coastline and our military personnel here are now subject to a national troop travel restriction of 20 miles. In their planning, the military chiefs need all the intelligence possible on the enemy's strengths and deployment and it is our duty to provide as much as we can. We know Rommel has been fortifying the German's Atlantic wall. That has led to highly important and much increased encrypted traffic which will doubtless increase further. Accordingly, a number of matters required addressing here. It has been decided that everyone will work a full six-day week, some sections do already, and until further notice, all leave is cancelled."

This last piece of news brought a gasp around the room as everyone considered the implications.

Gerry continued, "To some degree, the new machines in the Newmanry have been able to keep pace with increased volumes but the pressures have been most felt in the Testery. To help Ralph Tester, it has been decided to loan him five of our staff for the time being until he can recruit and train new people. That means we will suspend some of our activities. Necessary work on Japanese codes will, however, continue. These will move immediately to the Testery under Ralph: Alfred, Brother Stanley, Jim and Daphne. Please report to Ralph first thing tomorrow morning. Bill, you will join them when you have completed your write-up. Another Colossus is due to arrive shortly and Michael, your help will be needed in the Newmanry; meanwhile you can continue with the Sturgeon depth. I should emphasise all these arrangements are temporary and I hope we can resume normal working soon. Do you have any questions?"

The gravity of the situation weighed on everyone. No one spoke.

Gerry concluded, "Thank you all."

Small groups formed when the meeting broke up with much discussion but not dissention. It seemed everyone understood and supported the measures despite the impositions. There was much speculation about the invasion timetable. Was it imminent? Did Gerry know something but was not saying? Eventually, people drifted back to their work.

The upset that Bill had felt these last couple of days eased considerably. He did not like sudden change but the idea of a spell in the Testery had its attractions. If he had to work the night shift, that would be all right.

There was a letter from his mother on the hall table that evening which he opened before supper. It was not good news. She was concerned about his father who was very poorly and the doctor wanted him to go into hospital for tests. He was stubborn and did not want to go but the doctor said he must. An ambulance will come, she wrote, probably tomorrow. Mrs Mitchell has been very good and Lola has been over but not Joe yet. It would, she said, cheer up his father no end if he could come home, even for a short visit. Mrs Mitchell said Bill can telephone her at any time and gave her number.

His world was moving out of control, what with all the recent changes and now his mother's letter saying his father was ill and pleading for him to come home. Yet, it was not possible to get home and back on a Sunday and Gerry had just announced all leave was cancelled. What was he to do? He had leave due. Could he ask for an exception, for just one day given the circumstances?

In the morning, he consulted Michael whose opinion he had come to value. His response was if you don't ask, you don't get. Bill summed up his courage and went to see Gerry who was sorry to hear of his father's ill health but very regretfully said he could not make any allowances. In a strange way, Bill felt a little relieved. Even though he would have gone, he knew such a visit would be stressful in more ways than one.

Despite there being a public telephone box in the Park, he would write to his mother that evening rather than phone Mrs Mitchell with a message for her. He did not like to use public telephones; he found the experience nerve-racking and so avoided them.

After supper, he wrote quite a long letter home. Usually, his letters were concise, even when explaining some mathematical notion to Cedric. His style of letter writing was not quite brusque but neither was it free flowing but on this occasion, he felt he should try to be more open for his father's sake. He explained about the ban on leave and that he had tried, without success, to get an exception. He promised to visit as soon as he could. He wrote about how well he was looked after by Mrs Batchelor, about the Chess Club and the hike to Ashridge woods but failed to mention Grace. When he signed it as normal, 'Your ever-loving son, Bill', the sentiment held more meaning than usual.

In the Testery, Bill was paired with the genial 'Tubby' Roots who, according to Jerry Roberts, was a stalwart of the wheel-setters in Room 40. Jerry and his cryptographer colleagues occupied Room 41. Both were crowded and a hive of activity. For now, Bill and Tubby Roots were on the 9:00 A.M. to 4:00 P.M. shift with six other wheel-setters. Tubby was rather sheepish at having to show Bill the ropes knowing full well Bill's reputation. What slightly unnerved Bill was the military feeling of the room where nearly everyone, Tubby Roots included, was in army uniform; mostly barrack dress or shirt sleeve order. Nevertheless, Bill, never one to want to stand out, found himself standing out for wearing civilian dress. Tubby Roots explained the division of roles between Room 40 and Room 41.

"Once the chi and psi wheel patterns for the month had been worked out, the Newmanry strip off the effect of the chi wheels from the ciphertext using either Colossus or one of the Robinsons. The resulting letter stream is passed to the cryptographers in Room 41. With their skill, experience and sometimes, a little luck, they will find a break into the message producing, hopefully, at least 17 letters of psi stream, preferably more. We need a minimum of 17 to proceed as you will see. The results are then passed to us in Room 40. We work out the psi wheel settings, following which we can set the motor wheels as I will show you. With all the wheel patterns and settings the ATS girls plug that into a Tunny machine. They then type away at the original ciphertext and like magic out pops the German plaintext. Sometimes, Jerry or one of the other linguists will translate it but mostly, the plaintext goes straight to the Intelligence bods. Two of the most important links at the moment are Jellyfish, which connects Berlin with Paris, and Bream, between Berlin and Rome You're with me on Jellyfish."

He took Bill through the next message in front of him and then set Bill off on one on his own.

For Bill, the task of setting the psi and motor wheels was not difficult. The work was tedious and unexciting but he realised in the present pressured situation, he could not match the necessary expertise of the 20 or so cryptographers of Room 41 of whom eight or nine were on the 9:00 A.M. busiest shift. Occasionally, though, when a particular message could not be processed with the number of psi letters the cryptographers had supplied, rather than send it back, Bill would extend it himself forwards and backwards as far as necessary. Such small triumphs provided light relief.

On Friday afternoon, the last day of May, Bill had just completed a message when a voice said, "There you are, Bill." It was Jack Good. "If you can spare a few moments, come on over to the Newmanry. Tommy Flowers and his engineers are about to finish the installation of Colossus Mark Two."

Bill was glad of a change of scene and followed Jack. Gerry Morgan was there.

Colossus Mark Two looked the same as the first version but Tommy proudly pointed out the significant improvements. It had a thousand more valves, he said, and by some engineering design, could process tapes five times faster than Colossus Mark One.

Jack was excited about his new toy.

"Five times as fast!" he exclaimed. "And this is what I wanted to show you. This box here is an extra gadget Harry Fensom has made for us. A couple of months ago, Donald came up with a wonderful idea which we tested on Mark One, which it isn't really set up to do. Nevertheless, we proved Donald's idea worked. This gadget," he said pointing to it for emphasis, "enables us to set up Mark Two to do your Rectangling! Imagine, Bill, we can get the chi patterns in no time on just a single message."

Not given to over-excitement like Jack, Bill considered the development for a moment.

"Colossus must have the potential of even more," he said reflectively. "I still contemplate that one day a single message may yet be totally broken by a machine."

While Jack was enthusing about the power of this Mark Two machine, Gerry pointed to a growing pool of water creeping out from underneath it.

"Looks as though this machine has not been house trained," he observed sardonically.

"The valves generate so much heat that it has to be water cooled," chirruped one of the engineers from the back.

"Take no notice," said Tommy. "Actually, we have just discovered a radiator leak."

"Isn't it a bit dangerous, water and electricity?" warned Gerry.

"We can't stop," said Tommy busy with some connection. "We promised to have this fully functioning by tomorrow morning."

"Better leave you to it then," said Gerry ushering Bill out. When outside the room, he added admiringly, "That Tommy Flowers deserves a medal."

The following Tuesday morning, one of the ATS girls who had gone off shift rushed back into the Testery and called out loudly, "It's started. The invasion has started! It's just been announced on the BBC!"

Everyone stopped what they were doing. For a moment, there was silence while the startling news was absorbed, the news that had been expected for weeks but now that it was here, it could hardly be believed. Then a hubbub broke out. People pestered her for what else she knew.

"I don't know any more," she answered, excitedly, breathlessly. "Someone said there will be a news bulletin at ten o'clock."

Ralph came out of his room having heard the commotion. He knew everyone would be hungry for more news and to keep the Testery staff in their places, he despatched Tom Colvill, responsible for administration, to report back on the broadcast. Nevertheless, little work was done. Shortly after ten o'clock, Tom Colvill reappeared.

"It's confirmed," he announced. "D-Day has begun. Troops have landed on the coast of northern France. General Eisenhower has broadcast to the people of Europe saying the landings are part of the concerted plan for the liberation of Europe. There is no more at the moment. There will be a special bulletin at midday. I'm sure we wish all our troops and those of our allies Godspeed, good luck and a safe return."

Bill took the news in his usual reserved way and saw that the initial excitement was later tinged with sober reflection, as people's emotions became restrained realising the invasion troops faced extreme danger.

With Tubby Roots and a few others, he made his way over to the canteen at lunchtime. There were lots of people milling about outside the Main Building in the warm sunshine. Groups clustered discussing the news which had spread rapidly.

Suddenly, the chatter stopped and everyone stood still. At first, it was a dull noise in the distance but it became louder and louder until it became a deafening roar as wave after wave of RAF bombers came thundering low right overhead, so low that the roundel markings were clearly visible, the faces of the pilots could be glimpsed, the guns that bristled in the nose and the rear turrets glinting in the sun. The roar went on and on as more and more formations followed.

Even Bill found the sight and sound both thrilling and frightening. The ground under his feet shuddered, the air filled with a mixture of hot exhaust fumes and aviation fuel. People started waving, then cheering. From behind him a voice bellowed encouragement at a straggler, "Go on my son!" He had never seen anything like it. Nothing had prepared him for the rawness of the military might abruptly on display.

It seemed ages but it was only minutes. The crowd was left gasping, in awe at the show of sheer power, the threat of the devastation the planes could wreak on those below and the bravery of those flyers heading south into the teeth of the enemy. Everyone, including Bill, was left shaking but exhilarated.

The roar receded, the fumes cleared and the chatter resumed, even more lively than before.

During the afternoon, work continued. The mood was sober and determined, while everyone had half an ear for news which trickled through from visitors and those who found an excuse to go over to the canteen. The landings had been in Normandy with British, Canadian and American troops. Churchill made a statement to the House of Commons that was loudly cheered. He reported an immense armada of 4,000 ships and several thousand smaller craft had crossed the Channel. Eleven thousand aircraft were on hand to sustain the vast operation. Everything was proceeding according to plan. The King would broadcast to the nation at nine o'clock that evening.

"I think we will have our work cut out over the coming weeks," said Tubby Roots at one point.

Bill stayed on late to complete as many messages as possible. At supper, Mrs Batchelor was keen to recount her experiences of the day, the aircraft overhead, the latest reports she had heard on the wireless from correspondents with the troops. Churches were open, she said. Confiding she was not a regular churchgoer, she had, nevertheless, gone with her neighbour to a short service at the local church. She would be listening to the King later if Bill wanted to join her. He said he would.

At nine o'clock, Bill sat with Mrs Bachelor in anticipation of the King's address. In his slow, faltering voice, he recounted how four years ago, the nation had stood alone against an overwhelming enemy with our backs to the wall. We had survived that test but once more, a supreme test had to be faced. This time, he said, the challenge was not to fight to survive but to fight to win the final victory for the good cause. He called for a nationwide vigil of prayer as the great Crusade sets forth. He ended quoting Psalm 29, 'The Lord will give strength unto his people, the Lord will give His people the blessing of peace.'

Chapter 12
A Death in the Family

Bill's father had been admitted to hospital and letters from his mother talked of him getting weaker. Doctor Randall, she said, was not hopeful of much improvement. It was his heart; it was not strong. Lots of people were being very kind, she wrote, especially Lily Mitchell who regularly went with her to the hospital. Lola too visited when she could. But although his mother's correspondence was brief and prosaic as usual, Bill could sense from her most recent letters the growing strain all this was putting on her.

In his replies, he tried to be encouraging and supportive but he found writing on a profoundly personal level difficult; for him such words just did not flow naturally. He sent postal orders with his letters; it was the only practical help he could give in the circumstances. There were rumours the troop travel ban would soon be lifted and he hoped as a consequence, the ban on leave would be lifted too.

The atmosphere in the Testery was intense with grit and determination which allowed Bill to put family concerns to the back of his mind and concentrate on the constant stream of messages requiring his attention. He became adept at the techniques needed to tease out the required settings but he found the routine work not to his liking. He was used to sitting back and thinking deeply about a problem, to ponder on possibilities, to consider hypotheses without time constraints. Given the imperative of the situation though, he accepted he was needed in the Testery for now.

In a rare break, he went over to Room 40 to seek Jerry Roberts' help on a German word. Having given Bill a couple of possible words to try, Jerry was keen to tell him how in the run up to D-Day he had translated some messages that confirmed Hitler was convinced the invasion would be in the Pas de Calais area and was holding back his troops there. This, he said, must have given confidence to our military chiefs that they would have the necessary vital window to get a foothold in Normandy. Such was the tremendous importance of what they were doing.

"But," said Jerry, "we could be running into serious problems. On some links, the Germans appear to be changing wheel patterns daily instead of monthly. Where autoclave limitations are used, we haven't depths. Our only hope is your rectangling, Bill. By hand, though, it's impossible to cope with the change from monthly to daily patterns."

"Jack says he now has a rectangling gadget on Colossus. Is that going to help?"

"Yes, but the Newmanry is only just getting used to it. And of course, with only two Colossi, there is only so much machine capacity. I know Jack and Donald are working on improving rectangling routines though and Colossus Three is due any day. If the Germans change all their links to daily, your rectangling on Colossus may be our only hope."

"Let's hope the Germans are rather too busy to change their patterns," said Bill dryly.

Jerry noticed Bill glancing at someone sitting at the same table, a new face.

"Perhaps I should introduce you, Bill. This is Lieutenant Art Levenson of the US Army's Signal Security Service who has joined us in Room 40. He's one of your sort, a mathematician. Well, a mathematician first and a German linguist second so he's very useful to us."

Art gave Bill a wide smile as they shook hands.

"Exciting stuff you do here," he said, typically enthusiastic and positive like most Americans Bill had come across. "Have you met Captain Walter Fried, our Signals Corps liaison officer?" he asked, offering some polite conversation.

"Yes, I have met him," Bill replied.

"He has an interesting assignment," Art elaborated, "reporting back home on pretty much everything that's going on here. He's done some reports on Tunny, and Sturgeon too, I think. An excellent cryptanalyst is Walter, very experienced, very thorough."

On his way back to Room 41, Bill reflected that the two Americans he had met, Walter Fried and now Art Levenson, were pleasant enough. They certainly appeared capable cryptographers; perhaps he should not have doubted that.

"Bill, what are you doing here?"

Bill turned round, it was Grace.

"I was hoping to catch you in your break," he replied, having waited until late in the evening in the canteen to see her or one of her friends from Hut 6.

"But it's late. What is it?"

"I can't see you tomorrow. I have to go home. My father is unwell in hospital."

"Oh, dear!" Grace was both concerned at Bill's news and bitterly disappointed that their long-organised day out on Sunday was now not to be.

"I had a telegram from my mother yesterday saying he is quite poorly, so I must go home. He has not been well for some time. I haven't been able to get time off because of the ban on leave, but it will be lifted on Monday which means I can go tomorrow and stay a few days."

"I understand. Of course, you must go, Bill. I'm so sorry. I hope he will be all right. I'm glad you caught me," said Grace laying her hand lightly on his arm, an involuntary gesture of her concern. "Write to me when you get back. I finish late shifts this weekend but then have to do the night shift for two weeks. Please do write."

"I will. I had better go now." He made to leave.

"Good night, Bill, and go carefully," said Grace. "I do hope everything will be all right." Her hand lingered briefly on his arm as if she did not want to let go.

"I'll write," he said as he left, leaving Grace standing alone, her hopes for tomorrow suddenly dashed.

The encounter left Grace upset not only by his hasty departure but by his manner. He must have known that she would be disappointed about tomorrow; he could have said he was sorry. If his mother had sent a telegram, it must be serious yet he did not express concern for his father. She totally understood his need to go home but again, she felt frustrated at his lack of openness and empathy for her feelings. And surely, he did not need to have left her in such a hurry. She had hoped they were becoming closer but this episode rather belied that. Then, perhaps she was being too harsh on him. Was she being too self-centred and thoughtless, traits she knew she had but found difficulty suppressing at times? He had stayed to see her after all. It was late, and even if he didn't exactly show it outwardly, he must be worried about his father.

On the bus home after the shift, her friend, Connie, noticed Grace was quiet and asked what the matter was. When Grace explained, Connie was less than sympathetic.

"I've said before you are wasting your time with him. You are always going to be let down. Besides, he's no fun. I'd drop him sooner rather than later if I were you."

Connie's sniping annoyed her but Grace was too tired to react.

The only train the next day into Newmarket drew in mid-afternoon. On the journey, Bill could not help worrying about this particular visit home. He was not sure he had ever seen his father ill in bed before. What would he say? He worried the right words would not come. Just the idea of visiting the hospital was a concern with all those people and corridors. In his mind, the urgency of his work would provide a convincing excuse to catch tomorrow's train back, although he had not told anyone this was his intention. Unless, that is, the situation had improved and the doctors said his father could be allowed home. In which case, he would stay a day or two longer, all this alarm over, everything back to near normal.

He rehearsed his excuse as he walked along the platform to the way out. He turned into the booking hall and stopped immediately. There, sitting in the waiting area, was his sister-in-law, Lola. He had not expected anyone to meet him; the hospital was ten minutes' walk, no more. She looked up and when their eyes met, Bill knew something was wrong. She had a handkerchief in her hand and her eyes were red-ringed as if she had been crying. She got up slowly and came over to him, her eyes welling up.

"Oh, Bill," she wept. "I don't know how to say this, but your father died earlier this morning. Oh, Bill. I'm so sorry."

She hugged him as much for herself as to comfort him. He tentatively held her, the enormity of what she had just said gradually sinking in.

"He died in his sleep, Bill. He was not in any pain. His weak heart gave out. Doctor Randall said it could happen at any time." Lola blew her nose and dabbed her eyes. "We should go to your house. Your mother is there with Joe and Mrs Knights. Mr Knights has his car outside to take us." She took his arm to lead him outside.

Bill's reaction was hesitant. The alarming turn of events threw him, confused his thinking. He was so unprepared that his mind went into slow motion. He did not know what to say or do. It was only because Lola was leading him, that he followed her to the waiting car.

"My condolences, Bill. Your father was a fine man," said Mr Knights as he got in the car. Bill could not formulate a reply as his mind was reeling from the news. As they drove in silence, a growing awareness of the situation began to panic him. The dread of what might await him set his heart palpitating. Normally, flight trumped fight but this time though he knew there was no retreat from his predicament.

Lola led him into the house through the rarely used front door into the sitting room. His mother sat listlessly in an upright chair, her head resting on the high back. The armchair his father would sit in on the rare occasions the front room was used lay vacant. Mrs Knights sat on the pouffe next to his mother stroking her hand. They both looked up as Bill entered. He hesitated at the scene, his heart beating furiously. He had said nothing so far and could still not utter a word.

Nothing could have prepared him for the sight of his mother so utterly, utterly drained, her face drawn, pale, puffy with tears, her arms leaden on the arms of the chair. She was near to collapse; she did not even lift her head to him, just raised her eyes. This was his mother as he had never seen her before. She had always been alert, robust and busy. But now, her eyes, her face were almost vacant; almost, except she managed the merest of movements in recognition of her son.

Mrs Knights stood up and withdrew indicating Bill to sit next to his mother. He did and leant his head on her shoulder. Tears did not come but they were there inside him and his mother knew that. She slowly put her arm across his shoulder to draw him a little nearer. She knew her son. She knew to expect few, if any, words from him in the situation. For her, they were not necessary. For a few moments, the room was a silent tableau of mourning for a dearly departed.

Mrs Knights broke the silence and spoke quietly to Lola.

"Joe has gone to see Mr Rolfe about the funeral arrangements. Rolfes, the builders, do funerals as well, you know. Joe has the hospital papers and says he will go to the Register Office in the morning. I'll leave you to it now, but if there is anything you want, all you have to do is ask. I'll call round tomorrow in any case."

"Thank you for all you have done," Lola said sincerely. "And Mr Knights. I'll see you out."

Bill felt his mother's arm round him gently draw him a fraction closer.

"He went very peacefully," she whispered. "Very peacefully."

A few minutes later, Lola reappeared.

"Joe is back and Mrs Mitchell has brought across some supper, which was kind of her. I'll put the kettle on."

Joe came in.

"Bill, you've come," he said, not quite sarcastically but the words had an edge. He turned to his mother. "Mr Rolfe will make some telephone calls in the morning and come over to discuss arrangements. I'll come later when I've been into town. But I may have to do an extra shift to get someone to cover me for the funeral, we're so short staffed." He softened his tone. "You ought to eat something, Mother, you haven't had anything proper for days. Mrs Mitchell has brought some cold meat and salad. Shall I get Lola to get you something?"

"Maybe later," his mother sighed.

Ada King called round and sat with their mother for a while before Lola helped their mother to her bed. Joe and Bill took the opportunity to grab a bite to eat but despite the circumstances, the atmosphere between them was no better than in the past and Bill was quite relieved when his brother and sister-in-law left to catch the last bus. The children who had gone to Lola's parents for the day would go to school as usual in the morning. When the house fell quiet, Bill was at a loss as to what to do so he wrote to Cedric telling him the news. He would finish it when the funeral arrangements were known in the hope Cedric may come.

Bill went up to his room early. On his way, he stopped at the foot of the stairs. Unusually for him, he sensed something different. The house was different. It had changed. It felt strange, colder and emptier.

Although it was still early, he suddenly felt very tired. In the solitude of his room, he tried to think of his father because that is what he thought he ought to be doing. But when he closed his eyes, it was not his father that appeared in his mind. The image that dominated was that of his distraught mother, collapsed in the chair almost drained of life itself. The vacant, fearful, frightened look in her eyes haunted him. It was rare for emotions deep within him to surface into his consciousness but he became aware of a growing sadness. His sorrow, however, was not for himself or even for his father, it was for his mother. Convention, he knew, required him to grieve for his father, but all his grief, if it was grief, was for his mother.

The following two days saw a constant stream of visitors to the house. Joe called in on Monday lunchtime having registered the death and having placed a notice in the local newspaper. Mr Rolfe came over in the afternoon to say the funeral had been provisionally arranged for noon on Wednesday. He hoped to confirm it all later that day. Lola thankfully came and stayed until the children needed meeting from school. Bill found himself answering the door, inviting in visitors, accepting cards or taking messages, all of which he would rather avoid. Most of the people, he did not know and he managed only a brief perfunctory response to the many offers of condolence. Ada King sat with his mother for a while which gave him the opportunity to sidle off down the bridle path for a short respite from it all. His head was telling him repeatedly to make his escape but he knew in his heart he could not, although the temptation was great. One or two visitors tried to engage him in conversation but they soon politely withdrew. Between Joe and Mr Rolfe, the arrangements were made and flowers ordered. Bill was thankful he was not asked to take any responsibility over the arrangements and when asked, said he was content with everything if their mother was.

Even on Tuesday, Bill could see his mother was still very weak and frail and he wondered how she could possibly cope with the funeral. As for himself, he could feel a rising trepidation. He had not been to a funeral before and the whole situation was becoming overbearing. Notwithstanding it was his father's funeral, could he yet get out of it somehow?

Mr Rolfe called in late in the afternoon to reassure everyone that all was in place for tomorrow; all the family had to do was follow his guidance. A very nice young curate, Reverend Borrett, would conduct the service.

Mr Rolfe was a big burly man who, with his brother, ran the reputable building firm in the village set up by their father. The funeral business was a side-line. Bill could see his mother trusted Mr Rolfe implicitly and seeing the redoubtable Mr Rolfe take charge relieved Bill's anxieties somewhat.

In a quiet, private moment, his mother too sought to reassure Bill. Forever, his mother, she knew how anxious he would be.

"Are you all right, Bill?" she asked. "Your father knew you were coming to see him. That pleased him no end. You know, Bill," she said wistfully, "your father was very proud of you, wanted you to finish your studies. He had great hopes for you for the future. Your father," she reminisced, "took a great interest in your progress, you know, wanted you to succeed and only interfered when he thought necessary, like the time you passed the exam to go to upper school in Cambridge at the age of ten, a year early. He thought you were too young and went to see the headmaster who agreed to have you a further year. Of course," she said finishing the story he had heard many times, "you passed the exam the next year with flying colours and went." She paused. "Your father wasn't one to brag but everyone knew how proud he was of you."

Wednesday morning, Bill thought, was strange. He had expected when noon approached, the atmosphere to be heavy with grief and apprehension. Instead, everyone was quiet and slowly, pensively going about their preparations before the hearse and car arrived. Joe and Lola had come early and while Lola helped their mother get ready, Bill and Joe spent another awkward half hour or so in the back room interrupted only by the postman who offered his condolences as he delivered a telegram and a number of letters and cards.

Unknown to Bill and prompted by Lola, for once Joe made a conscious effort to rein in his ill feeling towards his younger sibling and tried to be a bit brotherly. He asked how Bill was, how was work, when was he going back? Bill said he would be glad when the funeral was over and expected to go back tomorrow. Work was particularly busy at the moment. Leave had been cancelled, which was why he had not been over recently.

Bill expected Joe would want to talk about their father, but their father was not mentioned. The conversation was stilted and the atmosphere between them remained tense.

"The car is here!" Lola called down.

Joe opened the front door to Mr Rolfe who said gently, "When you are ready, Joe. We have plenty of time."

As they made their way in silence to the car, Bill bowed his head. It was an unconscious avoidance of the reality in front of him, the coffin that lay in the waiting hearse. At the cemetery, under the archway between the little chapel and the cemetery offices, he and Joe stood on either side of their mother as the coffin was lifted onto the pallbearers' shoulders. It was a sight Bill could not avoid; he was close enough to reach out and touch it. Even at that moment, he was in a sort of denial. He knew it was his father inside the coffin yet it still did not seem real to him. Glancing round, there was his mother, Joe, Mr Rolfe, the pallbearers and the Reverend Borrett waiting patiently, clutching his prayer book. All this was real yet unreal. How could it be happening? Was it happening? In a haze, he followed the coffin into the chapel. He was vaguely aware of the dozen or so congregation standing as the pallbearers carefully set the coffin on a pair of trestles. Mr Rolfe ushered the family into the front pew and withdrew.

Bill paid little notice during the short service, his mind almost blank as he struggled to hold himself together. But it was not grief he was struggling with, it was his own self, the fight between selfishness and duty. He glanced across at the coffin and somehow, he sensed his father was watching out for him, protecting him, giving him strength, helping him see it through. It was then he accepted the reality, it was his father inside.

At the graveside Bill, his mother, Joe and Lola watched stony-faced as the coffin was lowered. The Reverend Borrett spoke the final words, "Earth to earth, ashes to ashes, dust to dust: in the sure and certain hope of the resurrection to eternal life."

That was the moment Bill's mother began to sob, the moment of her beloved husband's final departure. The Reverend Borrett came round and took her hands in his and offered a few quiet words of comfort.

The small party remained in thought a few more moments, Bill's mother reluctant to leave. Eventually, she looked at Mr Rolfe and said, "We had better go."

The rest of the day took a lighter note. The friends in the congregation had waited patiently outside the chapel for the party to return, for the chance to offer their own words of comfort to the family. Bill's mother wanted to see all the flowers and read all the cards. Several of those at the service came back to the house afterwards. Mrs Mitchell had made sandwiches and a cake. There was much small talk which Bill could not easily avoid. One repeated theme about his father was his kindness and his generosity. A number mentioned his father would regularly hand out produce from his garden, and what good produce it was too. Bill was asked a number of times what he was currently doing; politely he gave nothing away.

When everyone had gone, Bill's mother said she needed to say a few things before bed. They sat at the kitchen table.

"You don't need to worry about me, Bill. I will be all right. Really, I will. I have Joe and Lola and the children. I have lots of good friends. You go back when you want. I have some money in the Post Office so I will be fine. Your father provided as best he could. We own the cottage which will come to me so I will have a roof over my head. Aunt Ellen in Burnham said I could go over and stay with her for a while which I think I will do."

"But how will you manage?" asked Bill, concerned his mother was making light of her reduced circumstances. "Your Post Office money won't last forever. I can send you some postal orders regularly. I don't spend much. Can't Joe help? Maybe you could move in with them."

"No," said his mother flatly. "I don't think Joe would agree to that, not with all that's gone on. Besides, there is no room. No. I will be fine. You have your important work and when this war is over, you must go back to Cambridge. Your father wanted so much for you to complete your studies. He will still be watching to see you do."

"If you will really be all right, I should go back tomorrow. It's difficult to get over just at the moment, we are working six days a week. Hopefully, things will get better soon and I can come home more often. I will write. Oh, Mother! I don't know what more I can do, but you must let me know how you are."

"I will. Now, we've had a long day and I'm ready for my bed."

When he came down in the morning, his mother was already up and busy in the kitchen. Over breakfast, she showed him the cards that came with the flowers. She had told Mr Rolfe the flowers could go to the hospital but she wanted the cards and he had kindly brought them around first thing. Bill looked through them. It was odd to see his mother's name, Annie, alongside his own name. There were cards from Joe and Lola, the children Joey and Jeanne, Aunt Ellen who he vaguely remembered. There were some names he knew and some he did not.

"This one," his mother stopped him, "is from the Taylors who your father worked for over at Ashley. It was so kind of them to send flowers. Look, they even put their little daughter's name on the card, Josephine. Your father was fond of her. He used to teach her the names of the garden flowers and she used to help him pick the peas and beans and soft fruit. The Taylors were good to your father. I will have to write and thank them."

The postman delayed Bill's departure because amongst the cards and letters was an envelope addressed to both of them in Cedric's unmistakeable handwriting. He offered his sincere condolences and was clearly upset he would not make the funeral. He promised to write to Bill again soon.

"You must go," said his mother, "or you'll miss your train."

Here he was, heading back to Bletchley which he had desperately wanted to do ever since he had arrived, yet now, the high anxiety to leave was no longer there. Bill turned to wave goodbye at the end of the lane, as usual, but this time, the sight of his mother at the gate had a greater poignancy. This time, she was a widow, on her own.

Chapter 13
Silent upon a Peak

The news that Bill's father had died spread around the Testery and the Research Section. Everyone extended their sympathies. Jack Good came over from the Newmanry specially to offer his condolences. Mrs Batchelor was particularly understanding of his mother's situation, asking what she intended to do now, whether she would take in lodgers like she had to without a pension to rely on.

The attention Bill received on his return was, for him, rather two-edged. The situation made him even more self-conscious such that when his colleagues came to tender their well-meant sympathies, he found those moments distinctly uncomfortable. On the other hand, Bill could not help but recognise their genuine concern adding to his ever-growing sense of belonging to a much larger, much wider, yet no less close-knit group than at Trinity College. It began to sink in that he had a greater standing than he might have imagined and certainly never sought, and within a much more diverse assemblage than his close university circle of academic peers. No longer was he the student on a temporary placement but he was a valued member of a large organisation engaged in important, ground-breaking work. He began to perceive himself in a somewhat different light but this realisation did not inherently alter him.

Cedric's promised letter was very different from his customary light-hearted banter. The news had clearly shocked and saddened him and he was particularly upset at being unable to attend the funeral. His tone was sensitive and contemplative, expressing his sincere regard for Bill's father, for his warmth and generosity. He wrote that he always felt very welcome at the Tutte home which sadly will never be quite the same again. He finished by saying his parents joined with him in offering condolences to the family, adding he had written separately to his mother. Bill habitually kept all of Cedric's letters but this one was rather special, disclosing as it did a true friendship beyond their common interest in mathematics. Bill replied thanking him for his heartfelt letter and saying they must get together soon when they were both less busy.

Replying to Cedric prompted Bill to think about writing to Grace as he had said he would on his return. The reply to Cedric flowed relatively easily but composing a letter to Grace, who had not known his father, proved more troubling since she would not be expecting such tragic news. He hesitated. Although he had pen and paper ready, he set them aside putting off the task until the next evening. On the walk to work the following morning, Bill was reminded of what Cedric once jokingly said about his style of letter writing, that it was so stilted, that it was so cramped by years of writing theses, hypotheses and formal essays, that he had lost any ability to write an agreeable personal letter. He had to concede Cedric was right. In the end, the letter to Grace was unvarnished and in order to avoid writing at length, he said he would tell her more when they next met. Meeting might be difficult at the moment, he added, as he was helping a busy section, working shifts.

Grace's reply arrived a few days later. He opened it in his room and as he read it, he could not help sensing an emerging fondness for her, a step beyond a friendship to a relationship quite different from that with anyone else. Cedric's letter had been serious for once but it was still Cedric. Grace's letter was beautiful, not at all maudlin. It was her language that set her writing apart. She had a way of expressing herself through analogies and figures of speech; gently, evocatively and soothingly painting crystal-clear pictures of her thoughts; her sentiments conveyed exactly, sensitively. He marvelled at her command of language, at her understanding. Obviously keen to meet, she suggested organising a Sunday bicycle ride.

Her letter set him thinking. He was still confused about his feelings over his father's death; that he was yet to notice in himself any signs of grieving as he understood the word. During shifts, he was fully concentrating on the continuously increasing volume of work in the Testery but occasionally in quieter moments away from the Park, his thoughts did turn to home. His sadness though was for his mother still, not for himself. It was as if the loss of his father was not impacting on him directly, only indirectly through his mother. Would he experience true grief, personal grief, he wondered? If so when? Such questions lay unanswered.

What did emerge from his contemplations was a realisation that there had been a fundamental change in his life. It went back to that moment in the house when he had stood at the foot of the stairs. The house had changed, there was a void and perhaps that was the point at which the house ceased to be his home in the sense of his spiritual attachment to it. It had been relegated, relegated from the status of the family home to a place where his mother now lived alone. It was as though a last tie had been cut loose, that in death, his father had bequeathed him the final token of his independence, an independence he never actively sought but was now his by rite of passage. It had been coming, he reflected. At Trinity College, he went home regularly but gradually, since joining Bletchley Park, he had become more detached from his parents and from Cheveley. He was standing on his own two feet now, figuratively and financially albeit under the cloak of Bletchley Park which provided some measure of insulation from the world outside, an outside world which he was still inclined to avoid but with which, by degrees, he had learned to cope better.

Grace was waiting on Tickford Bridge as arranged. He had borrowed a bicycle and pedalled the nine miles from Bletchley in glorious sunshine. On the way, he so enjoyed the ride that he gave little forethought to his meeting with Grace which she had organised. Her idea of a bicycle ride together had to be abandoned as she had been unable to borrow a bike and the revised rendezvous involved Bill cycling over to Newport Pagnell and Grace walking to the bridge from her digs in Tickford Street. She waved energetically when he came into sight.

"Bill, it's so lovely to see you. Isn't it a glorious day? We can walk in Lovat Meadow by the river. It's nice to walk there. Not as interesting as the Embankment at Bedford but it's pleasant enough. How are you? Not too tired working long hours, I hope."

"I'm fine," said Bill with his traditional conciseness.

"This way," she said leading to a path at the side of the bridge that led to the meadows. "Look at the iron bridge, isn't it wonderful, so ornate and such a beautiful design. See how old it is, the plaque there says 1810."

He followed pushing his bike as she skipped down the path. Her obvious happiness was infectious and raised further Bill's spirits. He was glad she had not immediately brought up the subject of his father as he feared that might have started off the afternoon on the wrong note.

The grass of the meadow was lush and the river, which was more a deep, dark stream, pushed its way slowly through dense green rushes on either bank under willow and sycamore trees. Grace, enthused by Bill's arrival, chatted away about this and that as they ambled along the path. Occasionally, he looked across to her when he thought she would not notice and smiled at seeing her so happy and carefree. He wished he could be like her but he contented himself with her happiness and the lovely peaceful setting. She too glanced at him, looking for an opportunity to steer them to the river bank where they could sit close to each other.

"Let's go over there," she said eventually. "We can sit in the shade by the water."

They sat saying little for a while, taking in the peace and quiet, watching a moorhen busy herself amongst the green rushes. Grace idly picked a flower and not knowing what it was, offered it to Bill.

"Do you know what this flower is?" she asked innocently.

"Ragged Robin," said Bill taking it from her.

"What a funny name. I suppose the petals are a bit ragged. It's pretty though," she said.

As he took it, their hands touched momentarily, the accidental contact not lost on Grace. There had been no close contact between them since the dance evening, something Grace was desperate to correct. She had planned to link her arm in his on this walk but somehow, the bike got in the way. Discretely she hoped, while they both inspected the flower, she edged a little closer so their arms touched. She pointed to the other bank.

"There are some more pink ones over there, taller."

"Those are purple loosestrife."

"How do you know all these flowers, Bill?"

"My father. He taught me."

Grace had been biding her time for a suitable moment to bring up the subject of his father and now appeared fitting, particularly as they faced the same way looking at the river, a situation she thought might help him.

"Would you like to tell me a bit about your father, Bill? I seem to know little about him. What was he like?"

The question took Bill off guard. He bought some thinking time.

"What do you want to know?"

"Well, how did you get on with him? He was quite a bit older didn't you say."

Bill was never one to consider relationships in any depth and he had never been asked to talk about his father before in such terms. There was a long silence. Normally, he would brush off such questioning with a brief, vague reply. But in the circumstances and with Grace patiently letting him take his time, he decided he could, and perhaps should, gather some thoughts characterising his late father. He began hesitantly.

"Yes, he was quite a bit older, but I don't think that really mattered."

He paused.

"He was very good to me, always encouraged me. I don't ever remember him getting cross or telling me off. But then I suppose, I was quite a biddable child. I preferred books to getting into trouble." He stopped again to think. "He worked hard, my father. And he was proud of what he did. We were never well off, quite the opposite, but there was always food on the table. He believed in education. He wanted me to have the chance of a higher education, perhaps because he didn't have the opportunity himself. He always made sure I went in for scholarships, had the grants I needed."

"Were you close to him?"

"I don't really know," he said reflectively. It was a probing question. "He was always pleased when I passed exams. But then he was never in a position to help me with my work," he answered avoiding any deeper emotional analysis.

"He taught you about wild flowers though, you said."

"Oh yes. He loved the countryside. I suppose when I was growing up that was one subject where his knowledge was always superior to mine."

There was another long pause. Grace could see Bill thinking and held back.

"Some might say," he continued eventually, "he was a strong character. He was definitely the head of the household but not in a domineering way. We went to church on Sundays; that is except my brother, Joe. It was my mother who had the stronger faith though, so I suppose they complemented each other in a sense."

"What will your mother do now?" Grace enquired softly. "Will she move in with Joe and his family, do you think?"

Again, Bill considered for a moment what to say. He knew there were tensions between Joe and his parents and his mother had said only the other day that moving in with Joe and Lola would not work. Since he did not know the root cause of the tensions which were never spoken about, at least not in his presence, he was not sure he should allude to such family matters.

"I don't think they get on well enough for that," he decided to say. "She is going to stay with an aunt for a while. I don't think there is any hurry to decide anything."

Another pause told Grace that was as far as she should go and it gave her the chance to switch the conversation. There were common themes emerging in their backgrounds that she hoped could bring them closer together.

"I told you I went to university in Glasgow," she started wistfully. "When I went there, I stayed with a retired uncle and aunt who told me about the time my father died. I was only a baby so I knew nothing of my father. He died of pneumonia. Of course, it was calamitous in more ways than one. My mother was obliged to take in lodgers to make ends meet. It was hard for her but she had no option. Then the landlord dropped a bombshell; he wanted the house my mother rented from him for himself. Fortunately, one of her lodgers, a blind man, had some money and said he'd buy a house if my mother would live in to look after him. So, we moved and my mother looked after the blind man, as well as still taking in lodgers. When I was about 14, the blind man died and left the house to my mother. Soon after that we went to live in Crosby near her sister."

"Is that where you went to that school you hated?" said Bill interrupting her discourse, an interruption which pleased her as it meant she had his interest.

"Merchant Taylors', yes. The teachers were down on me from the start. I think my cousins who went there had been disruptive. Also, they did not expect me to be as clever as the English girls and held me back. In fact, most of the English girls were not as clever as I was and in the end, they had to put me in a higher class. And the uniform was silly. I was glad to leave. But rather like your father, my mother wanted me to have a university education so I could have a better life than she had."

"Didn't you say your mother married again?" Bill remembered from their walk at Bedford. "Was he not like a father to you?"

Grace hesitated.

"Debby, I called him. Erwin Debetaz was his real name. He was a Swiss travelling salesman who lodged with us when he was in the area. I liked him to start with; he had the appeal of a foreigner with a hint of mystery. He used to help me with my French homework. After they married, though, things changed. He wanted me to leave school and get a job to help with money. He could turn on the charm but he was hopeless with money. But my mother was adamant I should go to university. I think they argued about that. I thought my mother had made a bad bargain. From an early age, I had wanted her to marry someone who would look after us. With the right new husband, she would not have to worry about money anymore and I could leave her safely. I didn't want to give up my future to look after her. Was that selfish?"

Bill thought her question rhetorical and said nothing.

"Debby was never a father figure," she continued. "There were times I longed for a proper father. I was envious of my friends because they all had a father..." she tailed off, then added pensively, "but you can't change anything."

Of course, they were both fatherless now, something else they had in common but that, Grace thought, should be left unsaid.

They meandered along by the stream, their conversation idle and mostly one-sided. Grace talked of her love of reading and of history; topics she knew would hold Bill's attention. She was keen to delve into Bill's politics to see if he shared some of her staunch Liberal views but she resisted. It was far too early in their relationship to explore what could be a contentious and divisive subject, albeit one close to her heart. He had given no hint of his political philosophies or where his political loyalties might lie. That would have to be for another day.

They stopped again by some excited young children who, with their parents, were watching a mallard paddling against the stream ducking among the yellow waterlilies looking for food. They strolled on mostly in silence this time, both of them content to let the sublimely peaceful scene wash over them, Grace holding on to the handlebars of Bill's bicycle, a surrogate for his arm. Eventually, Bill said he must go soon because he had told Mrs Batchelor he would be back for supper as he was on early shift in the morning.

As they left the meadows heading towards Tickford Street, Grace asked Bill how soon he thought the war might be over now that the Allies had broken out of the Normandy bridgehead and were heading for Paris. Her mind was not really on the outcome of the war and she was loath to spoil the idyll of the afternoon but she had an ulterior motive. She wanted to steer the conversation to what the future might hold for them both when victory was achieved. Everyone, she said, was talking about the war ending soon, but typically, Bill was non-committal and Grace, treading carefully, decided the topic was best left for now.

They came to a terrace of neat houses each with a bay window, each with a tiny low-walled front garden and path leading to the front door. One had a large plaque high up on the wall with some initials and the date 1912 which Bill assumed had been placed there by the proud builder. Grace stopped.

"This is where I live," she pointed to the house next door to the one with the plaque.

Bill had been nervous of this moment, not knowing what he should do when the time came to leave. Grace saved him.

"Thank you for a lovely time, Bill. You must go. I'll write."

She leant up on tip toe and pecked him on the cheek then bounded up to the front door, turned and waved, grinning like a schoolgirl, her eyes sparkling. Bill hesitated.

"Go!" she called waving him away.

He straddled his bike and pushed off, one hand on the handlebars, wobbling as he looked over his shoulder waving goodbye.

Tickford Street was long and straight. After a hundred yards or so he thought he ought to look back. She was gone.

He pedalled hard, back over Tickford Bridge towards Bletchley, pushing himself, enjoying the effort, the breeze on his face, concentrating on pedalling, on keeping up a steady cadence. The exercise and concentration was a way of avoiding thoughts of the afternoon, of the somewhat awkward goodbye. He had planned to write to Cedric that evening but Grace trumped Cedric in his thoughts. Even from afar, she seemed to command his attention. Instead of picking up pen and paper, he lay on his bed and stared at the ceiling.

What was it about her that diverted him? Sounds and images of the afternoon came into his head. Her soft lilting voice, her twinkling eyes and her infectious happiness all led to an emerging sense that she was different from anyone he had met before. At first, he was slow to recognise this sense and to gauge how and why she was different. Yes, she was a young lady. Up to now, all his friends had been young men, undergraduates or graduates, their friendship based on a love of mathematics. The only female in his life was his mother. But Grace was young, vibrant and erudite. She displayed, however, some of his mother's traits; she was gentle, understanding and undemanding. His mother was always very supportive, anticipated his needs and he knew she was forever protective, shielding him whenever she could from the many causes of his anxieties. He could see that Grace, on the other hand, was very softly leading him into new experiences he would otherwise have turned away from yet he felt safe in her hands. To that extent, he had learned to trust her. She had drawn aside just a little the curtain he usually hid behind and he could see there might be more for him out there if there was a steadying hand. Like this afternoon when he had talked to her in ways he had never spoken to anyone, not his closest friend, Cedric, let alone his mother. But, and it was a big but—his emotions were still confused.

At Trinity and in and around Cambridge, he had seen young men and women together, confident and relaxed in each other's company. They all seemed to know the unwritten rules of relationships. But he was ignorant and gauche and he did not know what to do about it. Despite a very pleasant afternoon, despite Grace offering new possibilities, part of him still urged withdrawal to safe, uncomplicated ground. Still, his father's death had changed things and he knew he should turn to face the world, be more self-reliant however much that had its difficulties. It began to dawn on him that Grace could help him in this unsettling transition. Indeed, she appeared to want to help him; the peck on the cheek was evidence of that. What should he do? The mist that had hitherto confounded his emotions had not really lifted much, if anything. He would let her take the next step if that was what she wanted. She said she will write. He will await her letter.

Later that evening, Grace opened her diary and wrote she was going to bed that night blissfully happy, happier than she had been in a long time; the reason: Bill.

Jim Wyllie came into Room 40 and strode purposefully across to where Bill was sitting.

"Morning Bill. I have a message from Gerry Morgan. John Tiltman has called what, I think, can be termed a crisis meeting on Tunny for after lunch and Gerry wants you there. Two o'clock."

"Yet another meeting!" said Bill, mildly irritated. "I'm not surprised, though, daily pattern changes mean we're struggling."

"By the way, Bill. You know the cryptography dictionary I was working on? Well, Professor Vincent has sent my draft to the States, to William Friedman no less. Imagine; my piece of work sent to the Chief Cryptanalyst of the US War Department! Apparently, they don't have anything like it over there. It's thought useful to have some common terminology apparently since we are both working so closely together."

"Well done, Jim. That's excellent news. You were, of course, the right man for the job."

"I'm told Mr Friedman was over here recently to have a look around."

"I know," said Bill. "I met him. I gave him a précis on Sturgeon."

"Hey, when was that. I would have liked to meet him!" said Jim in mock offence.

"I think you weren't around. He only had a few spare minutes."

"What was he like?"

"Rather like you would expect. Very perceptive. It was all very brief. You didn't miss much really."

"Huh!" muttered Jim continuing his sham displeasure as he turned to leave. "Don't forget," he added with wink. "Two o'clock."

"Gentlemen, thank you for coming," said the Brigadier opening the meeting. Round the room were, Max Newman and Jack Good from the Newmanry, Ralph Tester and Jerry Roberts from the Testery and Gerry Morgan and Bill from the Research Section.

"We seem to have run into the sand somewhat with Tunny output just at this important time when our service chiefs are hungry for ever more intelligence. I thought we should all get round the table to see what can be done. Do we need more people? Do we need more machines? Do we need to up our game on attacking Tunny? The problems are I believe for us to address here. I'm told Knockholt are still able to send us all the traffic we have asked for. The logjam is in the Newmanry as I understand it. Perhaps, Max you could outline the situation."

"Harold Kenworthy's team at Knockholt are doing everything we want," Max began. "All the improvements we introduced are working well. The tapes they send are good quality. The only issue there is, I believe, some messages with the autoclave limitation do not transmit well. That, of course, is a problem for the Germans too. As you know, the recent issue for us has been the Germans introducing, particularly on the western links, daily wheel pattern changes instead of monthly changes. Up till now, the tedious and time-consuming work that yielded a link's patterns allowed us to concentrate for the rest of the month on finding the chi settings for each message. Now that effort, if successful, yields a set of patterns for a single day restricting us to message setting for that day only before we have to attack another day's patterns, and so on. Before the change, we would often have to try several messages from several days at the beginning of the month to discover the month's patterns because not all messages were suitable for one reason or another. You can see that over the relatively short period these changes have been introduced, some of our workload has grown progressively thirty-fold. Added to that, the western links have also been employing the autoclave limitation, meaning depths are no longer available."

"Max," said the Brigadier, "remind us how we got to this state of affairs."

"Take Jellyfish, Berlin—Paris. We noticed a change of patterns on 14 June. On 18 June, we broke in again via a crib from the Bream link; the patterns had changed again and only messages of that day could be set. The same situation arose on 24 June and as no other days could be set on those patterns, we concluded daily wheel pattern changes were being made. One more Jellyfish day was solved, 25 June, which confirmed our earlier conclusion. Progressively, we ran into similar problems with other western links. A new one, Grilse between Berlin and somewhere in northern France, was broken on 21 June but attempts on subsequent days were unsuccessful despite some suitable messages, although traffic on this link has been light. Gurnard patterns changed on 1 July and have not yet been solved despite heavy traffic and suitable messages. And so on…"

What about the eastern links?" asked the Brigadier.

"Because of our inability to solve other links, we started work on the Tarpon link between Berlin and Bucharest and a large volume has been read providing very valuable intelligence. But we suspect from operators' chat that daily change of patterns is coming into effect on this link too. The Whiting link between Königsberg and Riga and Perch, the link to Lyck in East Prussia have been statistically broken. The traffic though on both links has been quiet. The Stickleback link to South Ukraine has been virtually dormant for a while but is showing signs of life again. Tarpon is the only one of these to use the autoclave limitation."

"What effect is all this having on you, Ralph?"

"Well, we've been decrypting the Tarpon traffic but little else. We've turned back to hand methods but that is totally impractical with daily pattern changes and the wide use of the autoclave limitation, particularly in the west, restricting depths. We've also looked at our 'dead ducks', those failed messages put on one side for a second look when time allowed. Output has, therefore, been frustratingly slow. Machine breaking is the only answer."

"Have we enough resources…? Ralph?"

"We can cope with the increased volumes with current staffing. I've about 20 cryptographers, about 30 setters including those on loan from the Research Section whom I should be able to release shortly as new recruits arrive, 35 decoding machine operators and about 30 others mostly engaged on registration and control of traffic. I can always do with a few more decoding machines; breakdowns cause delays even though I have six mechanics covering the three shifts. On recent experience, we need two new decoding machines for each new Colossus which I'm told should not be a problem."

"What about you, Max?"

"As you know, we have four production Robinsons and the third Colossus is up and running. Colossus Four is due later this month. We could always do with more Tunnies, of course. Block H is nearing completion and will have a teleprinter room to receive messages direct from Knockholt. We are up to 20 cryptographers, about half mathematicians from Oxford and Cambridge, and we should build up to about 180 specially chosen Wrens by the time Colossus Four arrives. Colossi are the key and with the Post Office's factory in Birmingham in full swing, we expect one a month from now on; a total of 12 have been ordered. Frankly, we could do with all 12 now as we're feverishly trying to break in somewhere."

"How do we unlock this logjam then? There is urgency here."

Bill could see Max Newman getting a little irritated at the Brigadier's persistence in pointing to the Newmanry as the problem. Bill knew Jack Good and Donald Michie were continually improving the statistically based Colossus routines to increase productivity and there was not much he could add to the immediate debate.

"Firstly," said Max, "Colossus Four will have the special rectangling gadget; that will double our rectangling capacity. There is a proposal for Colossus Six to have a bedstead capable of taking messages 26,000 characters long which would be used almost exclusively for rectangling. The starting and converging of rectangles is taking a great deal of our time and energy at the moment. So, we're also looking at both ends of the rectangling routines, improving significance tests and convergence techniques. Colossus Six, when it's here, should be able to print a rectangle in about 15 minutes, a step change. In the meantime, crude convergence by hand still seems the way to go, although we're continually looking at our processes to improve our start points. As you know, the starting point for crude convergence is critical to success. I have also asked Walter Fried to see if Washington can possibly help operationally with rectangle analysis but I need to know more about their set up over there. Despite the setbacks, I believe, this month, we should get back to near May levels."

"Gerry," the Brigadier said inviting Gerry Morgan for his views.

"Well, with most of my staff on loan to the Testery, I have no capacity to devise alternative attacks. In any case, we don't have the luxury of time. Bill, do you have anything to add?"

Bill had half been expecting this.

"Nothing to help the immediate situation I'm afraid," he said, "but I expect, Jack, you have in mind converging rectangles on Colossus which is, after all, an iterative process ideal for a machine. Not for now," he added, "but for some point in the future when you have the capacity, I contemplate Colossus could be set up to find both psi and motor wheel patterns and settings."

"Indeed," said Jack. "We can converge on Colossus at the moment but given the exponential increase in our workload, until Colossus Six arrives, we are restricted largely to hand convergence at which our girls are very good. As to psi and motor breaking and setting, yes you know I share your view that that should be the ultimate goal of Colossus and I believe it is attainable."

"Gerry," said the Brigadier with a thought. "Could Sturgeon bridge the gap?"

Bill's ears pricked up.

"The short answer is no," said Gerry firmly. "There simply is not the time to develop from where we left it to making it routine. I gather that Max's team did run a statistical test to differentiate Tunny from Sturgeon but it needed about 40,000 characters to produce significant results but this figure might vary widely. A positive result, I understand, would safely lead to the conclusion that the traffic was Tunny. To conclude the converse, that random scores were Sturgeon, would be highly dangerous. That's about the only progress on Sturgeon. Is that right Max?"

"Yes. We have to stick with Tunny and mining the flexibility of Colossus is the only way forward."

There was a lull, the others expecting the Brigadier to close the meeting.

"You know," expressed Max to no one in particular, nodding his head slightly as though he had just thought of something profound, "this thing could do logical operations!"

Bill caught his breath at Max's prophesy. It was almost a throw-away remark but it struck home to Bill that Max was talking about applications for Colossus much, much wider than its current use, way beyond the confines of Bletchley Park and codebreaking. Logical operations could mean almost anything. Was he thinking of the universal computing machine that Bill had read about in Alan Turing's paper, *On Computable Numbers*?

For Bill, Max's remark was seminal, reminding him of the last line of a sonnet by Keats, 'Silent, upon a peak in Darien', a metaphor for an awestruck moment of revelation.

Chapter 14
End in Sight

Tom Colvill came into Room 40.

"Listen for a moment, please," he called out causing everyone to stop and look up at this unusual interruption.

"Some of you may know that Major Tester was taken unwell earlier. I'm sure you want to know he is all right. He passed out at his desk but came round quite quickly and was taken to sick bay as a precaution. I am glad to say it seems nothing more than exhaustion. He had been working a double shift today and had not eaten properly. I'm pleased to tell you that he is recovering well but understandably, the matron has ordered him to take a few days' rest. I'm sure we all wish him well."

Tom paused.

"Whilst I have your attention, let me say this. As we all know, for the last few months, the work has been more urgent than usual, demanding great concentration. Despite the recent encouraging news of tanks entering Paris and of Romania swapping sides, I expect our heavy workload to continue. Together, with the Newmanry, we are beginning to get on top of the daily pattern changes and I expect this month's decodes to be nearly back to May and June levels. And we have more wheel setters arriving which will help, even though we will see those from the Research Section gradually return. But I think the episode with the Major should serve as a reminder that over-working ourselves can be counter-productive. Some of you, I know, have been working 60-hour weeks. So, I encourage you to vacate your shifts promptly after handing over, to take proper breaks and get some fresh air, to eat properly and to look out for your colleagues. Anyway, the Major should be back with us in a few days. If his absence gives anyone any problems, come and see me. That's all everyone."

The word about Major Tester had, of course, got around.

"That's good news at least," said Tubby Roots. "He'll be back, imperturbable as ever no doubt. Looks, Bill, as though you are heading back to the Research Section."

"All good things come to an end," said Bill dryly.

"How is your mother?" enquired Mrs Batchelor at supper. "I hope you don't mind my asking but I couldn't help noticing one of the letters for you today was from Newmarket. I assumed it was from your mother. I think of her quite a lot and wonder how she is coping. It's so hard."

"She says she is managing," said Bill, "but then she always makes light of things. I wish I could get over to see her but it's difficult at the moment. Hopefully, we can have more time off soon. My sister-in-law visits her quite regularly as they are not far away and takes the children over at weekends and in the school holidays. But she writes the evenings are long."

"What will she do? Will she live on her own?" asked Mrs Batchelor who usually made a point of not being nosy with her guests. She was, nevertheless, kind-hearted and had taken to the quiet and respectful Bill whom she felt sorry for in his loss.

"I don't know," said Bill considering what to answer. "She says it's too early to decide."

"Of course," said Mrs Batchelor understandingly. "Please give her my regards when you next write."

Later in his room, Bill read his mother's letter a second time. Despite her words, it was clear she was struggling to come to terms with the loss of his father. Lola was being good visiting with the children, she wrote. But no mention of Joe visiting; was he reading too much into that? Interestingly, there was mention of Arthur Brett who was a regular lay preacher at the local church. His mother had often said how much she admired his preaching. Apparently, he had visited her several times which she said gave her great comfort. Prompted by the content of his mother's letter and now that he had returned to the Research Section, Bill felt he could perhaps ask for a day's special leave in order to go over to Cheveley.

That day, there had been two letters on the hall table when he had got in. The other one was from Cedric. At once, Bill felt a little guilty since he had not written to him for a while. Work had been draining and whilst he had thought of a few interesting maths topics to share with Cedric, he had not put pen to paper. Cedric began his letter with a tongue-in-cheek admonishment for the lack of correspondence from Bill and then rather surprised Bill with what followed. He wrote he was becoming deeply interested in the potential of scientific and academic approaches to the study of conflict. It was something he wanted to pursue. *Typical of Cedric*, thought Bill, *immersing himself totally in his ideas*.

The next day, Bill was in the site's Post Office to buy some stamps and some postal orders, intending to reply that evening to his mother's letter, when there was a tap on his shoulder. He looked round to see the cheery face of Jack Good.

"Bill. I'm glad I spotted you. Are you coming to the Chess Club tonight? I haven't seen you for a while?"

"Shift working, Jack, I'm afraid, but I'm back in the Research Section now. Yes, I'll come along. Be good to have a change."

"Excellent," said Jack. "Actually, if you have a few moments when you're finished here, we could take a stroll. I have something to ask."

"All right," said Bill intrigued as to what Jack wanted.

They meandered towards the lake. Jack politely enquired how Bill and his family were after his father's death before coming to the point.

"What I wanted to ask," he said, "is whether you have given any more thought to your rectangling technique? Donald and I have made quite a lot of progress on improving statistical tests for significance and convergence, often based on the study of language characteristics. Interestingly, the language characteristics of some links tend to make them more favourable than others; even one end of a link can have more favourable language characteristics compared to the other end of the same link. I wondered if you had any more thoughts on rectangling that could help us improve early selection of messages. We just don't have the time to devote to it ourselves. Oh, by the way," he continued in a hushed tone, "we've been told to keep ultra-quiet about rectangling on Colossus. I guess because it's so vital."

"Hmm," pondered Bill. "I've been thinking about some of the things Max said at that recent meeting. But I've not had time to develop anything since. I'll talk with Gerry to see if he is agreeable to me looking at it."

"No, no!" Jack said quickly. He was tempted to ask what Bill had in mind but held back knowing Bill would want to progress his ideas before revealing them. "Hold on. We'd better go through Max first. He's a bit touchy at the moment. Yesterday, some of the Post Office engineers setting up for the next Colossus were larking around and Max stormed out of his room and gave them a right tongue-wagging. Leave it to me. We'd better go through the proper channels but it's helpful to know you have something."

"I'll wait then," acknowledged Bill. "See you later at the Chess Club."

That evening, he was matched against a newcomer to the Chess Club who took white and opened with pawn to King four. Not sure how competent the newcomer was, Bill commenced with the Sicilian Defence, played cautiously and won quite easily in the end.

"Winning ways again, Bill, I see" said Jack coming over. "By the way, I forgot to tell you earlier some very disappointing news. I'm told the Bletchley Park Home Guard has been disbanded which means we won't be called upon to defend the realm. We all have to hope Mr Hitler doesn't hear the realm is defenceless!"

Gerry Morgan agreed a day and a half leave so Bill got home to Cheveley at dusk on the Friday. His mother, having received his letter saying he had been granted leave to come home, was expecting him and was obviously pleased and heartened to see him. Bill though was tentative, unsure how to deal with his now widowed mother, uncertain about referring to his father in case it upset her yet it seemed unavoidable. The house was tidy as always but Bill had misgivings whether his mother could manage the large cottage garden, the province of his father in which he had taken great pride.

The visit had an awkwardness Bill found difficult. They talked of mundane things, hardly mentioning his father. Lola came over with the children and Bill took the opportunity to escape for a while saying he was going for a short walk down the lane. Jeanne volunteered to go with him which he was happy with but Joey irritatingly moped about not wanting to do anything. Later when Lola and the children had left, Bill was able to raise the issue of money. His mother assured him she was managing for now and did not want to take any major decisions just yet. She had, however, been to see Mr Ennion, the solicitor, who would deal with the will and transfer the cottage deeds into her name. It seemed very grand, she said coyly, to be seeing a solicitor but his father had always insisted on dealing with financial matters properly. Interestingly, his mother mentioned again how kind Arthur Brett, the preacher, had been with his pastoral visits.

Going to bed that night, Bill rather dreaded leaving in the morning but he need not have worried. His mother insisted she was fine and he should make sure he did not miss his train. Asked whether his brother, Joe, would be coming over, his mother said she thought he was on overtime but her tone suggested she believed the excuse contrived. She reluctantly accepted Bill's postal orders as he left for the train; he said he felt better helping her with a bit of money as he could do little else for her as things stood. In the end, his mother made saying goodbye almost as easy as before and on the train, Bill was content, glad he had made the effort. He had planned to say nothing of Grace and kept to his plan. Mentioning Grace would only lead to a whole host of questions.

No instructions came to review rectangling, instead Gerry Morgan asked Bill to help Captain Walter Fried prepare a report on Sturgeon to send to Washington. Captain Fried had sent some earlier miscellaneous observations on Sturgeon but now Washington had asked for a more formal report. It was abundantly clear to Bill that Walter Fried had a strong grasp of the topic and needed little help. Nevertheless, it was interesting to work closely with Walter, a graduate from Harvard and Columbia Law School. He had a lawyerly penchant for clarity and detail of which Bill approved. They got on well, although Bill was a little annoyed he was left to do much of the drafting after they had agreed the structure of the report. Walter said he needed to continue writing his regular Washington reports, some of which, entitled 'Fish Notes', were updates on the progress against Tunny that Bill was able to read. They were very detailed and he found them a useful way of keeping abreast of Tunny developments. One set of regular statistics that particularly interested him showed that more than half the days solved were by his rectangling method but success appeared to be directly related to a high number of inactive pins on the small motor wheel, though not exclusively. When the dottage, as it was called, was low, other methods such as cribs and dragging appeared to succeed better. Could this data, he wondered, feature in his considerations on refining rectangling techniques?

"Bill, I'm over here!" called Grace.

Bill looked across the canteen to where the voice came from. He smiled at seeing her but was somewhat embarrassed making his way over, although fortunately no one in the busy canteen paid any attention to them lunching together.

"I'm so glad we can meet up like this now you are not on shifts," said Grace enthusiastically. "You got my letter then. I was afraid it might not be delivered in time. What do you want to eat? There's chicken pie today."

They met for lunch several days that week, afterwards strolling round the site perimeter. Grace had been making plans which she delicately dropped into the conversation bit by bit. There was another country dancing evening coming up; they could go together, she suggested. He bargained. He would accompany her on the basis he would only be required to join in two dances. Three, she countered. He gave in. Another day, she mentioned there was an organised hike due soon and could swap a shift if needed. The trip did not particularly appeal to Bill and he suggested an alternative day out in Cambridge, a Rolf Noskwith suggestion he remembered, just the two of them. He could show her the colleges and the other sights.

"That's a lovely idea," she said so pleased he had put forward an alternative outing of his own. They set a date for the next Sunday they could both make.

In Cambridge, Grace was utterly enthralled the whole day. They walked around the city, along The Backs by the river and spent an hour in the Fitzwilliam Museum which had managed to keep five galleries open despite the war. Grace was in awe at the gilded splendour of the Fitzwilliam's interior. Bill, however, was peeved to discover he had missed an exhibition of 'Greek Art from 3,000 BC to the Present' held at the Museum in May and June only. As they left the Fitzwilliam, Bill pointed to a building down on the other side of the road, saying it was Addenbrooke's Hospital where his friend, Cedric, worked. Grace immediately wanted to know more about Cedric and when Bill gave her a potted history, she promptly wanted to meet this conscientious objector hospital porter with a PhD. Hopefully, they could meet in the not too distant future, Bill had said dangling the possibility. They headed towards Trinity College where on arrival Bill pointed out the statue of the college founder, Henry VIII, above the arch of the Great Gate. Bill caught sight of Harry, the gate porter and steered Grace over to his lodge.

"Young Mr Tutte!" exclaimed Harry. "How wonderful to see you. I heard you had gone to do some war work. Are you back now? Who is this young lady?"

"Hello, Harry. This is Grace, a work colleague. I'm showing her around Cambridge. Sadly, my war work continues but I hope to be back as soon as I can."

"I see from my list you have been elected a Fellow, Mr Tutte. Congratulations!"

"May we just look around a little?" asked Bill politely. It always paid to be on good terms with the porter.

"Of course, of course. Nice to meet you, Grace."

"You too, Harry," said Grace smiling broadly. Harry too smiled; he enjoyed seeing his young men with a nice young lady on their arm.

Grace felt Bill's hand gently usher her forward. As the two of them moved under the archway of the imposing Great Gate, Grace was stunned into silence at the beauty and the elegance of the Great Court. The aura of the place was overwhelming. She looked up at Bill as if to say she could hardly believe her eyes and then gazed around again, taking in the large open court with its lawns and ornate fountain centrepiece. She hardly noticed the small knots of students in earnest conversation or others hurrying along with arms full of books and notes. They spent a few quiet minutes in the Chapel then crossed the Great Court, through a passage into the cloistered Nevile's Court where Bill pointed out the stunning Wren Library and where he had his room.

"You had rooms up there!" Grace could hardly believe Bill could have lived in such grand and prestigious surroundings.

"The rooms are quite spartan, actually," said Bill playing it down.

"But it must have been inspiring to study here," said Grace still breathless.

"I suppose so," replied Bill with predictable understatement.

On the train back to Bletchley, Grace was full of the visit, wanting to know more of everything, Trinity College, Bill's studies, Cedric, Harry the porter. Bill delighted in seeing Grace so happy that he did not mind her questions which he answered patiently. Recalling the meeting with Harry, yet another question formed in Grace's mind but one she hesitated to pose. Nonetheless, she felt driven to ask it because the answer, whatever it was, might be significant for her own post-war plans. When she judged the moment right, she made the question sound as casual as she could.

"You said to Harry that you hoped to return there as soon as you can. Is that what you plan to do? Do you know when?"

She held her breath.

"I don't suppose anything will happen before the war ends," Bill said thoughtfully. "The Fellowship makes it very easy for me to go back to finish my doctorate so I guess that is what I will do. I would consider, though, something along the lines of what I'm doing now, some sort of research role if there was one."

"Oh," said Grace not expecting the second half of his reply. Then regaining her composure, added, "I don't know what I'll do but I'll need to earn a living somehow. I have become used to having my independence so I know I don't want to go home. How much longer do you think the war will last?"

"It's impossible to say, hopefully, not too much longer. Perhaps, the end is in sight."

After that they passed the journey more in reflection of a day packed with raptures for her and pleasant distractions for him.

When the train drew into Bletchley Station, however, and the time came to say goodbye, Bill's deep-seated anxieties returned to the fore. But again, Grace made it easy. Hurriedly, she thanked him for a wonderful, wonderful day, leant up, pecked him on the cheek like before and skipped off to catch her bus.

On his way to his digs, Bill was surprised to find himself thinking about Grace, that without really realising it she had edged more and more into his consciousness, displacing to a degree his mother. He could not help thinking his mother was now a cause for his concern since his father's death rather than as hitherto a stable source of care and comfort. Grace, on the other hand, was undemanding, fresh and lively in an innocent sort of way. His confidence was boosted, like today, just by being with her. Her bright eyes and smile appealed to him, lightening his mood when she was around. She was on an intellectual par, knowledgeable on topics that interested him. Today, they had discussed art, history, architecture, the value of academic study and much else. And she had a command of English he envied. All so different from the conversations he had with his mother when he was last home. That Grace was affectionate was both flattering and a problem. Here was someone else who cared for him, albeit cared for him in a different way from his mother. But the idea of reciprocating, which he knew he should, made him freeze, his brain seemed to block all action and he did not know how to unpick the lock, to unfreeze. That was his only anxiety with Grace but an anxiety that loomed larger the longer the relationship went on. He somehow knew he had a responsibility to respond and that he risked everything if he did not but to him, it was an impenetrable emotional fog. Unable to find a way through this fog by himself, faint-heartedly, fatalistically he knew he was abrogating responsibility for their future; that their future lay in Grace's hands. He wished it was not so, but it was.

That night, Grace opened her diary wondering where to start as she had so much she wanted to record. She hesitated. The events of the day, so many, were still spinning around in her head. There was just too much to write tonight, she concluded, too much. It would be a jumble and a horrible mess. A considered account could wait till tomorrow; tonight's entry would be a distillation, the essence of the day. She thought for a few moments then wrote:

'Watershed day! Bill without doubt fitting my long-imagined cloak for him. Conducted me into his dreamy world with a gentle hand in the small of my back.

Truly believe our lives tessellate—a unity in joy of life, birth and death, the trinity of even the lowest human being. Dearest Bill, sleep very contented. I will.'

On Monday morning, Captain Walter Fried approached Bill's table accompanied by a civilian.

"Bill, meet Albert Small. He will be taking over from me and will nominally be with the Newmanry."

Albert Small was anything but small, as tall as Bill and confident looking as most of the Americans were. They shook hands.

"Albert had a big hand in our breaking the Japanese Purple code," said Walter endowing Albert with authoritative credentials. "I have to go to Paris tomorrow but I'll read your draft Sturgeon piece before I go and Albert can send it off. He's tasked with doing a full report on Tunny and I've said you are the man! Meanwhile, thanks for all your help, Bill. I may be back but can't be sure. I'll leave you with Albert."

"I'm really interested in this machine effort on Tunny, Bill. I gather you kicked the whole thing off," said Albert in his heavy accent.

"Sort of," said Bill modestly.

"Hey, a bit more than that, I'm told. Anyway, Bill I'll come and see you shortly. I was supposed to have a month's handover with Walter but that's been blown out of the water. Guess that's how it goes in this business."

Typical self-assured American, thought Bill, but being involved with Purple granted Albert Small immediate respect. It seemed to Bill that all the best American cryptanalysts were over here at Bletchley Park.

A few days later, the Sturgeon report was sent to Washington. Bill, still hoping for a resurrection of Sturgeon, suggested to Albert some wording for the covering memorandum to the effect that there was a great need for a statistical method of solution and for a test to differentiate Sturgeon traffic from Tunny traffic. Albert duly obliged.

Bill made his way over to the canteen to meet Grace. He put his coat on as the early November mild spell had been overtaken by weather more common to late autumn. To his surprise, Grace was waiting outside the canteen door, well to one side. He could not see her face properly as she was looking at the ground, her shoulders hunched. He sensed something was wrong.

"Grace, are you all right?"

She looked up. Her eyes were red, her cheeks blotchy and her expression sad.

"What is it?" asked Bill urgently. He had expected her all excited at the prospect of the dance at the end of the week. Now concerned, his own amiable mood drained away and his heart beat faster with apprehension, perplexed that what was wrong might be due to him in some way.

She reached a hand out.

"I don't want to talk here," she snuffled, taking Bill by the hand and leading him towards a bench overlooking the lawns. As they sat down, Grace still held his hand, the physical contact making Bill quite self-conscious but he made no move. His heart though beat erratically as the emotional fog started to come down. She looked up at him, her eyes welling.

"I've been promoted," she blurted out, then stopped to blow her nose.

This announcement puzzled Bill even more. This was good news surely?

Grace began to pour her heart out.

"But I have to move to an outstation in north London. I've been made a team leader to replace the civilian team leader there. I have to leave tomorrow. Oh, Bill. I don't want to go. I don't want to leave you. I don't want to leave my friends. I don't know what to do. Tell me I don't have to go. I don't even know where this place is. I'm supposed to report there tomorrow at one o'clock. What am I to do? I don't even know if I can be a team leader or want to be a team leader. Even if I do go, I might not like it there. Then what? And if the war is over by Christmas as people are saying, it will all have been a waste of time."

Fearing far worse news, Bill began to relax, found himself calming down, moving into analysis mode. What were the facts here, what were the options?

"What have they told you?" he asked as calmly as he could.

"They said I have to go."

"Have you said you don't want to?"

Bill sensed she was becoming a little less agitated. She sniffed and blew her nose once more.

"Sort of but they said I must go immediately. It's a requirement of my employment, they said. They have been very nice. They said the outstation is very good and I will be fine there. We all have to serve where we are needed, they said. It may not be for too long, they said, if the war ends soon but until then there is still a lot to do. I said, can't someone else go but they said no. What am I to do, Bill? I don't want to go."

"I suppose they are having to move people around all the time so I guess it is within their powers to do so. If you point blank refused, what would happen then do you think?"

"I presume they may ask me to leave or try to send me somewhere else to punish me. I knew they had these outstations but I've not been to any. Have you, Bill? Perhaps you don't even know about them."

"I was aware there were some but don't really know what they do," said Bill being circumspect. "I believe they're not far away; north London is not that far."

"I don't want to start all over again. I've come to value my friends here. And I don't want to be away from you. Am I being abominably egoistic and selfish?" she said looking up at him with doleful eyes.

"What choice do you think you have?" asked Bill getting to the crux of the issue but wanting her to come to the realisation herself that she had to go to north London or else face the possibility of an equally unpalatable sanction.

Grace sniffed and dabbed her eyes before answering.

"I suppose I must go," she said lowering her voice in resignation. "But if I go now, we will miss the dance. I was so looking forward to that."

Bill was relieved she was coming round to the only obvious solution.

"You will write to me, Bill? Won't you? We could still meet up, maybe in London."

"Of course," he said reassuringly.

He realised she was again holding his hand, now in both of hers as if doing so would prevent them from being parted.

"Oh, Bill. It will be all right, won't it? I guess some families are terribly split up so we must make the best of it, don't you think?" she added the last few words wanting his confirmation their relationship will continue.

"Of course," Bill repeated.

"I must get back. They have given me some time off to pack. I will write as soon as I get there. Dear Bill, I don't know what I'd do without you. Walk me to the bus please," she asked her eyes welling up again.

Grace linked her arm in his as they walked to the bus. On the way, as if to bolster her decision, Bill said that taking up a more responsible position would stand her in good stead for a post-war job. Begrudgingly, she expected he was right.

This time, the kiss on his cheek lingered a little longer than her previous pecks. She climbed aboard and sat at a window near him looking through the misty window pane. He waved as the bus pulled away. She looked back sorrowfully, managing only a feeble wave until the bus turned out of sight.

Bill looked at his watch. There was just time to run back to the canteen to grab a sandwich before he was due back. It was not until much later that he reflected on the emotionally charged lunchtime drama. In all, he judged, the outcome was as satisfactory as was possible. Grace quite obviously had no choice but to take up her promotion. For once though he had not shied away from an upsetting and fraught situation, indeed, he felt he had conducted himself commendably, unused as he was to dealing with someone as distressed and as tearful as Grace had been. He was not sure, however, what would happen now between him and Grace. Fate would have to take its course.

Grace wrote in her diary that night:

'This war with all its universal sorrows set Bill and me together and has now set us apart. Are we strong enough to overcome? The answer must be yes. But I set out tomorrow full of trepidation.'

At last, Bill was granted time to look at possible developments to rectangling. A request had come through from Max Newman to see if Bill could come up with something better than the current approach to rectangling, particularly the vital start to crude convergence. At last, he was reverting to his true vocation as he saw it, pure research, though within the tight brief given to him by Gerry Morgan.

Bill began by reviewing the current situation which was still based on his original rectangling discovery of recording data in the 1,271 cells of a rectangle representing 41 rows and 31 columns which in turn represented the first two chi wheels of the Tunny machine. He also studied a paper written earlier in the year by an American cryptanalyst, George Vergine before he came over from Washington to join the Newmanry, which proposed a purely theoretical, statistical approach to the problem. Some work had been done on it in the Newmanry but a fresh eye, it was thought, could be beneficial as Colossus was being used more and more. Not being a statistician, Bill was interested in the principle behind George Vergine's approach and immediately saw its potential.

It was well-known that for the convergence of a rectangle to be successful, a high degree of correctness was needed in that first set of delta chi two assumptions. The question was how could George Vergine's principle be applied to better the correctness of original assumptions? The issue ticked over in his mind as he walked to his lodgings in time for supper.

The expected letter from Grace had duly arrived letting Bill know her new address, some nondescript unit in Stanmore. He smiled when he saw how she had addressed him, changing from, 'Dear Bill' in previous letters to, 'Dearest Bill'. The body of the letter was by contrast downbeat. This place, she wrote, was more like a military base with uniformed Wrens on parade when she arrived. Her description was of a large site of depressing single story, utility buildings of zero architectural value. She admitted to being very nervous meeting her team but found them pleased to see her, as it became apparent her predecessor was not well liked. The whole unit was, she said, very busy and efficient with the Wrens doing the work and her team of young ladies supervising the shifts, helping solve any problems. We few civilians, she wrote, each have a room in a wing of the accommodation block but, she proclaimed, the place was soulless. The letter concluded in sombre tone with her expressing doubts she would be happy there.

Oh, dear, thought Bill, he hoped she had not set her mind against the move, determined not to make it work. What she described though was a significant change from the surroundings and atmosphere of Bletchley Park. When he replied, he wrote that he trusted her first impressions would not be lasting, recalling the experience of his first days at Trinity College.

In the morning, Bill set his mind to the convergence problem. He deduced the key to the issue would be to improve both the quality and the quantity of the data by selecting different parameters than was currently the case. Current practice was to select a row with a relatively large number of cells containing big scores, plus or minus, then secondly by selecting from that row six, seven or maybe more cells with the largest majorities. Depending on the plus or minus sign of a chosen majority score, a dot or cross assignment was made for the delta chi two sign for its respective column in order to commence the convergence. He was aware some variations on that method for assumed start points had been tried operationally.

Eventually, after much thought, pacing around, twiddling his pencil and staring out of the window, he devised a hypothesis based very largely on the theoretical fundamental of George Vergine's paper. Firstly though, to improve the quantity of data under initial analysis, he set his attention to the 41-cell columns instead of the 31-cell rows which immediately increased the initial set of data under scrutiny by a third. The second and most important element of his hypothesis aimed to improve the quality of data. His proposal was to pair columns, but to pair all 31 columns with each other was, he deemed, unnecessary and far too onerous. An initial selection of eight or nine columns could be made, again using high totals as a guide. By taking one pair of columns and multiplying each cell of one column by its corresponding cell of the other column, he could produce a product. Summing the products of pairs of columns produced an estimated numerical magnitude of the level of agreement between them. Entering these summations into a matrix representing the pairing of all the selected columns enabled the selection of the highest total, row or column, to provide a set of assignments for the delta chi two signs relative to those columns. Bill knew there was a mathematical justification for this treatment.

He set about testing it with a real example of a recent message of nearly 13,000 characters, the wheel patterns of which were certain. He laboriously created a rectangle by hand giving him ten elements within each cell, a favourable number for a successful rectangle. Next, he worked out the various summations and multiplications. For most people, such tedious work was boring but Bill was still content to apply himself to long periods of concentration. When he compared the result to the known patterns and to assumptions under the current method, he sat back with a quiet sense of satisfaction. The result was a definite improvement.

"What have you got?" asked Gerry Morgan.

"Well," said Bill knowing he was talking to a mathematician, "my hypothesis was to take pairs of rectangle columns, treat them as vectors and find scalar products to estimate the level of agreement between the selected columns. The result of an initial trial was satisfactory. More tests should be undertaken to validate the results but maybe these should be done in the Newmanry."

"Interesting," commented Gerry. "I agree it should be taken to the Newmanry. Excellent as usual, Bill."

"Any credit should really go to George Vergine," said Bill being typically unpretentious. "It was his paper that put me on the path."

"That and your graph theory, Bill; vectors, scalar products. Why don't you go over to the Newmanry and show George Vergine?"

"I will. His paper may have other applications."

Bill managed to get home for Christmas but just for a couple of days. It was not a happy time. He and his mother went to Joe and Lola's for Christmas Day. The adults made the best of the less than festive atmosphere; only the children were in the Christmas spirit eagerly awaiting the treats from Uncle Bill. Bill was glad to get back but in leaving his mother, it saddened him to think she must be anxious about her future. Nevertheless, he had a date with Grace to look forward to on the following Sunday, New Year's Eve in London.

They met outside Westminster Underground Station opposite Big Ben and walked along the Embankment under the bare plane trees. Despite the bright sunshine, it was bitterly cold. Grace linked her arm tightly in his, snuggling up to him delighting in being just like all of the other young couples strolling along in holiday mood. When they sat on one of the bench seats overlooking the river, Grace gave Bill a late Christmas present, a wrist watch in a presentation case. He said it was a grand present but she should not have spent so much money. He put it on. His old watch which he kept in a pocket had seen better days, the strap long lost, the glass discoloured and scratched. She said she liked giving presents. Gingerly, Bill pulled out from his inside coat pocket a little box of a similar size and self-consciously offered it to her. She smiled in surprise not expecting Bill to have thought of a present for her. It was a fountain pen in green. She looked into his eyes.

"It's beautiful!"

"For your poetry," he said hesitantly by way of explanation for his choice.

Originally, he had bought her a paisley-patterned, cotton scarf helped by a lady assistant in a shop in Bletchley. But seeing Grace today enveloped in a copious, multicoloured muffler, he was glad he had changed his mind and had given the scarf to his mother for Christmas. Grace had wrapped her bulky, woollen scarf several times round under her chin, trapping her shoulder length hair, pushing it up and giving her a different look. He smiled at seeing her so happy.

"I love it," she said. "It will be my special poetry pen. Thank you, Bill."

She pecked him on the cheek, pleased more than for the present itself but that Bill had been thinking of her enough to buy her something. Although she had a favourite pen for writing letters and her diary, she vowed to devote Bill's pen to composing poetry, endowing it with the prospect of inspiration.

They strolled on some more. Grace talked almost without stopping. She had settled more at the outstation but was still unhappy. It was not the people she worked with, more the place. It was totally devoid of any soul, unlike 'where you are, Bill', she said, which had a wonderful, academia-like feel to it where there was a sense of very important, even vital, work going on in the next room, the next hut, everywhere around you. It was not to say the work at the outstation was not important but having been 'where you are' she now felt out on a limb. She hated the way the unit was run on military lines, although one benefit, she said, was the few civilians were not required to contribute to their accommodation or food. That meant she could save a lot towards the time the war ended, which she hoped would be soon despite the German offensive in the densely forested Ardennes. On the way back to Westminster Underground Station, Grace wanted to ask Bill if he had settled his post-war plans but did not feel she should push the matter. Once more, Grace made their parting easy. She wished him a Happy New Year and after her usual peck on the cheek, quickly said she had a leaders' meeting 'at your place' soon so they could meet then. Before he could say anything, she had turned and disappeared into the crowds.

On the train back to Stanmore, Grace was floating on air. What, she mused, would she write in her diary later? Phrases came into her mind; 'New Year', 'new beginning; war ends', 'peace at last; et des questions pour moi?' 'A new job?' 'Where?' 'New friends?' 'And what of Bill???'

Bill too, on the train out of Euston, reflected on what 1945 might bring. For him, Cambridge probably; family-wise the picture was less clear. But when he thought about the future for him and Grace, the emotional fog descended once more.

"Ah, Gerry," said the Brigadier. "Take a seat and have a look at this."

Gerry Morgan took the telegram. It was from Washington dated 5th January 1945 signed 'Rowlett' asking for any help the Brigadier could provide in the urgent task of exploiting a breakthrough they had just achieved with the code called GEE.

"It seems at long last," said the Brigadier, "the Americans have had some success against GEE, the German Diplomatic one-time pad they had abandoned in 1940 but started to make some progress on last year. Frank Rowlett is Chief of the General Cryptanalytic Branch under Friedman. I've been considering Frank's request since his telegram arrived earlier today. I'm minded to offer him as much resource as we can muster, Gerry because I feel the potential intelligence value of this outweighs most if not all our present activities. This is, I think, particularly so for GEE traffic between Berlin and Tokyo in an effort to uncover all possible military information before the end of the Japanese War. I would be prepared to drop all my Japanese Naval code work. What can we do, and in a hurry?"

"Well, I guess we can divert practically everyone if needed. With your people that would be about 30 in all. Berkley Street would need to be on board and Freddie Freeborn too, his punch card Hollerith machines would be essential, I think, for us to be effective."

"I agree," said the Brigadier. "GEE is a five-figure additive code. Who have we got who is familiar with that?

"Well, Bill Tutte did some work on Floradora back in the beginning of the Research Section. There may be others. What is this American breakthrough, do you think?"

"The German Foreign Office use the same code book for GEE and Floradora with about 57,000 words, numbers, dates, etcetera allocated a five-digit number. We know pretty much all of that code book from earlier work on Floradora which has been read fully for about 18 months now. In GEE, they add another five-digit number, non-carrying. So, the breakthrough is on that additive. Originally, the Americans thought the additive was random but late last year, they appear to have identified some patterns. I'll talk to Berkley Street, Freddie and Commander Travis and let you know."

At the beginning of February, the Brigadier called Gerry and Bill to a review meeting. By then the GEE traffic had been divided between the Brigadier's team working on the traffic between Berlin and Tokyo and the Research Section who were looking at the European traffic, principally between Berlin and Madrid and Lisbon.

"Two major pieces of news," announced the Brigadier who was very obviously in a buoyant mood. "Firstly, I have been able to send to our Washington friends at Arlington Hall the first few wheel patterns which should lead to the solution of a large part of the material passing between Berlin and Tokyo. I got it before the Americans!" His eyes had a triumphal twinkle. "Now the other piece of my news is really quite remarkable. If you remember the Americans originally believed the additive to be random from a one-time pad. Well, you have to hand it to the Americans, they have all but worked out how the additive was generated. And now we can tell them exactly how it was generated," he said with glee. "Some clever soul in London has dug up an old record of an interview with a Mr Lorant of a London firm of engineers called Loranco Ltd. Apparently, he sold the German Government several machines between 1925 and 1932 that could produce the sheets of what the Americans thought were random five digit numbers, like those on a one-time pad found on an agent in the Panama Canal in 1940."

"Wasn't that Floradora material?" asked Bill recalling a conversation with Patricia Bartley just after he had joined.

"Yes," said the Brigadier, "that capture was mostly Floradora but there were also 3,600 pages of one-time pad, eight rows of six five digit numbers per page, just like Mr Lorant's machine with its 240 printing wheels could make. I have a copy of the interview for you. Have a read, it's a pretty ingenious machine but a machine nevertheless and the numbers must, therefore, be subject to a pattern. What progress with the European traffic, Gerry?"

"It has been slow going to start with but with the help of Mr Freeborn's team, we think we have identified five different arrangements of the same set of 240 wheels. We're looking at three at the moment, working on the wheel sequences and wheel arrangements. Cribs are being particularly useful as the German Foreign Office seems to insist on stereotyping the beginning and ending of messages; an example of the German mind-set helping us. For instance, all messages from Berlin end with a cipher made up of an additive and the number '00019' being the code for the plain text signature 'Foreign Office'. '00007' is another useful one meaning 'Period Paragraph'. Mr Freeborn's team also help us identify depths. It's a slog but once we have a start the work becomes quicker."

"We need to press on, Gerry. Keep me in touch please."

Bill took the interview report. Later as he read it, he did, indeed, think Mr Lorant's machine was ingenious. In essence, it was like a machine for printing consecutive numbers but with very marked differences. It could print on a page 48 five-digit numbers using 240 wheels, each embossed around the edge with the numbers 0 to 9, some with one, two or three numbers repeated. These ten or more numbers were in no particular order. The wheels could be interchanged both within the set of five and between the 48 sets. Once set up, it could print a batch of sheets of the same numbers before the wheels turned automatically to print the next batch of sheets with new numbers. But not all the wheels turned in the same manner. By a series of cams and notches, individual wheels within a set may not move, may move one place or two places. In addition to the automatic changes, individual wheels could be changed by hand. Sheets were not numbered so a pad could be made up of a sheet from each batch and then the sheets shuffled before being bound into a pad of tear-off pages. The report quoted Mr Lorant boasting the German Government had printed two million sheets without a breakdown. The report did not, however, say whether the British Foreign Office bought any of Mr Lorant's machines.

Hats off to the Americans, thought Bill, *for having reconstructed the additive generator machine without the benefit of this report.* It was clear there had been further enhancements to the machine because the cryptanalytic papers from Arlington Hall outlined the wheels turned or stopped on a dependence order rather than as Mr Lorant described. From captures, the Americans had also worked out the Germans developed several indicator systems using pad and sheet numbers to advise the recipient which sheets had been used for a message's encryption.

Even armed with the knowledge of how the additive was generated, there was much to do to reach the point of decryption. Different arrangements of the 240 wheels were used for traffic between Berlin, Madrid, Lisbon and Berne at different times. Once these arrangements had been identified, it was necessary to determine the dependence order of the wheels of a group and then the sequence of the numbers around the rims of the wheels. Finally, the point around the rim at which the machine began to print a page was needed to be worked out. Cribs, depths and the benefit of stereotyping of beginning and ends of messages were all possible ways in. Sometimes a circular from Berlin was sent out and even copied out a second time with the body of the circular all encrypted with the same additive, only the addresses being different. It was time consuming and exacting work but rewarding as the rate of successes was exponential as more and more basic data was stored and run through Mr Freeborn's Hollerith machines. Everyone had their head down recognising the urgency for results.

A note went round in the middle of April recording nearly 900 current-year GEE messages had been decoded, nearly half by the Research Section. Initial breakthroughs for the remainder had been sent to Berkley Street for them to decode. Brigadier Tiltman's group continued to work on disentangling pad families and setting messages in support of Arlington Hall.

Whilst the mood in the Research Section remained serious, the atmosphere noticeably lightened each time news of a further Allied advance was broadcast. The end of the war was surely approaching fast.

Grace finally came up to Bletchley Park for her delayed leaders' meeting. She had been writing to Bill regularly. He always looked forward to reading her letters written in her expansive prose. Now, she barely suppressed her delight at the opportunity of meeting Bill for lunch. The leaders' meeting, she said, was about preparations for the immediate post-war period but she did not say more, nor did Bill ask. As they walked afterwards, she deliberately steered the conversation to what would happen when peace was finally declared.

"They say there will be a list of post-war positions circulated soon. I will see what that offers, I suppose. I need to earn a living. Do you know what you will do, Bill?" she fished.

"Cambridge, very probably," he answered. "But there is talk of some work to record what has been done here over the last few years, maybe even some permanent work. I don't know yet."

His response disappointed Grace, who was hoping for a more concrete answer. Her fervent hope was that Bill would be settled in Cambridge and she could find suitable work there so they could be together. But she held back from being open and changed the subject, introducing the idea of a holiday. In her utility room at the soulless outstation, she often dreamed of holidaying with Bill in the Alps.

"I'd love to take a holiday after all this. I would go to Switzerland and hike in the mountains. I spent two months in Lausanne studying French just before the war, staying with Oncle Jean. At weekends, the whole family would go into the mountains on the 'funiculaire' as it was called for a picnic. It is breathtakingly beautiful. Have you been to Switzerland?" she enquired, fishing again.

"No. I've not been abroad," said Bill matter-of-factly without elaborating.

Grace left for Stanmore a little disappointed. She had wanted them to make some plans for the future, not necessarily firm plans but indicative at least but Bill seemed obtuse, not picking up on her thoughts, on her planted clues. But she was not downhearted having become used to his ways. He was still sweet. She would try again.

A few days later, Bill found four letters for him on the hall table. He recognised the writing on three, the fourth had Trinity College, Cambridge embossed on the envelope. He opened the latter first, hoping it was a positive response to his written request to return. To his great relief, it was; a room had been reserved for him. All he needed to do was to let them know a date. Pleased, he opened Cedric's letter next. Cedric was again cross with Bill for the lack of communication but the thrust of his letter was asking what Bill intended to do now the end of the war in Europe was approaching. His strong advice was Bill should return to Trinity to complete his PhD. As for himself, he would help voluntarily at the Friends Relief Service for a while before seeing what direction to take. Meanwhile, he was continuing his peace studies which interested him greatly. "I had better reply before I get into any more trouble," Bill said to himself. The letter from Grace recounted their meeting, brief though her visit to Bletchley Park was, but no other news. The last letter was from his mother. Suddenly, his mood changed. Unusually, she had written at length and the contents both shocked and worried him.

His mother had been to see her sister and Mr Ennion, the solicitor, on a matter of importance; she had wanted their advice before telling her sons what was on her mind. She was posting today letters to both Joe and to him.

Reading these uncharacteristic opening few lines, Bill became very anxious. What could this possibly be about? He became tense.

It was clear, his mother wrote, that she could not continue to live at the cottage. She could not manage money-wise on her own and in any case, she did not want to live on her own even though her friends were very kind. She had considered a lodger but there was no great call for lodgings in the village and what she could offer by way of accommodation would not command much rent. The last time Mr Brett, the preacher, came to see her, he wondered whether she would consider becoming his housekeeper. His wife, she wrote, had become very frail and Mr Brett had secured a room for her in a nurse-owned board-and-care home in the village but needs someone to manage the house and provide for him. 'He believes I would prove very suitable', she said. 'He has a large house', she explained, 'with some land, and I would have part of the house with a sitting room which I could furnish with my own things. And of course, I would be paid, she added. There would even be a spare room. Mr Brett says you can stay as often as you like. He lives only half an hour or so away in Glemsford which can be reached by train from Cambridge. You'll soon be going back to Cambridge, won't you?' she asked.

The news considerably troubled Bill whose mind was swimming with the many implications. This would mean the end of Cheveley for him, his childhood home, for their cottage would surely have to be sold or rented out. He would have no settled place, no home. He would be a 'visitor' when seeing his mother. What would happen when his mother got too old to cope or if Mr Brett should die? The consequences, should she go ahead, were profound.

Over the next few days, Bill became more and more stewed over the contents of his mother's letter, this bolt from the blue upsetting the equilibrium he had hoped would return very shortly when the war was over, which seemed imminent with the news the Russians were encircling Berlin. His Plan A was, indeed, to return to Trinity, but he was prepared to see if the Foreign Office in the shape of the Government Code and Cypher School had a sufficiently interesting research role to tempt him away from his PhD. But aside from what he decided to do, this totally upset the apple cart to the extent he became quite annoyed with his mother and his brother. His mother had said not long ago she was not looking to make any major decisions, yet here she was proposing an unexpected change with drastic and permanent repercussions for him. By extension, he was cross with Joe. He really should be helping their mother, maybe finding somewhere bigger so she could live with him and his family. But whatever happened in the past between them seems to rule that out, forcing their mother to move away.

From his mother's letter, the inference was her sister and Mr Ennion raised no objections to the idea. That appeared to place a responsibility on him, which he had not sought and did not want. His mother had ended her letter with a request he come home to talk it through; but that was not possible at the moment with the Section under such pressure. He disliked unresolved issues and he knew this one would only gnaw away at him until he could get home. In the end, he dashed off a few lines to say he would think it over and come home as soon as he could manage. He rattled off a similarly curt letter to Cedric then regretted it afterwards.

April gave way to May. Hitler was dead and the Soviets were at the centre of Berlin. Bill went to see Gerry to check on what was needed, to see if the work should stop as there had been no new GEE messages intercepted since the middle of April.

"Yes, I know," said Gerry, "but the Brigadier wants us to press on with unsolved messages for the time being. His side continues to work on setting Tokyo messages for Arlington Hall. He is not aware why the messages have stopped; it is more likely the end is nigh rather than they know their system has been compromised. By the way, you may not know Ralph Tester and one or two others are about to leave for Paris. There are teams set up under a Target Intelligence Committee, TICOM for short, to go into Germany with the front-line troops. The idea is to capture documents, equipment, even people, of the various German cryptography and signals units before any precious secrets can be destroyed or looted. And definitely to keep them out of the hands of the Russians. Anything too that will help in the war against Japan. Quite exciting for Ralph really; wish I'd had the chance to go. Let's see what they can grab."

"I'm glad they didn't ask me to go," said Bill under his breath.

Chapter 15
V E Day

As Bill walked into the Research Section on Monday morning, he was met by a heightened air of expectation. Over the last few days, rumour, speculation and talk had all been about the capitulation of the German forces, avidly anticipated for days now. Bill joined the periphery of a group in animated conversation.

"It's true," someone was emphasising. "They're saying it's been broadcast on German radio, earlier this morning. Winston Churchill is supposed to be speaking soon. We need to get hold of a wireless."

The waiting had been exasperating. The writing had been on the wall for weeks that Nazi Germany's death rattle was imminent. The Russians fighting street by street had now taken Berlin, the Reichstag had fallen. All day the rumours flew around but still nothing official was announced. People were, nevertheless, in high spirits, poised to celebrate. As Bill went back to his digs in the evening, he came across the Bletchley locals already in festive mood. Some were putting out flags. Bonfires built in readiness had been lit.

Mrs Batchelor greeted Bill with a broad smile saying she had heard Mr Churchill would make a statement tomorrow at three o'clock and a Ministry of Information announcement would be made that evening at twenty minutes to eight. He could come down and listen to it with her. In the event, the announcement was very brief merely stating that tomorrow will be treated as Victory in Europe Day and will be regarded as a holiday.

"That wasn't much!" said a disgruntled Mrs Batchelor. "But at least we can go to bed tonight knowing the war is finally over, so I suppose that is something. I hear there's a dance at the Welfare Hall tonight if you want to go."

"Thank you, but it's not for me. I'll write some letters. The announcement said it was a holiday tomorrow but I think I will have to go into work."

"Does this mean you will be leaving us?"

"I don't know. I may find out more tomorrow."

With that he went back up to his room. He could not work out how he felt about the war ending. Occasionally in recent months, he wondered how he would feel when this moment finally came but now it was here he could not put his finger on his feelings. In a way, he hoped tomorrow was not a holiday for him and others at the Park so he would not be jollied into joining the more raucous celebrations.

The overriding mood the following morning was one of relief that the waiting was over at last. Apparently, the teleprinters in the Newmanry ceased at one minute past midnight and Max Newman gave his Wrens two days' unofficial leave. There was no such leniency in the Research Section. But the day took on a strangely carefree and light-hearted aspect with much humour and joshing. Little serious work was done. Everyone was waiting for three o'clock when Mr Churchill was due to make his broadcast. A wireless had been set up in preparation.

Bill knocked on Gerry's door.

"Have you a moment while there is a lull?"

"Sure, come in, Bill. What is it?"

"I have a place confirmed at Trinity to pursue my PhD but I wondered if there was an opportunity to continue here in some sort of research role?" Bill asked tentatively.

"Well, that's a bit of a surprise, Bill," said Gerry somewhat thrown by the request. "I had imagined you would doubtlessly return to Trinity. And I must say, knowing you as I do, I would have thought a career in academia more in your line. That said, I don't know what the plans here are for when the war is finally over, but I'll see how the land lies for you, if that's what you want."

"Thank you," said Bill getting up.

Gerry thought about taking this opportunity to thank Bill for his contribution over these past four years but he let the moment pass as he had not gathered all his thoughts. In view of Bill's exceptional and outstanding work, not just in terms of the Research Section but for Bletchley Park and beyond, he wanted to be sure he had the right words.

As three o'clock approached, once more Bill looked forward to another splendid oration from the Prime Minister.

He was not disappointed. In his distinctive tones, Churchill announced the unconditional surrender of all German land, sea and air forces in Europe signed at Rheims yesterday. "It was", he said, "due to be ratified and confirmed in Berlin today but that should not prevent us from celebrating to-day and to-morrow as Victory in Europe days." He continued:

"The German war is, therefore, at an end. After years of intense preparation, Germany hurled herself on Poland at the beginning of September, 1939; and, in pursuance of our guarantee to Poland and in agreement with the French Republic, Great Britain, the British Empire and Commonwealth of Nations, declared war upon this foul aggression. After gallant France had been struck down, we, from this Island and from our united Empire, maintained the struggle single-handed for a whole year until we were joined by the military might of Soviet Russia, and later by the overwhelming power and resources of the United States of America.

"Finally, almost the whole world was combined against the evil-doers, who are now prostrate before us. Our gratitude to our splendid Allies goes forth from all our hearts in this Island and throughout the British Empire.

"We may allow ourselves a brief period of rejoicing; but let us not forget for a moment the toil and efforts that lie ahead. Japan, with all her treachery and greed, remains unsubdued. The injury she has inflicted on Great Britain, the United States, and other countries, and her detestable cruelties, call for justice and retribution. We must now devote all our strength and resources to the completion of our task, both at home and abroad. Advance, Britannia! Long live the cause of freedom! God save the King!"

Everyone cheered and clapped and shook their neighbour's hand. Bill was encouraged to join those who spilled out on to the lawns and pathways in the bright sunshine, even so he stayed on the side-lines steering clear of the more boisterous among them who burst spontaneously into noisy song. The word went round that a dance was to be held in the Club later on. And he caught mention that the King was due to broadcast to the Empire at nine o'clock that evening.

When Bill returned to the Section room, there was a copy of a memorandum on the table in front of each chair. He picked one up. It was a Special Order from Commander Travis expressing his personal thanks to everyone on this historic occasion. Bill read it a second time because oddly, his praise was a few sentences only, the rest of the memorandum emphasised their work was by no means ended, citing the continuing war in the Far East. And he stressed in the strongest terms the necessity of maintaining security. The last sentences were blunt:

'The temptation now to 'own up' to our friends and families as to what our work has been is a very real and natural one. It must be resisted absolutely.'

Even to Bill, the balance of sentiment seemed wrong, far too light on praise and too heavily biased on security but it was, he thought, just typical of how preoccupied still the big wigs were over secrecy.

No one was in the mood for picking up work again and most unofficially drifted off to join the celebrations in town. Bill tagged along for a while. Red, white and blue was everywhere. Houses and lampposts were adorned with bunting, shops had rosettes in their windows, children ran around with little Union Jack flags, elderly couples walked arm in arm sporting ridiculous red, white and blue paper hats and not caring and Bill even spotted a dog with a large tricolour bow tied on its collar. One middle-aged man with a glass of beer in one hand was waving a large American flag. Everyone was in high spirits. At one point, Bill was assaulted by two young ladies who hugged and kissed him and then, laughing and shrieking, moved on looking for someone else to pounce on. Bill had had enough and headed to his digs.

"You're home early," said Mrs Batchelor. "Good. They should give you some time off. I shall listen to the King tonight if you want to join me. He is due to broadcast at nine o'clock. Did you hear Mr Churchill earlier?"

"Yes, I did. Thank you, I'd like to join you later."

"Any news on how much longer you will be here?" Mrs Batchelor enquired again.

"I'm afraid not. I will let you know as soon as I know."

"My neighbour says there is a thanksgiving service at the church tomorrow lunchtime. I think I will go with her. It's funny," said Mrs Batchelor, "we've been waiting so long for this day and now that it's here, it feels very odd. Everyone was relieved last month when the last of the blackout restrictions was lifted but I expect rationing will continue for some time. Now we want the war in the Far East to end and all the boys to come home. Will you be going home when the time comes?"

Her question reminded him of the issue surrounding his mother but it was not a topic he wanted to discuss with her.

"I will probably go back to university."

"Of course, of course," she reminded herself that her very nice young paying guest was also very clever.

The King spoke slowly in his rather monotone voice, his stammer making it almost embarrassing to listen to, and at times, he sounded not unlike Winston Churchill. For nearly ten minutes, Bill and Mrs Batchelor listened in silence as he gave thanks for a great deliverance, saluting those who had brought victory and remembering those who would not come back. Some passages stood out for Bill for their historical resonance:

"The knowledge that everything was at stake: our freedom, our independence, our very existence as a people…

"In the darkest hours, we knew that the enslaved and isolated peoples of Europe looked to us, their hopes were our hopes, their confidence confirmed our faith. We knew that, if we failed, the last remaining barrier against a worldwide tyranny would have fallen in ruins…

"…then, let us turn our thoughts to this day of just triumph and proud sorrow, and then take up our work again, resolved as a people to do nothing unworthy of those who died for us."

He ended:

"In the hour of danger, we humbly committed our cause into the hand of God and he has been our strength and shield. Let us thank him for his mercies and in this hour of victory, commit ourselves and our new task to the guidance of that same strong hand."

"Oh, poor King George with his stutter," said Mrs Batchelor. "But what a grand speech. With Mr Churchill, their broadcasts on the radio were just right to mark this day, don't you think? I wager the festivities will go on long into the night. I'm too old for all that but you go and join them," she urged but Bill gave his excuses.

"I have some letters to finish and work tomorrow. No day off for us."

Mrs Batchelor gave a wry smile. She hoped he would let his hair down for once but was not surprised he headed up to his room.

Mrs Batchelor was right, he thought, as he lay down and turned out the light, it had been an odd day. The mood inside Bletchley Park had been strangely subdued compared to the streets of the town, maybe due to the fact that inside the Park, the war against Japan was still immediate. For the townsfolk, that war must seem far away except for those with family and friends involved out there. Lying in the dark, he supposed the thanks of Churchill, Commander Travis and now, the King did to some extent apply to him, a very strange thought indeed. He found it more of a stretch of the imagination, though, to directly relate to Churchill's more strident words, 'the evil-doers, who are now prostrate before us'. It was, indeed, a historic day. No doubt about that; his considerable knowledge of history told him so. But what did he think of his role, of his time at Bletchley Park? No answer came before he succumbed to sleep.

"Bill, have you got a minute?" called Gerry.

Bill followed him into the room.

"Shut the door."

Bill stiffened wondering what was to come.

"First, some TICOM captured material has just arrived. GEE one-time pads," he said tapping a large pile of bound books of sheets. "There are more, 650 in all, a whole crate load and more on the way. They are thought to be from a reserve stock and have dates from 1941 to 1944. Take this first batch and hand them round. There must be some that will help us with 1944 traffic. We also want to find any that are on a machine we don't already know about."

He paused.

"Now about your request to see if there might be a post-war role for you, I've asked around and at the moment, a new structure for GC&CS has yet to be worked out. But the general feeling is there will necessarily be a considerable down-sizing once the Japanese war is over and anyone who wants to leave will be allowed to go. So, I think your best option is to take up your place at Trinity. My view, for what it's worth, is you have more to offer the academic world than a post-war Government Code and Cipher School. Think it over; you don't have to decide anything just yet. There is, however, some work about to be started with which you could help us in the short term. It's been decided to write a comprehensive report on Tunny. Jack Good, Donald Michie and Geoffrey Timms will be leading it. I'm sure they would welcome a contribution from you."

He paused again, this time for a little longer, gathering his thoughts.

"That brings me to say a few words of personal thanks, Bill. Actually, whatever I say will be wholly inadequate in the light of your very considerable achievements here, particularly on Tunny of course. They say it's better to be a lucky general than a good one; well, I think I have been lucky to have had you join my Section and I think the real generals would echo that if only they knew where their precious intelligence came from. It is difficult to quantify what your original breakthrough on Tunny has led to. Of course, the intelligence value has been incalculable. But I saw a review memo the other day, some of which may surprise you. It quoted the Testery and the Newmanry had grown to about 450 staff with ten Colossi, four Robinsons and dozens of other machines housed in a purpose-built block. From the registers, it is estimated on average over 100 Tunny messages per day were decrypted last year. Then there are some 800 or so intercept staff at Knockholt. Over 1,200 people, all working flat out on Tunny, three shifts a day. And you can add to those numbers the doubtless hundreds of GPO engineers building and maintaining our machines. You gave birth to quite an industry.

"We all tend to understate our achievements and my sense is you are more modest than most, Bill. Of course, Tunny was just part of your overall contribution. But it does no harm to recognise what you have achieved; indeed, I would call Tunny a triumph. Sadly, only a few here will know the whole of your work but believe me those that do know fully appreciate what you have done these last four years, and they would all wholeheartedly join with me in what I've just said."

"I don't know what to say," said Bill, embarrassed and struggling for words. "There were lots of others. Tommy Flowers for instance needs much of the credit."

"But you opened the door for them, Bill. You led them through and showed them the way."

"I suppose so," said Bill weakly.

Gerry rather gave up at that point not getting much response from Bill. But he had said what he had wanted, what needed to be said. He stood up and came around the desk. Bill stood up too. They shook hands firmly.

"Now get these one-time pads distributed," he said kindly. "There's still work to do."

"Come quickly," a voice called from the doorway. It was Tubby Roots. "They have captured a Tunny machine! Art Levenson is telling us the story."

Chairs were hurriedly pushed back as people rushed to Room 40 to hear the news. They crowded at the back of the throng already surrounding Art Levenson who had started the tale of his odyssey into Germany.

"The TICOM team I was with spent VE Day in Paris, a great, great excitement as you can imagine. Major Tester's team had already set off a couple of days earlier heading for Augsburg. Capturing a Tunny machine was high on our wish list. Major Tester's team spent several days ferreting around in southern Germany and in the Salzburg area. They were looking for Field Marshal Kesselring's final headquarters. The trail led to just over the border into Austria where his Chief Signals Officer, a General Würster no less, very helpfully told our lot that Kesselring's communications trucks were in a farmhouse at nearby Dorfheim. A spearhead team found them, all in full working order still with its signals unit, a dozen of them. You all know the link they formed as Jellyfish."

The mention of Jellyfish drew a collective intake of breath from the enthralled group as they recognised a direct connection with their day-to-day work.

"We met up with Major Tester at Berchtesgaden just over the border in Germany. Bizarrely his team were holed up at the impressive Hotel Deutsches Haus, a favourite of Hitler and other Nazi Party top brass we were told. But having located the trucks, no one had permission to move them. So, the day after I got there, someone went to Augsburg to send TICOM a report and to persuade the Americans who were ostensibly in charge of the area to allow three trucks to be moved up to Berchtesgaden. I say ostensibly because the situation was strange. The Germans appeared to control the area, they were still armed, and even Kesselring and his staff were said to be acting like they were not convinced the war was at an end, believing the Americans wanted their cooperation against the Russians."

He looked around the room at a sea of unconvinced expressions.

"Yes, really! It seems they did not understand, 'unconditional surrender'. We were told they were quite truculent at times. Anyway, we got permission to bring the other three trucks up to Berchtesgaden. So, we had six ten-ton diesel trucks, an officer in charge called Oberleutnant Wurm, and his unit of eleven operators and technicians. The decision was that under Major Tester, the whole convoy would set off for the UK with me riding shotgun in the rear truck. Oberleutnant Wurm and his men were only too willing to man the convoy when they were warned to stay might mean they ended up in the hands of the Russians. Essentially, of course, they were POWs."

"You mean the Germans drove their trucks to England for you?" asked someone.

"Oh, yes," said Art, "only too happy. Just as well as it took two weeks and was not easy. The biggest problem was the trucks were obviously German driven by Germans. For some reason, the trucks had not been painted with capture numbers. They had a white star painted on the side but still looked for all the world like German trucks. In Belgium particularly, the German crews got really scared; thought they'd be lynched or something. At one place, the convoy was even pelted; I got hit by a tin can thrown by one very irate Belgian lady. It was pretty eventful. We had to stop for all sorts of reasons sometimes for several days. Diesel was hard to get. Getting permissions to move on took time. We got to know Oberleutnant Wurm and his men, and even became quite friendly. In some places, they were treated roughly and we had to intervene. They were afraid if we left them. I let Oberleutnant Wurm have my gun. We knew they wouldn't try to escape because they would be far worse off. Besides they weren't hardened combat troops, they were signals people. There was an odd interdependence; we needed them to drive the trucks, they needed us for their safety. Eventually, we got to Ostend and were loaded onto a Landing Craft built to carry tanks and after spending the night in the Thames Estuary, finally docked at Tilbury."

"What happened to your POWs," someone asked.

"It's funny," said Art, "at Liege they couldn't believe it because they had been told Liege had been totally destroyed by V-bombs. One of the older men said before the war, he hoped to see London and now, he never would because of the V-bombs. I told him he'd see it well enough with his own eyes when we got there. They said they didn't necessarily believe everything they were told but now they knew they were told a load of propaganda lies. So, the POWs were handed over to the Military Police who escorted them to Kempton Park, I think. Some British drivers brought the convoy up near here somewhere. Major Tester is, at the moment, trying to set up a demonstration."

Bill's ears pricked up at that remark. He was very anxious to see the machine he had toiled against, had metaphorically battled against. He was determined to be at that demonstration.

A week or so later, Bill made his way across to the Newmanry to meet Jack Good.

"Ah, Bill. Thanks for popping over. Let's use this side room."

They sat down. Jack was his familiar engaging self.

"I've been meaning to ask you what you are going to do next. Are you going back to Trinity for your PhD?"

"Almost definitely," said Bill.

"Excellent!" said Jack. "I'm sure that's the right decision. Now listen, I want to ask you a favour. Donald, Geoffrey and I have to write this major Tunny report. We've done some preliminary planning, but none of us joined until the Newmanry was formed so what we want is a draft of events leading up to that point. You know the sort of thing. You have a file in the Research Section I'm told and there must be a lot in your head. Maybe you could also write introductory pieces on your one plus two routine and your rectangling and anything else you think will be useful. Gerry is prepared to release you from what you are doing now. It's important we get your input; after all, you were its progenitor."

"I was warned you might ask. I'll have a go but I'm not very good at that sort of thing."

"Not to worry, Bill. Just in draft is fine. We'll be asking a number of people and we'll have to stitch the whole thing together. Excellent! Now, I have saved the best till last. At least I think it is the best."

Bill wondered what was coming knowing Jack could be a bit of a tease.

"You, Max and I have shared a dream for a while now, have we not—a dream that Tunny could be broken entirely by machine. Well, Bill, I think we are there, we're there! With your one plus two routines, we started to set the chi wheels, then the psi wheels. With your rectangling and our statistics, we found we could break the wheel patterns too. Just the other day, Shaun Wylie discovered how the motor wheels could be broken on Colossus without any modifications. With the Tunny decoders, our dream of total mechanisation has been realised. Just think, Bill, just think what else we could do with Colossus!"

Bill felt a glow he had rarely felt. His face lit up like never before. This was, indeed, the best news. Tunny totally tamed.

"That's just wonderful news, Jack! I knew it was only a matter of time. You and the others must be very pleased. Thank you for telling me." He paused, pensive for a moment.

"You were there, Jack, when Max said he believed Colossus could do logical operations. For me, that was a seminal moment—my 'Silent, upon a peak in Darien' moment, if you know what I mean. I believed him then and I'm even more convinced now. Colossus should continue to be developed, not just for codebreaking." He paused again and changed the subject.

"What are you going to do after the report, Jack? Will you stay on here?"

"I'm not sure yet. There's quite a bit to do on the report so there is plenty of time to see, but I may follow Max. He hopes to move up to Manchester University. He wants to pursue a vision, researching applications for electronic computing machines like Colossus for use in the field of mathematics which sounds really interesting."

The next day, Bill and about a dozen others assembled in a room in the Main Building. Everyone was excitable; they were due to see a Tunny machine for the first time. Bill was talking to Jack Good.

"Finished your drafts for me yet?" Jack joked. "By the way, this should be good, but I've no idea what to expect."

The door opened and in came Major Tester and Brigadier Tiltman.

"Gentlemen," Major Tester addressed the expectant group. "We are about to see a demonstration of Field Marshal Kesselring's mobile communications unit incorporating the Tunny enciphering machine. But first, some polite requests.

"The demonstration will be carried out by the German officer in charge, Oberleutnant Wurm and his signals unit. They are, of course, POWs but they were very helpful in bringing their trucks over here. They proved cooperative and trustworthy, and did not try to damage or destroy their highly secret equipment giving us the unique opportunity to examine and understand it. I'd ask you to respect them.

"In talking to them on our journey across Europe, it is quite clear they believe their Tunny system to be totally unbreakable. We do not want to disabuse them of this belief. They will obviously be in some POW camp and talk to other POWs. We do not want the slightest hint to get out that we have broken it and have been reading their traffic. Please be very mindful of what you say in their earshot; some of them have a smattering of

English. Best of all, pretend you know nothing about their machines. One link was being pushed down from Berlin and the other eastwards from Paris as the Allies advanced. Finally, both ends came together near Salzburg where we found them. Both communications units were in full working order, complete except for a power unit which was carried on a trailer. We managed to get hold of a power unit from the Ministry of Works for this demonstration.

"We have an hour's bus ride now. Please, no discussion of this on the way there or on the way back for the driver to hear. Your carriage awaits, gentlemen."

Eventually, the bus turned into a heavily guarded entrance gate to a parkland estate, the only identification being a sign, 'War Office Camp 300'. Everyone was checked after which the bus headed along a driveway towards a large three storey Palladian mansion house. To one side was a series of Nissen huts, to the other side was a wire-fenced compound with guard towers, inside which could be seen some low flat-roofed brick and concrete buildings with interconnecting corridors. A few men could be seen walking slowly inside the compound; outside there was much evidence of a considerable military presence.

"What is this place?" Jack whispered to Bill.

"Some sort of POW camp perhaps."

The bus skirted the buildings and came to a halt in a large open space to the rear but out of sight of the wire-fenced compound. There they could see two groups of three large German military trucks about 100 yards or so apart, each guarded by armed soldiers. The Bletchley Park party alighted full of curiosity. Ralph Tester escorted one half of the party including Bill to one group of trucks and Art Levenson took the rest to the other group. On the way, Ralph outlined the purpose of each truck. One was obviously the transmitter with a tall antenna, the one they were going to was the operations unit and the third one was a central unit that listened in to the transmitting tone and was connected to the operations unit by field telephone.

They clambered up into the operations truck which barely had room for them all. Seated at their stations were two German signallers. To the surprise of the visitors, Ralph shook hands with them, one of whom he introduced as Oberleutnant Wurm. Neither looked nervous. In front of them, Bill could see what he had come to see, the Tunny enciphering machine.

'It is a brute,' he said to himself. It was large, very large compared to the Hagelin hand machine and many times larger than the Enigma. He could see clearly a row of toothed grip-rings protruding from a lid, presumably for turning the wheels; on the housing above each wheel position was its number, 1 to 12. On top was a staggering array of levers, switches, motors, dials, electrical components and connections. It stood on a heavy iron base, speaking volumes of solidity and superlative German construction.

Bill fixated on it, rationalising his thoughts. For him, his foe was not the Luftwaffe who had dropped bombs on him. The enemy had not been the U-boats or the feared Panzers and their Blitzkrieg tactics. Even this machine in front of him was not his adversary per se; but it was the physical embodiment of his adversary representing as it did the intellectual concept that he had fought against and overcome, not by the sword or by the gun but by logic and mathematics. Here it was; captured, silent, inert, yet carrying with it still an air of invincibility. He smiled recalling Churchill's words, seeing no intellectual concept prostrate at his feet. Not that he saw himself as some victorious gladiator lauded by a baying multitude; curiously those who conceived the Tunny machine knew nothing of him or of its undoing. Satisfaction not glory sufficed.

As Bill's mind wandered, the others were listening to Ralph as he explained the other equipment in the truck, teleprinters, a tape reader, a second Tunny enciphering machine, two telegraph connection devices and a voice frequency modulator.

Ralph spoke in German to the Oberleutnant who opened the lid on his Tunny machine to expose the wheels. Bill returned to the moment. The wheels glinted of precision milled steel. Each wheel had its setting positions in clear white numbers against a black rim with visible in/out cams opposite each setting number. Although all the wheels were the same size, Bill could see how the different number of cams on each wheel had been cleverly arranged. He could not help but admire the engineering.

"They will run through a typical transmission for us," said Ralph. "I will translate as we go along. The other unit will reply. Then we'll do it in reverse."

As the demonstration unfolded, the visitors did not find it difficult to feign ignorance. They found it fascinating.

When the Oberleutnant began, Bill heard him use the phrase, Schlüssel-Zusatz, which Ralph translated as 'cipher attachment'. The Oberleutnant explained that the cipher attachments at each end of the link must be set up exactly the same way. Each wheel of the cipher attachment had a series of cams which had to be set, either 'nocke', operative, or 'keine', inoperative. There were 501 cams on each machine which had to be set each day. He held up a sheet of paper with a serial number and a series of noughts and plusses for each of the 12 wheels. A plus meant 'nocke' and a nought meant 'keine' or none. Both transmitter and receiver must use the same sheet identified by the serial number, he emphasised. He and his Unteroffizier then demonstrated how the cams were set. Ralph said ten wheels were already done and the two remaining wheels with the lowest number of cams would now be set. The Oberleutnant started to call out from the sheet and his Unteroffizier used a stylus to flick the cams, up for operative and sideways for inoperative. Bill thought it was amusing and quite impressive how they did this. As the Oberleutnant rattled off 'drei nocken', 'zwei keinen', 'nocke', 'keine', 'drei nocken', 'drei keinen', the Unteroffizier flicked the cams with the stylus turning the wheel as he did so by the toothed grip-ring. When the two wheels had been completed, the Unteroffizier called them back from his wheels to the Oberleutnant who checked them against his sheet. *No wonder they were expert at it*, thought Bill, *if they had to go through all 501 cams every day, no wonder in the early days they had changed the chi and psi patterns only monthly or quarterly.*

Ralph then translated as the Oberleutnant explained that before they sent a cipher message they checked the other end was ready and that the transmission signal was strong enough. The Unteroffizier tapped a short message on the teleprinter and a few moments later, a message printed out, 'QSA 5' meaning the signal strength was excellent, explained the Unteroffizier.

Next, the Oberleutnant picked up a pad with rows of numbers. These, he explained, were called QEP numbers and by each number of the left-hand column on each page was a string of 12 double-digit numbers. He chose the next free number from the left column and then called out the numbers across the page. The Unteroffizier turned each wheel in turn to the number called out and then called them back for the Oberleutnant to check from his page. Then the Unteroffizier sent a message on the teleprinter quoting the QEP number. This, it was explained, was so the receiver who had the same pad of numbers could set the wheels of his cipher attachment to the same starting positions. An acknowledgement came back; everything was ready.

Again, Ralph translated that a message had been pre-prepared on a tape which asked what the weather was today. The receiving unit had not been told what to expect. A final message, 'Um', was sent and then the cipher attachment was switched to 'in' and the tape fed into the tape reader. The unit hummed, wheels turned, dials quivered, levers moved.

While everyone waited for the response, the Oberleutnant addressed the group through Ralph. The message in cipher form, he explained, was not seen by them or the receiver; it existed only in the air. He proudly announced that because of the number of patterns of 'nocke' and 'keine' that can be created on the wheels, changed daily, and the number of starting positions available, a different set used for each message, the cipher cannot be broken.

A number of heads nodded sagely.

A few minutes later, the receiving teleprinter clattered spelling out the reply directly in German. The Unteroffizier tore off the gummed strip and stuck it on a sheet of special message paper and handed it to Major Tester.

"The weather is fine," Ralph translated. "But it is not as hot as in Germany. We hope it stays fine for our holiday in England."

"Very droll," murmured Jack Good. He nudged Bill. "See that," he whispered pointing to a small open tin on the table next to the printer. "If I'm not mistaken that is tree bark, I bet used for tobacco. Germany must be in a poor state if it can't get tobacco for its troops."

The Oberleutnant was giving a quick résumé of transmission options. Operators, he said, can transmit to each other in cipher or in plain language according to whether the cipher attachment is switched to 'in' or to 'out', and either hand mode, that is simply typing on the teleprinter keyboard or in auto mode like we did just now by running a pre-prepared tape. It was also possible if reception was favourable for both operatives to send and receive at the same time. There were heavy penalties for sending the initial operator exchanges in cipher.

"Ask them what would happen if they sent two messages in cipher on the same setting," asked Peter Hilton of the Testery team. Ralph translated.

The death penalty, came the answer.

"Really!" responded Peter rather sarcastically. Ralph shot him a thunderous look as if to say he wanted no more remarks like that.

"What's behind those curtains at the end of the truck?" asked the young and curious Donald Michie.

Sleeping quarters for two was the answer. The crew slept in their trucks.

A few more questions followed but Bill had switched off having seen enough of the machine. He was contemplating the cryptographic minds behind the machine, what they understood of its vulnerabilities and what they would think if they came to Bletchley Park and saw Colossus.

The visitors watched as the roles were reversed, then with the demonstration over the visitors made to leave. The Oberleutnant stood and shook hands with everyone as they turned to clamber off the tuck.

"Danke, danke," was even offered by some but not Bill who avoided the officer's eyes, nervous and uncertain how to act towards a prisoner of war. He had only seen prisoners of war on newsreels or in the newspapers. He had expected them to be gaunt and cowed but these two appeared quite the opposite in both respects.

On their way back to the bus, Jack asked Bill what he thought of the Tunny machine.

"I would like to meet the German cryptographers who devised it and who saw the need to continuously tighten its security," said Bill not really answering Jack's question. "We sort of played a game of chess with them."

"I found it very interesting," said Jack. "I'm not sure what I expected. The machine was much bigger than I had imagined but I guess what surprised me most was the size and organisation of the unit. Six huge trucks and a dozen men. A pretty sizable outfit. But then Kesselring was a very important man, I suppose. Wasn't it difficult to keep shtum though!"

He turned to Ralph Tester.

"What will happen to those men?"

"They'll go to some POW camp in England. They hope our camps will be better than the pens we saw on our way across Europe, all out in the open, teeming with German POWs. Our prisoners called those pens, 'dust bins'."

As the bus drove out of the park, Bill looked across to the barbed-wire enclosure. The image was too powerful to ignore. It brought home to him what peace looked like for some and what a huge task lay ahead to restore normality.

Chapter 16
Farewell

Grace was in reflective mood. Life was about to change in so many different ways. Her time at Stanmore, the soulless Stanmore, was thankfully coming to an end. But that forced changes on her. She wrote in her diary:

'With meeting Bill tomorrow, I have been thinking about our relationship. Being apart does not make it easy but then I suppose many couples separated by duty remain firm so there is no reason to believe we should be different. Questions: Does our present relationship make us a couple? Do we see our relationship in the same way? Does his lack of response mean he regards me with platonic affection only (a concern)?

'I don't know if I truly believe in platonic affection between a man and a woman. It is rare in literature and I suspect even rarer in life. It never truly is if one half pretends a relationship is platonic when deep down that half wants more. And I do want more, much more—but does Bill?

'I trust him—and his lack of forwardness tells me his intentions are honourable and so he earns my respect. I feel secure with him but I have kept secret from him my true feelings for fear of losing him. Yet, how long can I keep this up?

'I have convinced myself underneath he is very shy of women, naïve, innocent and inexperienced, hence his unresponsiveness. I can help him, shepherd him; we can journey together. I could do it if he would let me, would trust me to. If only we could spend more time together, just the two of us. There must be time for a holiday together before I take up my new job and before he returns to his studies—walking in the Lake District or North Wales (the Alps will have to wait). That would elevate our relationship, open it, cement it, make us a couple.

'Tomorrow, I will suggest it. There, I have written it down so it is much more likely to happen!

'P.S. Why am I drawn to men much cleverer than me? They are far more difficult to fathom. I just am.'

They met as usual at Westminster Underground Station and strolled along the Embankment in the dappled sunlight beneath the plane trees in full leaf. In care-free moods, they decided to take a river trip from Westminster pier. Her big news, she told him, was she had been for an interview at the Ministry of Transport for a situation with the European Central Inland Transport Organisation. They had offered her a position as the personal assistant to the Secretary-General. The Organisation, she told Bill, was being set up to co-ordinate the restoration of transport across war-torn Europe, but the appointment would not be available till the Autumn because they had to raise money from a number of countries. Excitedly, she told him the role may involve some travel. In the meantime, she said, Stanmore was being wound down, the equipment dismantled, and the Wrens would shortly be transferred to Woburn Abbey. After that the place would become a military dispersal centre. So, she would probably have to go home before starting her new post.

Bill was pleased for her. He had already told her in a letter he would return to Trinity College but did not know yet when he would leave Bletchley Park. He wanted to get established at Trinity College as soon as possible after he departed but he also needed to go home. At this point, he decided to confide in Grace his concerns about his mother's plans, knowing she would have some understanding.

Grace quickly realised the importance to Bill of this revelation, sympathised but was careful not to pass any comment. Nonetheless, sensitive to his need to see his mother, her earlier resolve to raise the idea of a holiday together went overboard into the River Thames. 'That will have to wait a little longer', she decided. She was, however, so pleased he had shared his family complications, a real testament to his trust in her, that in her contentment, she turned her head to the sun, closed her eyes and laid her head on his shoulder.

Feeling her hair brushing his cheek in the breeze was an unusual yet agreeable sensation for Bill. Gradually, very gradually, he had become comfortable with her, trusting her and passively allowing her more and more into his life. The Goddess Peitho in her was still working her charms.

Bill avoided goodbyes whenever he could but was not always successful. Max Newman had already left and Alan Turing was in Germany as was Jerry Roberts who had been sent to report to a War Crimes Investigation Unit. Other permanent staff like Gerry Morgan and the Brigadier were staying. Bill had delivered his draft texts for Jack Good's report and had posted home most of the accumulated gear from his digs. When the day came for him to leave, the motherly Mrs Batchelor was saddened at losing her nice young lodger. As a token, she gave him a copy of her fruit cake recipe for his mother.

Rolf Noskwith spotted Bill in the canteen and made a beeline for him.

"Hear you're leaving, Bill. Just came over to wish you luck. Returning to Trinity, I gather."

"Yes, be glad to get back to my graph theory. What about you?"

"I'm staying on for a bit, perhaps to the end of the year. Having a crack at some different codes. I quite like it here; it's like an extension to university. Then I suppose my father will want me to join his firm."

"Best of luck, then," said Bill as they shook hands.

Rolf reached the doorway, half turned and said loud enough for almost the whole canteen to hear, "Saw you the other day with that rounders young lady. Don't forget to invite me to the wedding!" And with a broad smile and a wave, he disappeared.

Bill had received a message that Commander Travis wished to see him after lunch before he left. He went upstairs in the Main Building to report to the Commander's secretary who ushered him in.

"Ah, Mr Bill Tutte. Thank you for coming over. Take a seat. I gather you leave today and I wanted a few words."

He drew a breath as though embarking on a soliloquy.

"As you know much has happened here during the last few years, much of it of great significance to the war effort. It has been a tremendous contribution from all concerned. We have grown from a few hundred at the beginning to some 10,000 souls working all hours. Not only have we needed people but to attack the enemies' ever more sophisticated codes and ciphers, we needed machines. I think one of the most significant developments in cryptography has been the recent innovation of complex electronic machines to take on the work load we humans could not possibly complete in a timely and useful fashion. That impressive Colossus is a prime example. In tandem with these new machines, I think the other significant shift in our approach to the art of cryptography has been the employment of mathematics, principally the branches of statistics and probability. Not a strong suit of mine, I might add.

"Now, as I understand it, we have a great deal to thank you for in the attack on Tunny. Without your insight, we still might not have broken it. Rotor machines like the Enigma and the Hagelin, we knew all about at the beginning; even had the machines and captured material to help us. Not so the Tunny machine which, as you well know, until a few weeks ago we had not seen, and which in pure intelligence terms turned out to carry the highest grade over its teleprinter links. I would pick out three important series of Tunny messages which you may or may not know about. The first is around the Battle of Kursk when we provided the Russians with vital intelligence enabling them to rebuff a major German attack. That was a turning point on the Eastern Front. The second was the Italian campaign where we knew Hitler continued to commit significant troops to the defence of the Italian peninsula thereby reducing his defensive capability on the Atlantic seaboard. Thirdly, and arguably the most important, was the run-up to D-Day when we knew from Tunny decrypts Hitler's defensive strategy, that he had swallowed the Allied deception of an attack based on the Pas de Calais. Not only that, but before D-Day, Rommel sent a comprehensive and detailed report of the whole Western defences including the Normandy beaches. If I remember correctly that decrypt was some 70,000 characters, the size of a small pamphlet, I might tell you.

"Launching an invasion is a tricky business, Bill. If the Normandy landings had not succeeded it would have been a long time before another invasion force could have been assembled; some say another two years. Who knows what would have happened during that long delay.

"I wouldn't be telling all this to just anyone, Bill, but I wanted you to leave here understanding just how important your work has been.

"Now, tell me, what, in your opinion, were the German mistakes and the flaws within the Tunny system which let you in?"

"Well," said Bill launching into an explanation he had run over in his mind a number of times, "there was the major blunder of the August '41 depth read by Brigadier Tiltman. That was a bad error. The second critical mistake at that time was made by the German cipher officer who made up the wheel patterns. He did not put enough changes between dot and cross in his psi patterns, so in the stretched-out psi impulses, two consecutive symbols were more likely to be the same than different. Had he arranged the patterns so that two consecutive symbols were more likely to be different than the same, then my method would have failed.

"With the system itself, I would say the first main weakness was the separation of the five impulses, each effectively controlled by only two wheels. The second main weakness was the psi wheels moved in step. If they had been controlled independently, the later work by Alan Turing, the statisticians and myself would not have been applicable."

"Mmm, interesting," reflected the Commander. "Nevertheless, a remarkable achievement by all concerned. Now, what I have to say next I find most difficult."

The Commander pushed up his portly figure from his chair, took a pace over to the window and stared outside composing his words.

"Over the coming months, Bill, you will no doubt find many people being recognised for their contribution to the war effort, from prominent Generals to the ordinary foot soldier, to the deserving civilian, all awarded medals and honours and nationally applauded. Quite rightly too."

He paused again and turned round to engage Bill directly.

"But for us here, there can be no recognition, no reward. Our work is too secret. I regret, sincerely regret, I have nothing to offer you, Bill, nothing other than my personal gratitude for your very significant contribution. I am only too aware this is wholly inadequate. And to add insult to injury, we are obliged to ask everyone when they hand in their pass to sign the Official Secrets Act again to emphasise the importance of protecting our secrets for those who follow.

"So, as you leave us, Bill, very regrettably there can be no commendation, no award; I can confer no privileges only place upon you the heavy burden of secrecy."

The Commander then lightened his tone.

"Now, tell me, Bill, what you have gained from your time here?" he asked, expecting something along the lines of the satisfaction of 'doing one's bit'.

Bill thought for a moment.

"I believe I have grown as a mathematician," he replied.

Rather stumped and almost dumbfounded by Bill's completely unexpected reply the Commander spluttered, "Well, well good luck with whatever you are going to do. Cambridge, isn't it? Well, good luck again."

They shook hands and as Bill made for the door, the Commander reflected that these mathematicians were a rum lot.

A little while later as the Cambridge train drew out of Bletchley Station, Bill pulled out a letter from Grace that had arrived the previous day. He re-read it. In it, she had suggested a holiday together; a suggestion that presented a potentially pivotal moment in their relationship. But with her letter was a folded piece of paper that she asked him to open only after he had left Bletchley Park for the last time. On it, she said, was some poetry she had written for him based on one of her favourite poems by W B Yeats; written with her special poetry pen. It was rather too long, she remarked, but she had decided to leave it rather than edit it to a better length. Bill opened up the piece of paper and read:

When we are old and grey

When we are old and grey
Sitting by our firesides one day
We shall have known a special time
We've sworn to keep secret for always.

When we were still so very young
Our lives were altered when just begun
Our hopes and dreams were all deferred
Our days of heroism left unsung.

    Even when we're old and grey
    No one will have told
        no one else will say.

There will be hidden memories
Each time we sit and chat
There'll be awkward taciturnity
Times when we'll need to be solitary.

I'll never know all you'll recollect
You'll never know my reminiscences—
On the verge of peace my retrospect

Stretches back as I struggle to connect.

> Even when we're old and grey
> No one will have told
> > no one else will say.

How can I begin to tell you
Of watching bleary-eyed long past midnight
Of feeling life is like a crossword clue
Its meaning only clear to the talented few?

Of queuing shivering for the late-night bus
Exhausted ashen faces at early dawn
Keeping our own counsel each of us
Never letting a careless word escape us.

Of waking late from fitful sleep
Forgetting the dark tunnel our life's become
Dreaming of Mont Blanc's glistening peak
Wandering its slopes for an entire week.

Of cleaning the crumbs in my dusty billet
Sitting in its doorway to catch the sun
Writing letters home sounding steadfast
Savouring my landlady's meagre breakfast.

Of weekends in London visiting a friend
Waking to the sirens—running for the shelter
Sitting for hours cradling her neighbour's bairn
Emerging to sunlight and new ruins at night's end.

> Even when we're old and grey
> No one will have told
> > no one else will say.

How can I convey the complexities
The mix of feelings we all felt
The canal-side walks on sunny days
The laughter and games under such blue skies?

The solitary moments of anguish
Poring over each news dispatch
Thinking that war is simply hellish
Wondering if evil will ever be vanquished.

> Even when we're old and grey
> No one will have told
> > no one else will say.

And yet—the constant camaraderie
That buoyed us up when times were tough
The sense of youth and hope and possibility
That pulled us through incredibly.

Even when we near life's end
We'll share our best kept secret still
We'll know that youth and intellect did lend
Their hand to fight determined for war's end.

     Even when we're old and grey
     No one will have told
                     no one else will say.

Post Script

In the autumn of 1945, Bill Tutte resumed his studies at Cambridge being awarded a PhD in October 1948. His ground-breaking thesis was entitled *'An algebraic theory of graphs'*.

He was then invited to join the Faculty of the University of Toronto where he rose to pre-eminence in the field of combinatorics. During his early days there, he married Dorothea Mitchell, whom he met through the Youth Hostel movement. They had no children. One form of recognition in that period was his election as Fellow of the Royal Society of Canada.

In 1962, he joined the University of Waterloo where, as Professor of Mathematics, he made a major contribution to establishing the identity and reputation of this young university, attracting high-calibre mathematicians from all over the world. Here, he and Dorothea much enjoyed the nature and outdoor life the area offered, hiking being a great favourite of theirs.

Over his professional career, Bill Tutte published more than 160 papers and books becoming a dominant figure in graph theory, many of his theorems carrying his name.

Following his retirement in 1985, he continued to be a significant member of the Faculty of the University of Waterloo as Professor Emeritus.

Dorothea died from cancer in 1994 and not long afterwards, Bill returned to his Newmarket roots living with his great niece, Jeanne. But he missed academic life and returned to Waterloo where he died in 2002.

It was not until around his 80th birthday, when the Tunny story began to emerge, did Bill, for the first time, feel able to open up about his involvement.

Among the many other honours he received were the Jeffery-Williams Prize in 1971, the Henry Marshall Tory Medal in 1975, the Isaak-Walton-Killam Award in 1982 and the CRM-Fields-PIMS Prize in 2001. He was elected a Fellow of The Royal Society in 1987 and an Officer of the Order of Canada in 2001.

In 2009, the Tutte Institute for Mathematics and Computing was established in Ottawa, Ontario, named after Bill Tutte. A world-class mathematical and computational institute, the first of its kind in Canada, it conducts classified research into cryptology and knowledge discovery.

The following are extracts from a letter Prime Minister David Cameron wrote in 2012 to his great niece:

'We should never forget how lucky we were to have men like Professor Tutte in our darkest hour and the extent to which their work not only helped protect Britain itself but also shortened the war by an estimated two years, saving countless lives.

I understand that, partly owing to the secrecy of his work, Professor Tutte was never honoured officially in his lifetime, although he undoubtedly held the respect of those in his field. Whilst the only honours that can be awarded posthumously are for those of gallantry, I can say, without doubt, that Bill Tutte deserves the thanks of the British people.'

The town of Newmarket in Suffolk, Bill Tutte's birthplace, honoured his memory in 2014 with the unveiling of a monument in the centre of the town, a modern sculpture with symbolic installations set into the surrounding open space. At the same time, The Bill Tutte Scholarship was announced, an annual award open to outstanding candidates from the Newmarket area who wish to study Mathematics or Computer Science at University.